Death Penalty Jurisprudence in Nigeria

ADENIYI OLATUNBOSUN

Death Penalty Jurisprudence in Nigeria

GALDA VERLAG 2018

Bibliografische Information der Deutschen Nationalbibliothek
Die Deutsche Nationalbibliothek verzeichnet diese Publikation in der Deutschen Nationalbibliografie; detaillierte bibliografische Daten sind im Internet über http://dnb.ddb.de abrufbar.

ISBN 978-3-96203-013-1 (Print)
ISBN 978-3-96203-014-8 (Ebook)

PREFACE

This book evaluated the underlying principle of retributive theory of punishment behind the application of death penalty for the offenders and appraised the practice of death penalty by assessing the administration of death sentence through the mode and manner of execution. It reviewed the perception of the public and appraised the constitutionality of the practice in Nigeria and other countries in Africa, Asia, Europe and America. The study found that death penalty met some objectives of punishment; retribution and deterrence, although there are divergent public views and opinions on the subject. Some argued that it has been capable of actually deterring prospective criminals from committing capital crimes and that the system is unable to correct mistakes where innocent ones are wrongly executed. Some advocated for its retention as it is meant to keep away those whose conducts are inimical to the lives of the good citizens in the society. They have also argued that through the commission of murder and other capital crimes the dependants and relations of the victims of these heinous crimes borne the trouble and hardships arising from the loss of their loved ones, and felt that it would be most unfortunate and disgusting for the murders walking freely on the streets while the victims had gone on a journey of no return. The book also considered the use of the alternatives to death sentence as complimentary forms of punishment. The author concluded that Nigerian society still needs death penalty system against the backdrop of incessant brutal killings, violent crimes, insurgencies, hate crimes so rampant and prevailing in recent times while identified shortcomings in its operation should be addressed in order to make it more functional; and that it is the system of trial rather than the punishment is prone to errors.

Adeniyi Olatunbosun
Department of Jurisprudence and International law
Faculty of Law
University of Ibadan
Nigeria

1

INTRODUCTION TO DEATH PENALTY

Death penalty is the supreme penalty paid under a legal system as punishment for murder and other capital crimes. Death penalty is the same as death sentence, which is the punishment of death imposed by a judge. In other words, capital punishment is the punishment by the legal killing of a person found guilty of committing a capital crime[1]. However, capital crime is one for which death penalty may, but need not necessarily be imposed.

Obviously, there must be something inherently wrong about the imposition of the death sentence, which pricks the conscience of the civilized world[2] hence with almost periodical regularity, the question of death penalty keeps coming up for consideration or reconsideration in different countries of the world over the years. Putting to death people judged to have committed certain heinous crimes is a practice of ancient standing but in many countries of the world, Nigeria inclusive. In the latter half of the twentieth century, it has become a very controversial issue.

In recent times, the Nigerian government through the National Assembly is being pressurized by international communities to examine the question of capital punishment with a view to abolishing the system. Perhaps, one needs

---

[1]Black's Law Dictionary defines death penalty as supreme penalty exacted as punishment for murder and other capital crimes; held not to be, under all circumstances, cruel and unusual punishment within prohibitions of 8th and 14th Amends., U.S. Const. 5th ed. (St. Paul Minn West Publishing Co. (1979) referred at pg. 360 *Gregg v. Georgia,* 428 U.S. 153, 96 S.Ct. 2909, 49 L.Ed. 2d 859

[2]Gabriel Wells; Capital Punishment (London, William Heinemann Ltd, (Double day, New York, Doran & co., Inc. 1929) at p. 3. Anthony James, A New Look at Capital Punishment (1977) at p. 26. See also, Gerald Gardiner (1956), Capital Punishment As a Deterrent: And the Alternative (London, Victor Gollancz Ltd.)

to recall that the consideration of the subject-matter has been going on for ages in Europe and America and all efforts, this time around, is not likely to differ greatly from those of previous occasions which have produced stimulating and interesting arguments in support and against its application[3] based on multifarious factors among whom are logic, religious norms, doctrines, political, socio-cultural, moral and legal reasoning.

For centuries, no appreciable change has been made in the attitude towards death penalty. The study of the retention or abolition of death penalty in international law could not have been relevant years ago because its subject matter did not exist.[4] Crimes were then treated as subjects of municipal jurisdictions having no extra-territorial application.[5] Though its scope has been gradually restricted at international level, nevertheless its validity has never been completely or successfully impugned. International norms addressing the question of death penalty are essentially a post second world war phenomenon. The quest for abolition was promoted during the drafting of the Universal Declaration of Human Rights in 1948 as it found expression only implicitly in the recognition of what international human rights law[6] describes as the "Right to Life". Even as at that time all but a handful of states maintained the death penalty and in the aftermath of a brutal struggle which had taken hundred's of millions of lives, few were contemplating its abolition.

The idea of abolition gained momentum over the last two decades with the

---

[3]In Britain, several views and opinions have been expressed in both Houses of Parliament during the last 200 years and several reports of Commissions and Committees have been compiled and published. The Royal Commission Report is the most significant in this field of study. CMD 8432 (1953). The Howard League for Penal Reform published a book; The Hanging Questions, edited by L.B. Lom Cooper (1969) (Gerald Duckworth & Co.) (London) (1969). See also Roy Calvert; Capital Punishment in XXth Century quoted by Gerald Gardiner Q.C., Capital Punishment and the Alternative (The Camelot Press Ltd.) (London and Southampton, 1956). The literature is enormous. The most illuminating American work is selling, the Death Penalty (Report for the Model Priminal Code Project 1959) and Bedau, ed. Death Penalty in America 1961. See also Welsh, Capital Punishment in South Africa. (Duckworth & Co.)

[4]William A. Schabas, The Abolition of the Death Penalty in International Law, (2nd Ed.) Cambridge University; 1997 at p. 2.

[5]Graveson R.H., Conflict of Laws Private International Law (7th Ed.) Fourcet & Maxwell Ltd. 1974.

[6]See Universal Declaration of Human Rights G.A. RES 217A (III 1948) (This Declaration was adopted by the U.N. General Assembly on December 15, *1948*, 48 states voted in favour, none against and 8 abstained including Saudi Arabia, South Africa, (Union of Soviet Socialist Republics, Yugoslavia).

international law makers urging the limitation of the death penalty to very serious crimes in countries where it is being retained[7] excluding juveniles, pregnant women and the elderly from its scope. The international law makers while recognizing the principle of sovereignty of each country requested for enhanced procedural safeguards wherever death penalty still obtained. Eventually, three international instruments were drafted that proclaimed the abolition of the death penalty,[8] as at present about 49 countries have ratified these treaties and perhaps, the number is likely to grow rapidly. Four European states have pledged to ratify protocol No. 6 within 12 months as a condition for joining the Council of Europe. The trends and patterns of crimes are circuitous and that a position on any aspect of criminality is relative at any given point in time.[9] The events at international level in the past and very recently support this viewpoint. The United Nations during the Korean War formally provided for imposition of the death penalty on prisoners of war for post-capture offences.

About 57 (now 65) years after the Nuremberg trials, the international community has now ruled out the possibility of capital punishment in prosecutions for war crimes and crimes against humanity by the enactment of statute of International Tribunal for the former Yugoslavia[10] and Rwanda[11] and the establishment of the International Criminal Court (ICC).[12] The objective of the International community towards setting international standard is aimed at attaining a situation when the abolition of the death penalty becomes a universal norm entrenched not only by convention but also by custom and qualified as a pre-emptory norm of *jus cogens* in the foreseeable future. The trend is intimidating and ravaging too, from a handful

---

[7]In 1946 a Norwegian Court ruled that the death penalty was actually prescribed by International Law and thus could be legitimately imposed despite the fact that it was inapplicable under the country's ordinary criminal law.

[8]See (1) Protocol No. 6 to the Convention for the Protection of Human Rights and Fundamental Freedom Concerning the Abolition of the Death Penalty. ETS 114 (See Appendix 10 p. 338).

[9]See Adeniyi Olatunbosun; (2002) Constraints in the Administration of Criminal Justice in Nigeria M. Phil. Thesis (unpublished) p. 6.

[10]Established by S.C. Res. 827, U.N. SCOR, 48th Sess; U.N. DOC. S/RES/827 (1993) and 1.

[11]Established by S.C. Res. 955, U.N. SCOR, 49th Sess; U.N. DOC, S/RES/827 (1994).

[12]Rome Statute for the International Criminal Court, U.N. DOC. A/Conf. 183/9, July 17, 1998. See also Justice Louise Arbour, The Prosecution of International Crimes: Prospects and Pitfalls in Washington University Journal of Law and Policy, Vol. 1, 1999, Adeniyi Olatunbosun, The Reprehension of International Crimes and the Challenges Ahead in Faculty of Law Journal Olabisi Onabanjo University, Ago-Iwoye, Ogun State, Nigeria (2001).

abolitionist countries in 1945, the list grew steadily and by 2000, considerably more than half the countries in the world had abolished the death penalty *de facto* or *de jure.*[13] Those that still retain it, find themselves increasingly subject to international pressure in favour of abolition, Nigeria is a typical example. The mode of pressure being exerted on Nigeria is divergent; sometimes coercive and at times persuasive.[14] In the field of foreign policy, it has been canvassed by power blocs that abolition of the death penalty is an important element in democratic development and sustenance for Nigeria breaking with a part characterized by terror, injustice and repression. Nigeria is also being encouraged to explicitly refer to constitutional instruments and policy statements and to the international treaties prohibiting the death penalty. The sensitization of the public through the print and electronic media on the desirability of considering the relevance of death penalty in the administration of criminal justice system is being adopted by the government in collaboration with international bodies[15] with financial aids and support. While all these approaches are permissible under international law and foreign diplomacy, it must be employed cautiously as the question of public opinion relevant as it is probably a danger for any government to try to go too far ahead of public opinion,[16] rather it is the responsibility of the leaders to ensure that they are not pushed to the wall. The Nigerian government must discern "the voice of the people" from the "morbid state of public feelings" and "the voice of the uninstructed mob". In other words, we must try to ascertain to what extent public opinion is well informed and instructed. Legal issues must not be hinged on sentiments.

[13]Argentina, Australia, Bolivia, Bosnia, Brazil, Chile, Colombia, Costa Rica, Czech. Republic, Denmark, Dominican Republic, Ecuador, El Salvador, Finland, France, Germany, Guatemala, Honduras, Hungary, Italy Licctenzlein, Luxemburg, Macedonia, Malta, Mexico, Mozambique, Namibia, Netherlands, New Zealand, Nicaragua, Norway, Romania, Paraguay, Peru, Portugal, Romania, San Marino, Seychelles, Slovenia, Spain, Suriname, Sweden, Switzerland, Uruguay/ Venezuela.

[14]The Federal Government of Nigeria has set up a Committee to organize national debates and workshops on Death Penalty.

[15]Special mention must be made of The Amnesty International, its secretariat is located at 1 Easton Street London, WC IX 8D J U.K. http: //www.amnesty.org.

[16]The opening of the National Campaign for the Abolition of Death Penalty at FCT Abuja promised to accommodate divergent views of eminent jurists, government officials, technocrats, legislators, seasoned professionals and stakeholders on this highly controversial subject.

Foundation of Death Penalty

It is difficult to say precisely when death penalty came into use but death penalty has a long and gruesome genesis over the years. The ancient societies have almost put criminals to death for a variety of offences. The theological reasonings prevalent at that time held that innocents would emerge unscathed as God and heavenly forces would protect them, while the guilty ones would perish. But certainly more words have been uttered in public and in private – over the issues of capital punishment than over any other single-issue of public or social policy. Everything that can be said both for and against this heavy penal sanction has been said *ad nauseam.* Yet the debate rages on.

In Britain, several views and opinions have been expressed in both Houses of Parliament during the last 200 years and several reports of Commissions and Committees have been compiled and published. The Royal Commission Report is the most significant in this field of study. Indeed, the literature is enormous as the debates on death penalty seem to be one of the most controversial, emotionally laden and intriguing discussions carried out by eminent scholars, human rights' activists, politicians, religious leaders, psychologists, academia, medical practitioners, psychiatrists, sociologists, philosophers, legal practitioners and public stakeholders. Also, in United States of America, illuminating works on the death penalty sentence has been recorded.

Unlike Britain that has considered the abolition of capital punishment as far back as 1868. Nigeria has very little about it. Perhaps, the only Nigerian research work first recorded was that of Aguda, other eminent scholars such as Milner, Adeyemi, and Ijalaye have also made enviable contributions in this field.

However this work evaluates death penalty as a mode of punishment and assesses the constitutionality of the practice with a view to having a balanced position, taking into consideration the peculiarity of Nigerian society with the introduction of sharia law in some States of the Federation which is likely to create a conflict of law problem under the Nigerian Legal System. This work will further examine the legal implication that would result from whatever decision the National Assembly will arrive at the status of capital punishment in Nigeria as to the retention or abolition of death penalty, this situation would create a mixed status of the nation being classified as abolitionist *de jure* and *de facto* by Islamic nations.

What is important is to arrive at a balanced position on the issue of death penalty whether the prevailing situation justifies the propriety of retaining the practice or the imperative for its abolition.

Historical Development

Death penalty has existed since antiquity. Anthropologists even claim that the drawings at Valladolid by prehistoric cave dwellers showed an execution.[17] In the history of mankind all of earth's creatures kill, but only man punishes, and the highest rung on the ladder of punishment which man has evolved for breach of societal laws is the death penalty. This mode of punishment has a deep root in the Mosaic Law based on the Hammurabi Law, which has in it the principle of retribution and legal revenge.[18]

In the primitive societies where punishments were savage and violent, death sentence had a pride of place. The Persians practiced burning alive, boiling, drowning or burning at stakes. The Athenian society around 200 BC practiced stoning of the convicts. The Ancient Greeks adopted the use of poison derived from the hemlock trees. The Romans adopted a variety of method like crucifying, beheading, burning alive, submerging in cold water and dumping in boiling oil.[19]

Even in England, in spite of her acclaimed civilization and sophistication there were an amazing 220 capital crimes at the beginning of the 19th century for variety of offences such as impersonating a Chelsea prison and damaging London Bridge.[20] However, by 1861, the number of capital crimes had been

---

[17]It is difficult to say precisely when death penalty came into use. But certainly more words have been uttered in public and in private – over the issues of capital punishment than over any other single-issue of public or social policy. Everything that can be said both for and against this unique penal sanction has been said *ad nauseam*.. Yet the debate rages on. See also Darwin, Charles (1859), on the origin of species by means of natural selection, London Watts. Brace, C.L. (1967), the stages of Human Evolution: Human and Cultural Origins, (Englewood, Cliffs, NJ. Prentice-Hall).

[18]In positive law, capital punishment can be traced back as early as 1700 BC, in the Lex Talionis.

[19]Death Penalty has a long and gruesome genesis over the years. The ancient societies have almost put criminals to death for a variety of offences. The theological reasonings prevalent at that time held that innocents would emerge unscathed as they would be protected by God and heavenly forces, while the guilty ones would perish

[20]Perhaps, the display of insensitivity became manifest in 1801, when a child of 13 years was hanged in Tyburnn, England for stealing a spoon. See also Judicial Hanging – Timeline of Capital

reduced to just four (high treason, murder, piracy and arson in Royal dock yards) by the Criminal Law Consolidation Act.

In the United States of America, the use of capital punishment has undergone numerous changes and reforms in the past two centuries falling in and out of public favour.[21] In 1846, the Michigan legislature made that state the first government in the world to remove the death penalty; some other states have abandoned the death penalty while some have laws permitting capital punishment, but have not executed any one under them. Changing views on this issue and many legal challenges to capital punishment resulted in a halt to executions in the United States in 1967. Eventually, the Supreme Court placed a moratorium on capital punishment in 1972 but later upheld it in 1977.A few years ago, it was reported that one Michael Royce, sentenced to death for killing eight women about twenty years ago sought for his own execution on the ground that members of his family have undergone traumatic experiences while on the death row awaiting the news of his execution. The court accepted his request and he was executed on the 12th May 2005 at New England, U.S.A. thus becoming the first person to be executed in this century in that country.[22]

Punishment in Britain. See facts about Deterrent and Death Penalty – http/www.essential.org/dpic/deter.html.

[21]See Williams S. Mcfeely; Trial and Error; Capital Punishment in United States History (2001). See also Louis Masur; Rites of Execution, Capital Punishment and the Transformation of American Culture 1776 – 1865. Stuart Banner; The Death Penalty: An American History. Harvard University Press, March 2002; Some books convey the report that children were routinely hanged for minor crimes such as theft during the 17th and 18th centuries, though there is little hard evidence to support this view. But in Richards book titled 'King's Lynn' published on 1907, an account of possibly the youngest children ever executed in Britain were Michael Hammon and his sister, Ann, whose ages were given as 7 and 11 respectively. Although the English Press did not consider the execution of Michael and Ann newsworthy, even that followed their executions attracted news headline, as it was reported 'There was violent thunder and lightning after the execution and that their hangman, Anthony Smyth died within a fortnight of it. Obviously, the execution attracted the wrath of God! Hence the proximate revenge of the inflictor of the most barbaric and ruthless administration of death sentence in the history of mankind. During the post three decades the issue of the capital punishment has been very controversial inside the United States. During 1972 the U.S. Supreme Court decided in *Furman v. Georgia op. cit.* that the death penalty was unconstitutional because it was a form of 'cruel and unusual punishment'. However, this decision did not last long; in July 1975 the Supreme Court ruled that capital punishment did not violate any parts of the Constitution. Executions as they had before 1972 resumed again since then 180 prisoners have been executed. See also *Gregg v. Georgia op .cit.*

[22]According to C.N.N. news on 12th May, 2005 reported in Guardian Express Newspaper.

The state of New York is a state that practiced capital punishment since its colonial days, but abolished it in 1965. But now, the death penalty is back in the books. Indeed, in U.S. restoring capital punishment is the will of the people, yet many voices are raised against it[23].

Today's modes of execution seem almost merciful. In ancient Persia, condemned prisoners were often eaten alive by insects and vermin. During the Middle Ages, common execution methods included mutilation, amputation, impaling, flaying, crucifixion, boiling in oil, drawing and quartering, breaking on the rack, and burning at the stake. Just as appalling, in a way, were the crimes that exposed offenders to such torture. Under the Code of Hammurabi, selling beer illegally carried the death penalty. The ancient Hebrews inflicted death on anyone found guilty of cursing his mother or father or breaking the Sabbath. The Persians executed anyone who accidentally sat on the King's throne. From the late Middle Ages until the 18th century, the number of capital offences increased greatly in many European countries. In the 16th Century Britain, eight offences were punished by death, including treason, murder, and rape. But the number of capital crimes ballooned to about 350 by the mid-1700. Public executions were festive and frequent, and hawkers sold refreshments and programmes.

Meanwhile, a movement to abolish capital punishment was gaining support throughout Europe.[24] In 1753, Russia became the first nation to ban the death penalty. American colonies prescribed death for fourteen offences, but the number for which death was actually imposed varied from colony to colony. For example, in 1936, the Massachusetts Bay colony listed thirteen capital crimes. A century and a half later, only nine such offences were recognized.

Many death penalty opponents also considered life imprisonment more

---

[23]D.B. Davis, Movement to Abolish Capital Punishment in America, 1787 - 1861, (1957) 63 American Historical Rev. 23.

[24]Bedau, Hugo Adam, Radelet, Michael L. Miscarriages of Justice in Potentially Capital Cases. Stanford Law Review, November 1987; Bend avid, Naftali, What Ever Happened to Habeas Reform? Legal Times, May 16, 1994; Dicks, Shirley, ed., Congregation of the Condemned: Voices Against the Death Penalty, Prometheus Books, 1991; Monk, Richard C. Taking Sides: Clashing Views on Controversial Issues in Crime and Criminology. Dushkin Publishing Group, Brown & Benchmark Publishers, 1996; Sack, Kevin, Strict Rules on Death Penalty Are urged by Lawyers' Group. New York Times, December 31, 1994, p. A28; Spertzel, Jody K. Government Officials Support Alternatives. Corrections Today, October 1993, p. 16; White, Welsh S. The Death Penalties in the Nineties: An Examination of the Modern System of Capital Punishment. The University of Michigan Press, 1991.

effective than executions as a crime deterrent. While the cost debate still swirls on, a nationwide consensus is emerging on execution technology. Just as electrocution once was hailed as more humane than hanging, lethal injection is now the execution method of choice in most death penalty states.

The practice of Death Penalty in Nigeria

Capital punishment has a long and storied history in many societies that later formed the continent of Africa, Nigeria inclusive.[25] Aspects of death sentence existed under customary criminal justice system for certain categories of crimes like witchcraft, murder, adultery, profaning the gods and repeated thefts etc. In all these communities, various forms of executions were adopted ranging from hanging, beheading, stoning, drowning, burying alive or killing by the identical means used by the offenders. Executions continued under the customary criminal justice process until its abolition under the 1963 Constitution and subsequent constitutions. The Islamic Personal law that existed in the Northern communities of Nigeria provided for the practice of corporal punishment.

The advent of the British rule brought along the application of death penalty under the Criminal Code and Penal Code in the Southern and Northern Nigeria respectively[26]. The Colonial Government strictly limited the crimes, which carried the sentence of death. In the Colony and the Southern protectorate,[27] the received English Criminal Law and then the Criminal Code reduced capital crimes in theory to four, though in practice to one i.e. murder.

---

[25]See A.K. Ajisafe, (1996The Laws and Customs of the Yoruba People (Lagos) (K & K Bookshop,) S. Ojo, The Origin of the Yoruba (Part I) Their Tribes, Language, Native Law and Custom NP 1953, O. Onwubiko: African Thought Religion and Culture. Snaap Press, 1991. See also Akin Ibidapo-Obe; Death Penalty and African Tradition Lesson for Modernity, paper presented at the National Dialogue on Death Penalty in Nigeria, organized by the Federal Ministry of Justice on 17th October, 2003. T. O. Elias: The Nature of African Customary Law (Manchester University Press, 1954). J.B. Danquah, Akan Laws and Customs, (London Routledge 1928); T. O. Elias: British Colonial Law (Stevens, 1958).

[26]See Political Memoranda 1913 – 18, Memo. VIII. para. 34, until complete standardization was achieved in the mid. 1930's two methods – hanging and decapitation were common.

[27]Annual Colonial Report, Northern Nigerian, 1900-1911. See also O. I. Odumosu, The Nigerian Constitution: History and Development of Its Laws and Constitution, 1967, pp. 15-72. B. O. Nwabueze; Constitutional Law of Nigerian Republic, 1964.

In the North[28], Moslem and customary criminal laws co-existed with the Code until 1959 but the effect of the Northern administration's policy was to allow the execution of only those offenders whose crimes would have been capital under the Criminal Code. As at then, murder was the only crime in respect of which death sentences were ever carried out.[29] Though the Penal Code of 1959 extended the liability to suffer death to a wider range of offenders, executions remained restricted to those convicted of murder.

The contemporary Nigerian criminal laws under the two Codes show little similarities in their spheres of operation. Only three offences are capital in both Codes; murder[30], (culpable homicide)[31], treason, directing, controlling or presiding over an unlawful trial by ordeal which results in death, though the Penal Code extends liability to anyone who is present at such a trial. Another offence which may in some circumstances be capital under both section 302 of the Penal Code makes brigandage[32] punishable with death for all the participants if a culpable homicide punishable with death occurs during it and it is certainly possible to see circumstances in which this would create joint liability for murder under the Criminal Code.[33]

In 1959, Northern Nigeria adopted the death penalty for three other offences, exclusively on the basis of the Indian model for its new Penal Code. These offences are: giving false evidence in a trial which results in the conviction and execution of an innocent person, abetting the suicide of a minor, a mentally abnormal or drunken person; and attempting to commit culpable homicide by a person already serving a life sentence.[34] Indeed,

---

[28] *Tsofo v. Gubba* (1947) 12 WACA 141 for a brief history of British acquisition of Nigeria; see Kala Ezera, Constitutional Development in Nigeria, 1960 pp. 12-15.

[29] Bohannan; African Homicide and Suicide (1960) at p. 31. Where he commented, "Among the Tiv there was what one can only call amazed wonder than Europeans executed a man whose only fault was killing another". For a more detailed account by the Colonial system of government; see T. O. Elias, Nigeria: The Development of its Laws and Constitution (1967) pp. 1-72 (London Stevens & Sons).

[30] Section 319 C.C.;

[31] Section 221 Criminal Code.

[32] Defined by S. 297 as five or more persons conjointly committing or attempting to commit a robbery, or where the whole number of persons conjointly committing or attempting to commit a robbery and persons present and assisting amount to five or more. It is based on the Indian offence of dacoit.

[33] Section 8. See also *Alagba v. R.* (1950) 19 NLR 129.

[34] See sections 159(2), 227 and 229 Criminal Code compared with SS 118, 326 and 321, Criminal Code that carry life imprisonment as the maximum punishment.

Milner has rightly observed that there is nothing whatsoever to suggest that these additional capital offences have any special relevance to conditions in the Northern states; which he further described as being simply copied from the model used for the Code.[35]

From 1960-1965 few executions took place under the Balewa Administration. The Army struck on the night of 15 January 1966.[33b] The emergent Aguiyi Ironsi regime added a further crop of capital offences. Serious public order offences[36] and ammunition and possession of explosives were made capital as a purported deterrent to those who opposed the 1966 coup d'etat and then the Federal Military Government. Although a spokesman for the Ironsi regime threatened the death penalty for a wide range of behaviour,[37] but eventually only one limited type – the offences of planting, cultivating, importing or knowingly selling Indian hemp – became capital.[38]

The state of emergency, which existed from 1966 to 1970 during the Civil War era, yielded more capital crimes.[39] Following public disorders in most parts of the country in subsequent years produced extensive trends of theft and robbery cases, which were traced to the activities of former soldiers who had used their military weapons and uniforms to cause further violent crimes. The first reaction was the repressive robbery legislations in 1967.[40] The post Civil

---

[35]See Constitution (Suspension & Modification) Decree NO. 1 of 1966.

[33b]At a meeting between the Armed Forces and the remaining members of the civilian cabinet the next day, an attempt to constitute a valid cabinet failed. The upshot was a quiet coup d'etat by the Armed Forces, Legislative effect was given to this in the Constitution (Suspension and Modification) Decree No. 1 of 196.

[36]Suppression of Robbery Decree 1966, Public Security Decree 1967.

[37]Looting, arson, homosexuality, rape, embezzlements, bribery, corruption, sabotage and false alarm will be punishable by death . . . " Major Nzeogwu, Radio Nigeria, Kaduna, January 15, 1966 by Luttwak, *Coup d'etat,* 175 (1969). The Ironsi Regime suffered a counter-coup in its seventh month, July 1966 this brought in Gen. Yakubu Gowon. See also Adeniyi Olatunbosun, Coup d'etat in Nigeria Can Law Forestall It? accepted for publication in University of Calabar Law Journal.

[38]Indian Hemp Decree 1966.

[39]Suppression of Disorder Decree *op. cit.* The Law and Order (Maintenance) Edict 1967 (E.) had a similar provision and also made serious subversion criminal. It was repealed after the end of the Civil War in 1970.

[40]Suppression of Robbers Decree 1967 (Fed.). Robbery (Summary Trial and Punishment Edict 1967 (W); Penal Code Law (Amendment) Edicts 1968 (N.C); 1969 (N.E); 1969 (Kwara); 1970 (Kano).

War era witnessed unprecedented upsurge in the incidents of armed robbery operations leading to the extensive revamping of theft and robbery laws.[41]

---

[41]Robbery and Firearms (Special Provisions) Decree 1970.

[39a]In the United States, about 13,000 people have been legally executed since colonial times. By the 1930's up to 130 people were executed yearly. Lack of public support for capital punishment and various legal challenges reduced the execution rate to near zero by 1967. The U.S. Supreme Court banned the practice in 1972. In 1976, the Supreme Court authorized its resumption. Each state can now decide whether or not to have the death penalty. As of the 2002, Oct, only the District of Columbia and 12 states do not have the death penalty. The states which have abolished executions are: Alaska, District of Columbia, Hawaii, Iowa, Maine, Massachusetts, Michigan, Minnesota, North Dakota, Rhode Island, Vermont, West Virginia and Wisconsin. However, seven jurisdictions have the death penalty but have not performed any executions since 1976: Connecticut, Kansas, New Hampshire, New Jersey, New York, South Dakota and the U.S. Military. In almost all states, the death penalty is limited to cases involving aggravated murder. The U.S. Supreme Court ruled that whenever a sentencing jury has the ability to impose capital punishment, the jury must be informed in advance if the defendant would be eligible for parole. Almost all states have an automatic review of each conviction by their highest appellate court.

There are a number of federal offences that can lead to the death penalty. About 21 prisoners are housed in a death row at the federal Terre Haute, facility. One was executed in 2001. This was the first federal execution in 36 years. Texas holds the record for the largest number of executions since the death penalty was reinstated in 1976. Virginia executes a larger percentage of its population than any other state over 1 million in populations. About 30 to 60 prisoners are currently killed annually, most by lethal injection. About two out of three executions (65.6%) are conducted in the states: Texas, Virginia, Missourt, Florida and Oklahoma. Texas leads the other states in number of killings (256 killings; 34% of the national total). There were about 3,690 prisoners sentenced to death in 37 state death rows, and 31 being held by the U.S. government and military. About 1.5% are women. Recent laws have expanded the number of crimes for which capital punishment can be applied. Other legislation has reduced some of the appeal mechanisms available to those on death row.

Public approval of the death penalty is currently about 70%. About 90% of those executed could not afford a lawyer when they went to trial. They had to rely upon a court-appointed lawyer. The homicide rate in those states with the death penalty is almost double the rate in states without the death penalty. It is not known whether this is due to: People in high homicide states demanding the death penalty as a perceived deterrent, or use of the death penalty by the state cheapens the value of life, and causes a higher homicide rate. Essentially, all of the persons executed are male since 1976 when executions resumed, there have only been three women executed These were: 1984: Velma Barfield, put to death in North Carolina for poisoning her fiancé; 1988-Feb 3: Karla Faye Tucker, 38, in Texas. She was convicted of killing two people in 1983 with a pickax. She was the first woman since 1863 to be executed in that state. She had repented of her crimes, and been 'born again' during her 14 years of imprisonment. Her case received a great deal of publicity. Many individuals and groups pleaded for clemency. This included fundamentalist Teleminister Pat Robertson; Ron Carlson (brother of victim Deborah Thomton); Peggy Kurtz, (sister of victim Jerry Dean); Paul Ward, a juror who convicted Tucker; and even her arresting

Executions were relatively low in respect of murder convicts, while robbery convicts faced public firing squads. But the rate of robbery incidents became increasingly common and it appeared that the deterrent effect of the death penalty was inadequate to control its rampaging impact. Unlike Britain and even America,[39a] there are no comprehensive empirical records of sociological and legal studies of the death penalty in Nigeria.[42] Though there were few scattered records of executions in widely separate states of the country.

The Gowon Administration between 1966-1975 recorded many instances of executions, mostly for offences of murder. The peculiarity of Nigerian political history saw the emergence of counter-coups even among the Military administrations[39b.] Just like war, which has its own psychology and its own morals, military law has its own as well. At the inception of military rule in Nigeria, people freely shared death sentence for aborted coup like that of D.S. Dimka, Bisalla and others in 1976. There was nothing about the condemned persons to arouse tender feelings as people publicly demanded for executions by firing squad of those implicated by the Military Tribunals. However, the succeeding military regime of General Obasanjo added little or nothing to the death penalty statistics, except that few executions were carried out. It is worthy of note to state that relatively few executions took place during the civilian regime of Shehu Shagari between 1979-1983. However one execution that attracted public awareness was that of Nosiru Bello who was convicted

officer, J.C. Mosier. 1998-March 30: Jody Brentano aged 54, in Florida. She was called the 'Black Widow' for poisoning her husband, drowning her son and trying to blow up her fiancé. She was the first woman to be executed in Florida since 1848.

Canada does not have a death penalty. In most cases the most serious sentence for murder is life imprisonment with no possibility of parole for 25 years. However, if a person has a long history of violent crime, then he can be declared a 'dangerous offender'. With this classification they are given an indefinite sentence with little chance of ever being paroled.

Public opinion polls show that over 70% of the adult population would like to see a return of hanging for first-degree murder. The Roman Catholic Church and liberal churches wish to continue the present status; conservative protestant denominations are overwhelmingly in favour of a return to capital punishment. The homicide rate in Canada has been gradually dropping since executions were stopped. This phenomenon has been observed in many other countries that have abandoned the death penalty.

[42]See Annual Reports of the Nigeria Police Force 1985 – 1965 – 1974, 1974-1984, 1985-1994, and 1995-2004.

[39b]The Gowon administration lasted until 1975 when it was overthrown in another coup resulting in the Muhammed-Obasanjo regime, which handed over the administration of the country to the civil rule in 1979.

for armed robbery in 1981 and while his appeal was pending, he was hastily executed.[43]

The military regime of Major-General Mohammadu Buhari[44] re-introduced mandatory death penalty provision by the promulgation of Robbery and Firearms Decree No. 5 of 1984 with no right of appeal though clemency could be exercised by the military Governor of a state after consultation with the Advisory Council on the Prerogative of Mercy. The regime also passed the Special Tribunal Miscellaneous Offences Decree No. 20 of 1984. By Section 6(3) of the Decree, death sentences by firing squad for a number of offences including the following; arson, tampering with oil pipelines, tampering with electrical and telephone cables and dealing with cocaine or any similar drug. In April 1985 three persons, Bartholomew Owoh, Bernard Ogedengbe and Lawal Ojuolape were publicly executed by firing squad having been convicted for miscellaneous offences of drug trafficking.

The Babangida regime[45] that toppled the Buhari's administration promulgated the Special Tribunal (Miscellaneous Offences Amendment) Decree No. 22 of 1986, which allowed appeal to a special tribunal. Though, the Babangida administration did not abolish the death penalty for armed robbery offences but for miscellaneous offences that carried death sentence under the Buhari regime. Invariably, this regime set up a special appeal court, which commuted seven outstanding death sentences to life imprisonment. At the state level, the then Military Governor of Niger State Col. Mark in July 1986 introduced a new dimension on the mode of executing convicts of armed robbery when he directed that those convicted should be wounded slowly so that they could die installmentally and thereby the death could take a longer time. This approach attracted public outcry and condemnation following the execution by firing squad of two convicts in this manner. Some state officials reported that it was a traumatic experience with serious consequences.

---

[43](1986) 5 N.W.L.R. 826 at p. 860.

[44]In the night of December 31, 1983, the Armed Forces took over the administration of government from the civilian administration. It declared itself to be an offshoot of this last Military administration under Generals Muhammed and Obasanjo. The first decree enacted, the Constitution (Suspension and Modification) Decree No. 1 of 1984 suspended certain provisions of the 1979 Constitution.

[45]The Buhari regime was itself overthrown in a bloodless counter coup on August 27, 1985 by Major-General Ibrahim Babangida, who emerged as the new leader under the style and title of President, Commander-in-Chief of the Armed Forces.

The Babangida administration experienced aborted coups of Maman Vatsa and Gideon Orkah, despite the gravity of the offence people received the events with ambivalent reactions, nevertheless the culprits were executed.

Available records show that most of those sentenced to death were men, though there were few instances when women were executed. But in January 1988, it was reported that a woman convicted of armed robbery subsequently escaped hanging because the gallows at the prison in Jos, Plateau State was defective. The Tribunal that passed death sentence had directed that being a woman, she should not be executed in the public but be hanged in a prison out of public view. The point whether age is a factor in the application of death sentence came for consideration in the verdict of death sentence of 12 kid robbers by the Lagos state Armed Robbery Tribunal having been found guilty of violent robbery of a business woman in Ikorodu, Lagos State. There were large numbers of pleas to the Military Governor, Colonel Raji Rasaki, to commute the death sentences to imprisonments. While the kids were on the death row, one of them died. The kids remained in the prison awaiting execution when the civilian administration of Governor Michael Otedola that came in granted the kids clemency and they were eventually released and set-free. Another positive impact of public opinion on the application of death penalty was recorded in the trial of Major-General Zamani Lekwot (Rtd) and five others that were condemned to death by a special Tribunal headed by Justice Benedict Okadigbo having been found guilty of culpable homicide during the Zango-Kataf Communal disturbances. The passionate pleas of eminent Nigerians like General Olusegun Obasanjo and The Anglican Archbishop Adetiloye among others impressed on General Babangida and the Armed Forces Ruling Council to commute convictions to jail terms. The head of the Military junta eventually exercised prerogative of mercy in their favour when the convictions were commuted to terms of imprisonment.[46]

The successive military era of General Abacha had a similar issue for consideration in the trial of Ken Saro Wiwa and seven others charged for murder of four Ogoni Chieftains, they were convicted and sentenced to death but before they could exercise their right of appeal to the Provisional Ruling Council (PRC) they were executed. The incident caused uproar and condemnation nationwide and internationally leading to expulsion of Nigeria

[46]For a detailed account of Military Rule in Nigeria, see Abiola Ojo: Constitutional Law and Military Rule in Nigeria (1987, Evans Brothers (Nigeria Publishers) Ltd.) Eweluka, D.I.O., Constitutional Aspects of Military Take-over in Nigeria, 1967 2 Nig. L.J. No. 1 pp. 1-15.

from the Commonwealth of Nations. Under that regime another controversial aborted coup of Oladipo Diya brought about deep in people's hearts, the enormity of inflicting death penalty upon human beings thereby arousing public sentiments against application of military law which imposed the death penalty. There were many agitations nationwide against the execution of the alleged offenders based upon an inborn repugnance to taking human life coupled with the general public perception that the military regime of Abacha had lost its relevance and credibility in political administration through great atrocities, extra judicial killings, human rights violations, mis-management, ineptitude and large scale corruption.

The hard earned civil rule of the fourth republic, which ushered in General Obasanjo, has brought sanity to the manner of execution by reviewing the plights of condemned persons on the death row in the various designated prisons nationwide. Consequently, the death penalty imposed on many convicts was commuted to life imprisonment and terms of imprisonment. However, the death penalty is still retained under the existing criminal laws in the country.

The application of the death penalty has been expanded in its scope with the introduction of sharia law in some states of the federation. Several crimes ranging from apostasy, adultery, rape, and theft attract corporal punishments. The sharia legal system permits capital punishment by the authority of prescribed law both at municipal and international levels. The declaration of sharia as the state religion in some parts of the country and Nigeria being a member of Organisation of Islamic Countries further complicates the likely outcome of the on-going debate on the abolition of the death penalty.[47] The Islamic states advocate for the death penalty and corporal punishments in obedience to Islamic law and the structures of sharia. Thus without prejudice to what would be the final recommendation of the National Assembly on this matter, the abolition of capital punishment in the country, would create a mixed status, as Nigeria would then be classified as abolitionist *de jure* by the International Communities and *de facto* by the Islamic nations.[48]

---

[47]See Prof. Prof. Yahdudu's comments in The Guardian, Sunday August 24, 2003. S. Idris "Sharia and the 1999 Constitution: Is there a Cause for Alarm? In Law, Human Rights and the Administration of Justice in Nigeria, Essays in Honour of Justice Muhammed Lawal Uwais (M.T. Ladan, ed.) (Dept. of Public Law Ahmadu Bello University, Zaria) (2001) at p. 396.

[48]A.A. Adeyemi, The Death Penalty on Criminological Perspectives, Nigerian Situation, paper delivered at a National Conference on Death Penalty, 1990.

Thus, a strong case can be made in principle for and against capital punishment. The argument in favour is based on justice and the nature of a moral community, which requires that each person respect the life and liberty of others. Those who commit vicious crimes destroy the basis on which a moral community rests and forfeit their rights to citizenship and even to life itself. On the other hand, the argument against is based on love and the nature of an ideal community in which forgiveness and the hope for redemption are guiding principles. The protection of the innocent requires that criminals be isolated, perhaps permanently. Just punishment is appropriate, but love never gives up even on those who show no love.[49]

The Administration of the Death Sentence

The death sentence is mandatory for persons found guilty of murder and other capital crimes. Before accused persons are sentenced, they would be asked if they had anything to say why sentence of death should not be pronounced upon them. Occasionally, a woman convict would "plead her belly" i.e. that she was pregnant, and up to 1827 men could demand "benefit of clergy" which was a permissible excuse put up by the church to ensure that clerics could not be executed for most offences. However, if neither of these excuses were available, the judge would place the "black cap" – a 9-inch square of black silk, on his head and proceed to pronounce the death sentence. The judge would say:

> "That (full name of the convict) you are sentenced to be taken hence to the prison in which you were last confined and from there to a place of execution where you will be hanged by the neck until

[49]Kenneth Cauthen: Capital Punishment, Death Penalty, in Toward a New Modernism, (Lanham, M.D: University Press of America 1997) 151-165 and in The Ethics of Belief: A Bio-Historical Approach, 2 vols. (Lima, OH. CSS Publishing Co. 2001).

dead and thereafter your body buried within the precincts of the prison and may the Lord have mercy upon your soul".[50]

That was the practice up to 1947. But in 1948, The Royal Commission on Capital Punishment recommended that the sentence be modified slightly by the substitution of the words "suffer death by hanging" for "be hanged by the neck until dead". It should be noted that the sentence did not end public execution or the introduction of the long drop. By practice, execution took place two days after sentence, unless the third day was a Sunday in which case it would be held over until the Monday. From 1834, the practice changed, a minimum of three Sundays had to elapse before the sentence was carried out. From 1902 this was reinforced and the Home office suggested Tuesday as the day for execution. By the 20th century, prisoners spent longer on the condemned cell due to awaiting the hearing of an appeal, but many condemned chose not to appeal and their execution was frequently carried out within the three weeks.

Methods of Execution

Capital punishment is the infliction of death as a penalty for violating criminal law. Throughout history, people have been put to death for various forms of wrong doings. Methods of execution have included such practices as stoning, drowning, burning at the stake, and beheading. Today capital punishment is typically accomplished by lethal gas or injection, electrocution, hanging, or shooting. The death penalty is the most severe practice in the

[50]Judicial Hanging – Timeline of Capital Punishment in Britain. See Ss. 366-400 C.P.A. on provisions relating to sentences of Death, whipping and other corporal crimes. Furthermore, upon pronouncement of death sentence by a judge, a condemned person will be taken to the designated condemned prisons e.g. Abeokuta for Southwest of Nigeria and Kirikiri for Lagos, Nigeria. Such condemned persons are placed on death row. Thereafter death warrant will be issued from the proper execution authority appointing time and place for the execution of the sentence of death upon s convict judicially condemned to suffer that penalty. Then the deathsman who is the executioner, hangman or person that executes capital punishment will then carry out the executions. In Saxon law, a fine for illegal hanging of a thief or for allowing him to escape is called hangwite. However, an executioner has immunity from such fine. An executioner is authorized to execute a condemned criminal and such killing is not unlawful provided it is carried out in the manner prescribed by law.

modern world. In the majority of countries, contemporary methods of punishment, such as imprisonment of fines, no longer involve the infliction of physical pain. Although imprisonment and fines are universally recognized as necessary to the control of crime, the nations of the world are split on the issue of capital punishment. About 80 nations have abolished the death penalty and an almost equal number of nations retain it. Crime definitely cannot go unpunished; killing a prisoner is just going too far. If we kill a criminal for killing someone it makes us so bad as the criminal. People who support the capital punishment will argue that it is cheaper, it gets the justice "everyone" wants, and that it deters potential murders, but this is not true.

Hanging

Hanging was the principal form of execution from Anglo-Saxon times until the death penalty was abolished in 1964 in England.[51] This method is being used in Nigeria and a host of other countries up till today.

The Gallows

The gallows up to the beginning of the 20th century comprised of a tree with prisoner being either handed up manually by the hangman or turned off from a ladder or the tail of a cart. There are still some hanging trees in existence today. The trees with a beam between them formed the gallows.[52]

By 1571 the famous "Triple Tree" was set up at Tyburnn to replace previous smaller structures and was at least once, used for the hanging of twenty-four

---

[51]Hanging as a form of capital punishment means suspension by well until dead. Hanged drawn and quartered. It is methods of executing criminals have been introduced in England 1241 against traitors. The traitor was carried on a sled or hurdle to the gallows, (formerly dragged there tied to the tail of a horse) hanged till half-dead and then cut down, his entrails, cut out and burnt, his head cut off and his body to be divided into quarters, with which his head were hung in some public place. In practice, the executioner usually cut out the heart and held it up to view.
[52]See the account of Mary Blandy's execution at Oxford on April the 6th 1752, when she altered the famous words "for the sake of decency, gentlemen, don't hang me high". She had been persuaded to poison her father by her lover, captain Cranston, who presumably hoped to get her inheritance.

prisoners simultaneously.[53] Tyburnn gallows remained in use until the end of 1759 and consisted of three tall (approximately 12 feet high) uprights joined at the top with beams in a triangular form to provide a triple gallows under which three carts could be backed at a time. The structure was removed as it had become a cause of traffic congestion and was replaced by a portable gallows, which had a raised stage under the beam, which collapsed giving the prisoners a small amount of drop.[54]

The design of the new gallows was on wheels and was brought out especially for each hanging by a team of horses. It had two parallel beams from which a maximum of a dozen criminals could be hanged at once.[55] This mechanism was called the "New Drop".[56] Towards the middle of 1820's, hanging became slightly less frequent; the double beam gallows were replaced with a single beam pattern, which could still accommodate three prisoners side by side.[57] In some parts of Britain, like Dorchester, Bristol and Nottingham, gallows had far more steps up to the platform. In other prisons a balcony type gallows as in York and Lancaster where the prisoner was; brought directly onto the platform through the first floor French windows. Some countries like Gloucester and Burham used two uprights with a cross beam and with the single or double trap doors set over a brick lined pit in the yard. The trap doors were released either from underneath by with-drawing bolts or latterly from the platform by pulling a lever.

After the passing of the capital punishment within Prisons Act of 1868, all executions had to take place within the walls of country's prisons. The existing gallows was generally used, set up in the prison yard rather than in public.

---

[53]It was reported that on the 23rd June 1649, twenty-three men and one woman were executed for burglary and robbery having been conveyed there in eight carts. Another mass execution took place on March 18th, 1740 when the famous pickpocket and thief, Jenny Diver, was hanged before a huge crowd, together with 20 other criminals.

54Executions were transferred to Neugabe Prison and the first executions took place on the 9th December, 1783, when 9 men and a woman were hanged simultaneously by Edward Dennis and William Brunskil for a variety of offences. See also Kenneth Wolpin, "Capital Punishment and Homicide in England: A Summary of Results, in American Economic Review, 1978, May.

[55]The prisoners stood on a platform,10 feet long by 8 feet wide, released by moving a lever or 'pin' acting on a draw bar under the drop. They now fell some 12-18 inches, roughly to knee level.

[56]It claimed 96 convicts between February and December 1785, with 20 men being hanged on the 2nd February of that year. All of the prisoners were aged under 30 and *not one* was convicted of murder.

[57]The platform was usually about 5 feet high and shielded by either wooden boards or black cloth drapes to conceal the legs and lower body of the usually struggling prisoner.

The prisons that regularly carried out hangings mostly had execution sheds built in one of their exercise yards.[58] Until 1884 each country was responsible for providing the gallows for carrying out the death sentence passed in that country, and therefore all sorts of designs were in use. For example smaller prisoners with fewer executions usually erected their gallows in the open air in one of the yards. In 1885 the Home office commissioned Lieutenant Colonel Alton Beamish to design a standard gallows for use throughout Britain.[59] This was regarded as a great improvement over some of the designs then in use and considerably speeded up the process. This pattern remained in use in most prisons until after the Second World War. From the gallows in the execution shed at Wandsworth Prison in 1900, which happened to be one of the very few to have been actually photographed, a lever, open trap and one of the boards laid across the drop for the warders to stand on whilst holding the prisoner. As part of its design, some of these gallows had the Royal coat of Arms displayed on the beam, which in the thoughtful way of the Home office must have been a great comfort to the condemned!

The 20th century recorded the replacement of the Victorian pattern single beam by two beams of about '8' x '3' section Oak, running parallel to each other about 2 inches apart, there being no uprights. The trap doors were reduced in length as multiple hangings were no longer favoured and normally consisted of two leaves each of 4-8 feet in length and 2 feet wide. The one

---

[58]e.g. Newgate, Wandsworth, Durham, Armley, Kirkdale, (Liverpool) and Strange ways in Manchester. The execution sheds typically had the trap doors installed over a 12 feet deep brick lined pit, as drops of up to 10 feet were not unusual, consisting of two stout uprights with a cross beam. Normally only one iron band was fitted to the cross beam in the center and from it 6 links of circular chain dangled, to which the rope was attached. Additional iron bands could be added for multiple hangings. On each of the uprights was a pulley for raising the trap doors which were operated by a lever on the platform and fell against three bales of cotton in an attempt to muffle the noise. All the woodwork was painted a dull buff colour. See also the History of Executions at Newgate Prison. See also the progress of execution by hanging in Britain, the list of cases of those executed and the prisons in which their hangings took place in Chronological Order from 1741 to 1955. See also the History of executions at Newgate Prison. The progress of execution by hanging in Britain, the list of cases of those executed and the prisons in which their hangings took place in chronological order from 1741 to 1955. In Timeline of Capital Punishment in Britain http/www.

[59]This consisted of two uprights with a cross beam in 8 inch section oak. The beam was long enough to execute three prisoners side by side and was set over a 12 foot long by 4 foot wide two leaf trap set level with the surrounding floor. The trap doors were made from three inch thick oak and were released by a metal lever set into the floor of the execution chamber.

nearest the lever being conventionally hinged while the other had extended hinges that run under the first leaf and are held on top of an iron drawbar which has three slots.

In the early 1900's there was a move to reduce the number of hanging prisons and in those where executions were to continue, purpose built condemned suites were constructed within the prison itself, having a condemned cell(s) and an execution room with a cell below for the drop and often an autopsy room. This pattern continued as the standard form with minor improvements until the abolition.[60] In other jurisdictions more conventional gallows were built, having either a single upright with a projecting beam cross braced to it or two uprights and a cross beam where more than one person could be hanged at a time. Both types still required the use of a ladder or a cart to get the criminal suspended. In many places, these gallows were not permanent and were dismantled after each execution. In other places the gallows was erected near to the scene of the crime so that the local inhabitants could see the outcome.

The Noose

A simple noose consisting of a loop worked into one end of the rope with the other end passed through it. It was later improved on by passing the free end of the rope through a brass eyelet instead of just a loop of rope, which made it more free running. The execution rope was made from a 13 foot length of ¾" diameter Italian silk hemp rope, bind with chamois leather to avoid marking the skin. It was stretching before use, by dropping a sandbag of approximately the same weight as the prisoner through the trap and leaving it suspended overnight. The purpose was to reduce any tendency of the rope to stretch during the actual hanging, which would reduce the force applied to the prisoner's neck. The use of hemp was preferred material as it is both soft and strong with a smooth surface. The condemned eyelet was positioned under the angle of the jaw in order to allow the head to be thrown backwards

[60]The last working gallows was at Wandsworth prison and was last used on the 8th of September, 1961 before it was eventually dismantled on July 31st, 1992 at the Prison Service Museum in Rugby. The rope is suspended from a chain, attached to an adjustment mechanism bolted to the beams above the ceiling. This device was accessed from the room above where the drop could be set in safety, without the need for step ladders.

by the rope so that the force was transmitted into the neck vertebrae rather than being thrown forward and the force taken on the throat, which tended to cause strangulation. It was crucial that the noose was put on the right way round so that it rotated in the correct direction with the eyelet ending up under the jaw.

The Hood

In the practice of execution it has been customary to "hood" the prisoner with a white hood. For over 300 years, the "hood" was an ordinary nightcap rather than a purpose made execution hood and it was generally white and by practice it presumably became the traditional colour as nobody is certainly sure why white was the chosen colour. When the prisoner had finished praying, he would be allowed to see the gallows, the trap, the executioner and officials and the noose dangling before them, the hangman simply pulled it down over their face. Typically in most cases women might chose a bonnet with a veil instead and in other cases the prisoner possessed or chose neither. Thus it would seem that the nightcap was optional and provided for the prisoner to hide their face from the crowd. The idea of hooding immediately prior to the noose became normal practice rather than hooding them earlier and assisting to lead them to the gallows, as they would be more frightened by not knowing what was happening. By 1850 a white cotton hood was provided by the authorities, which was similar to a small pillowcase and was applied as part of the execution process.

Pinioning

The prisoner's hands were pinioned in front of them until 1892. Thereafter, the prisoner's wrists were tied with a cord and often a second cord passed round the body and arms at the elbows. This was done to allow them to pray on the gallows, however this made it easier for them to resist and fight at the end so pinioning the wrists at the sides to a leather body belt became conventional until abolition. This significantly reduced the time taken in the pinioning operation. With the advent of the long drop the prisoner's legs were usually pinioned with a leather strap around the ankles to prevent them getting their feet onto the sides of the trap when the doors fell. The legs of female prisoners were tied to prevent their skirts billowing up and exposing their underwear. As women's skirt got shorter in the 20th century an extra strap could be placed round the lower thighs, to prevent their skirt rising up as they dropped. Where a prisoner was in a state of collapse at the end they were sometimes tied to the chair sent through the trap.

The Condemned Cell

It comprised two standard cells knocked into one and had fairly minimal facilities. Later in the 20th century condemned cell block consisted of the prisoner's living quarters, visitor's area and proximity to the gallows. The living area was normally two or three standard cells knocked into one and then usually no more than 15 feet from the gallows itself. The hard robe concealed the door to the execution chamber and was pushed out of the way by a warder at the last moment. Not all prisons had the condemned cell in such close proximity to the gallows; some required the prisoner to walk some distance down a corridor to it. In others, the cell was on the first floor to obviate the need for the pinioned prisoner to climb steps to the gallows. The average time a prisoner would have spent here was two to three weeks and they would have been watched round the clock by teams of two or three wards.

Places of Execution

Before 1800 almost anywhere could be used as a place of execution and it was often the practice of the court to order that the hanging be carried out as near as possible to where the crime was committed, apparently so that "justice could be seen to be done" especially by the relations and neighbours of the victims of the crime as well as by other people as there were very little mode of effective publicity in those days like the present electronic and print media. But most executions were carried out in recognized places, like on markets days in the country towns, so as to draw the biggest audience. Also, prisoners were hanged at Execution Dock in warping (on the north bank of the river Thanes) their bodies were left on the shoreline gallows until three tides had washed over them. What the use of this was is unclear – perhaps the water cleansed their souls. In London, Tyburn and New gate are the most well known, execution sites, although other places within and outside London were used. The first recorded place of execution was Tyburn in 1196.

Electric Chair

The late 1800's saw the coalescence of two growing trends: the dawning market for electricity and the growing public apprehension that executions could unduly torture and maim those condemned for capital crimes. The electric chair had a bizarre origin, mainly from a New York dentist, Alfred Southwick. He had the unfortunate opportunity to witness the death of an elderly hobo in 1888, when the indigent man accidentally stumbled upon an electrical generator Southwick was fascinated by the apparent swiftness and painlessness of the man's death and thereby suggested to a New York state legislator that electricity might alleviate the traumatic results from judicial hangings.[61] A metal skull cap-shaped electrode is attached to the scalp and fore head over a spring moistened with saline. An additional electrode was attached to a portion of the prisoner's leg that has been shaved to reduce resistance to electricity. The prisoner was then blind folded. After the execution team withdrew to the observation room, the warder signalled the executioner, who pulled a handle to connect the power supply. The first jolt of 1700 volts lasted for five seconds, followed by 1000 volts for seven seconds, then a 208 – volt close for almost two full minutes. The doctors wait a few seconds for the body to cool down and then would check to see if the condemned man's heart was still beating – if it was another jolt would be applied. This process continued until the prisoner was dead. On more than one occasion, the executioner had to apply more than one dosage of electricity to ensure that the condemned man had passed away.

---

[61]Consequently the New York government set up a special commission to investigate how electricity might be used as an alternative to hanging. On August 6, 1890 Kemmler became the first person ever to be executed via electrocution. After the execution of William Kemmler, many states quickly adopted electrocution as a primary means of execution. The first public electrocution was that of Ruth Syder in New York in 1928, when a Journalist apparently stuck a small camera within the death chamber. Electrocution as a means of execution reached a climax stage in 1949, when twenty six of the then forty eight states in America had explicit Statutes adopting the method though no state has formally adopted electrocution as its preferred means of execution. Each prisoner was shaved and strapped to a chair with belts that cross his chest, groin legs and arms.

Lethal Injection

In 1977, Oklahoma became the first state to adopt lethal injection as a preferred means of execution. Since that time, many states have changed methods or added an alternative method of execution – lethal injection. Most capital punishment states, in an effort to move away from the media frenzy over botched electrocutions adopted lethal injection as the sole means of execution for capital crimes.[62]

Gas Chamber

The advent of the gas chamber has waned greatly in recent years, the state support for electrocution in US five states have adopted this method though retained lethal injection as an alternative method. This method drops cyanide, into acid producing hydrogen cyanide, a deadly gas and takes many minutes of agony before a person dies.

Guillotine

A famous French invention, named after the inventor, which was in use during the French Revolution. This method severed the neck and death came quickly.

Stoning

By this practice the prisoner is often buried up to his neck and pelted with rock until he eventually dies. The types of rocks chosen are meant to cause significant injury to the victim but are not so large for a single rock to kill the prisoner. This

[62]For example, Florida, in the face of a likely appeal to the United States Supreme Court over the unreliability of its electric chain chose instead to scrap electrocution in form of lethal injection. Reports had it that most condemned methods of condemned prisoners elect lethal injection over other methods of execution. As at year 2000, 36 states authorized lethal injection in America. By this method, lethal drugs are injected into the prisoner while he lays strapped down to a table and the injection is administered into this body, the prisoners fades quickly into unconsciousness. If the dosage of drugs is too low, the person may linger for many minutes experiencing paralysis. The breakdown of preferred methods is starkly weighted toward lethal injection.

method is used in Rome and in Nigeria, under the Sharia law as penalty for murder, adultery and other classified capital crimes. Also, under the customary law, witches that make confessions publicly were stoned to death. Although customary criminal law has been abolished, this practice of stoning still thrives on in some communities in Nigeria where the sharia law has been adopted.

Firing Squad

The prisoner is bound and tied with strong ropes to the stationed drums and shot by multiple marksmen from a close range. Death comes quickly by this method. In the US, only the state of Utah used this method. Though this method is not popular in America, four convicted prisoners on the death row chose death by firing squad recently. This method that has been abandoned in favour of lethal injection in the US is in use in Nigeria and applied to prisoners convicted of armed robbery.

Other Methods

In addition to the various modes already discussed above, there are other methods being practised in many jurisdictions but which are not known or publicised. For example, beheading is practised in some Arabian countries like Saudi-Arabia. Thus, the list of methods of executions are expansive, and over the years as society evolved, various punishments have been prescribed for the breach of societal law of all forms of punishment proscribed by man for the breach of societal law, the highest magnitude of such punishments is capital punishment; it is said to have a deep root in the evolution of mankind in view of its genesis as traced above. Thus its existence is rooted in law and as such cannot be attacked as illegal or unlawful rather it is the continual use of death penalty in a form of punishment for crimes that has generated a repeated and continuous debate. The legal and other related issues will be evaluated in this work.

Chinese Method

Apart from the common modes of execution highlighted above, a new method has evolved in China. With the on-going campaign on crime control launched in 2001 tagged "Strike hard" has led to a rise in executions. From the 2001/2002 Amnesty International Report, more than 5,900 death sentences have been implemented worldwide out of which more than 3,500 executions were carried out in China. The China provincial authorities have introduced "mobile execution vans" to replace the conventional method of execution by firing squad. According to officials in Yunnan Province, this new method required only four people to carry out the execution in the mobile vans viz: the executioner, one member of the Court, one official from the protectorate and the forensic doctor. The newspaper Beijing Today reported that the use of the vans was approved by the legal authorities in Yunnan province on 6 March, 2003 and the President of the Yunnan Provincial High Court praised the new system in this way:

> The use of lethal injection shows that China's death penalty system is becoming more civilized and humane.[63]

However, members of China's legal community have voiced their concerns that it will only lead to an increase in the use of the death penalty. The relevance or otherwise of death sentence will be further examined along relevant international treaties on human rights with specific reference to right to life and right to dignity of person and Conventions outlawing the practice of the death penalty.

---

[63] *Ibid.*

Table of Methods of Execution Worldwide[*]
(Countries in italics are abolitionist de facto, underlined countries are abolitionist for ordinary crimes only).

Countries	Methods adopted
Afghanistan	Firing squad, hanging, stoning
Albania	Firing squad, hanging
Algeria	Firing squad
Antigua and Barbuda	Hanging
Armenia	Firing squad
Bahamas	Hanging
Bahrain	Firing squad
Bangladesh	Firing squad, hanging
Barbados	Hanging
Belarus	Firing squad
Belize	Hanging
Benin	Firing squad
Bermuda	Hanging
Bolivia	Firing squad
Bosnia-Herzegovina	Firing squad
Botswana	Hanging
Brunei Darussalam	Hanging
Burkina Faso	Firing squad
Burundi	Firing squad, hanging
Cameroon	Firing squad, hanging
Central African Republic	Firing squad
Chad	Firing squad
Chile	Firing squad
China (People's Republic)	Firing squad, lethal injection
Comoros	Firing squad
Congo (Democratic Republic)	Firing squad, hanging
Congo (Republic)	Firing squad, beheading
Cote d'Ivoire	Firing squad
Cuba	Firing squad
Dominica	Hanging
Djibouti	Firing squad
Egypt	Hanging, firing squad
El Salvador	Firing squad
Equatorial Guinea	Firing squad, hanging
Eritrea	
Ethiopia	Firing squad
Gabon	Firing squad
Ghana	Firing squad
Grenada	Hanging

Countries	Methods adopted
Guatemala	Lethal injection
Guinea	Firing squad
Guyana	Hanging
India	Hanging
Indonesia	Firing squad
Iran	Firing squad, hanging, stoning
Iraq	Firing squad, hanging
Israel	Hanging
Jamaica	Hanging
Japan	Hanging
Jordan	Firing squad, hanging
Kazakhstan	Firing squad
Kenya	Hanging
Korea (North/Democratic People's Republic)	Firing squad, hanging
Korea (South/Republic)	Hanging
Kuwait	Hanging, firing squad
Kyrgyzstan	Firing squad
Laos	
Latvia	Firing squad
Lebanon	Firing squad, hanging
Lesotho	Hanging
Liberia	Firing squad, hanging
Libya	Firing squad, hanging
Madagascar	Firing squad
Malawi	Hanging
Malaysia	Hanging
Mali	Firing squad
Mauritania	Firing squad
Mongolia	Firing squad
Mongolia	Firing squad
Morocco	Firing squad
Myanmar	Hanging
Niger	Firing squad
Nigeria	Firing squad, hanging
Oman	
Pakistan	Hanging, stoning
Palestinian Authority	Firing squad, hanging
Papua New Guinea	Hanging
Philippines	Lethal injection
Qatar	Hanging, firing squad
Russian Federation	Firing squad
Rwanda	Firing squad

Countries	Methods adopted
St. Christopher and Nevis	Hanging
St. Lucia	Hanging
St. Vincent and The Grenadines	Hanging
Saudi Arabia	Beheading, stoning
Senegal	Firing squad
Sierra Leone	Firing squad, hanging
Singapore	Hanging
Somalia	Firing squad
Sri Lanka	Hanging
Sudan	Hanging, stoning, crucifixion, firing squad
Suriname	Firing squad
Swaziland	Hanging
Syria	Hanging, firing squad
Taiwan (Republic of China)	Firing squad, lethal injection
Tajikistan	Firing squad
Tanzania	Hanging
Thailand	Firing squad
Togo	Firing squad
Tonga	Hanging
Trinidad and Tobago	Hanging
Tunisia	Hanging, Firing squad
Turkey	Hanging
Turkmenistan	Firing squad
Uganda	Firing squad, hanging
Ukraine	Firing squad
United Arab Emirates	Firing squad, stoning, beheading
United States of America	Lethal injection, electrocution, Lethal gas, hanging, firing squad
Uzbekistan	Firing squad
Vietnam	Firing squad
Western Samoa	
Yemen	Firing squad
Yugoslavia (Federal Republic)	Firing squad
Zambia	Hanging
Zimbabwe	Hanging

Method of Execution	Practiced in . . .
Firing squad	73 countries (sole method in 45 countries)
Hanging	58 countries (sole method in 33 countries)
Stoning	6 countries
Lethal injection	5 countries (sole method in 1 country)
Beheading	3 countries
Electrocution	1 country
Lethal gas	1 country

Platform for Death Penalty

It is important to evaluate death penalty by considering the underlying principle of retributive punishment for the offenders in accordance with the concept of "an eye for an eye and a tooth for a tooth". The prevailing trends demand for assessment of the application and administration of death sentence through the mode of execution to determine whether manner runs contrary to human dignity or amounts to torture, inhuman or degrading treatment which have been prohibited by the Nigerian Constitution. This is imperative in order to evaluate the perception of the public and appraise the constitutionality of the practice with a view to having a balanced position or determine the proprietary of retaining or abolishing the death penalty in Nigeria. The jurisprudential analyses of arguments for and against the practice of death penalty shall be undertaken in determining the extent of its deterrence potentials.

Historical Sketch of Debate on Death Penalty

Before now, any talk about the need to expunge the death penalty provisions from our statutes was isolated and conserved to private debate. Unlike Britain, that has considered the abolition of capital punishment as far back as 1868, Nigeria has very little about it. Perhaps, the only Nigerian discussion first recorded was that of Aguda's paper, which was almost exclusively in terms of the experience of the rest of the world and not that of Nigeria *per se*[64]. Everywhere, the debate whether to abolish or retain capital punishment is held. It is controversial, divisive and acrimonious. Just like the issue of

[64]A paper delivered at NBA Ibadan branch on Death Penalty in 1964.

abortion, capital punishment is an emotive issue. It is man's nature; life is not just mankind's most precious gift, which can never be replaced once taken. No doubt, this kind of irrevocable lurks in every heart. The vengeful urge may be natural to man and capital punishment is only the collective expression of it. Still, everyone seems to recognize that there is something inherent if awkward about revenge especially when it comes to human life.

The genesis of public debate on capital punishment in Nigeria began unknowingly when the Federal government made a last minute diplomatic effort to save the lives of a Nigerian, Nathaniel Jackson Ikpato Notibo and three Ghanaians sentenced to death in Libya. They were tried and found guilty for the murder of a Libyan, Mohammed Mustapha in Ghat in 1995. They were to be executed on Friday 28, 2002 by the Libyan authorities but the Nigeria's plea that the death sentence passed on them be commuted to prison terms yielded positive response, when the Libyan government acceded to this plea. Unknown to the Federal government, it has provoked a debate among its citizens over the retention or abolition of capital sentence in the country. On the 21st January, 2003 in Abuja, Federal Capital Territory under the auspices of the National Human rights Commission, Legal Resources Consortium, Human Rights Law Service and Vanguard, Lawyers, Journalists and sociologists met to discuss on the need to abolish capital punishment in Nigeria. Thus we have not only begun a public debate on capital punishment but that President Obasanjo has gone even further to set up a committee to examine and advise him on the issue. This step shows that Nigeria finally inclining into the social mainstream of the 21st century. The government stance is viewed as pondering to the degenerate Liberalism of Europe and America where anything goes, including gay bishops. This national assignment has begun to generate suspicions and fears on its likely outcome going by the then President Obasanjo's pledge to a delegation of the European Union of his determination to seek for the abolition o capital punishment in Nigeria. It is difficult to convince the public that the government will not unduly influence the debate to tilt towards the promise already made to the European Union to abolish death penalty, a theme so clear to Europe's heart. That was one of the conditionality, which Turkey had to meet in order to qualify for European Union membership.

The issue of capital crimes is enormous; we must not take chances with our well-being, safety and security of our lives. The incidents of violent crimes are increasing on daily basis in Nigeria. We have had series of political assassinations, politically motivated murders, armed robberies resulting in brutal and cruel deaths, ritual killings, ethnic cleansing deaths, communal killings and religious murders unresolved, charade arrangement and burgled trials. Many times, governments have played politics with celebrated murders thereby making the public feel indignant and lose confidence in the judiciary. Improper handling of public debate on the death penalty has the potential of even bringing down political leaders and their governments. Even great religions seem to endorse the vengeful instinct in affirming the principle of an eye for an eye and a tooth for a tooth.

If the President and the National Assembly with the support of certain Human Rights group are inclined to expunge the death penalty provisions from our statute books, then constitutional conformity is imperative. The Constitution of the Federal Republic of Nigeria, 1999 does unequivocally recognize capital punishment. In this regard, Section 33(1) provides:

> 'Every person has the right to life, and no one shall be deprived intentionally of his life, save in execution of a sentence of a court in respect of a criminal offence of which he has been found guilty in Nigeria.'

Thus any law that runs contrary to the provision of the Constitution is null and void and of no effect whatsoever. The first step towards abolishing capital punishment is to amend this constitutional provision but first subjecting the matter to a referendum for the public to approve or disapprove it. If this is done, conflict of laws situation will however arise from the position that is invariably arrived at the end of the day, in view of the fact that the application of Shariah law in some states of the Federation would retain death penalty in their respective jurisdictions.

Emerging jurisprudential issues

The subject offers stimulating issues of jurisprudence and legal theory for discussion among the stakeholders in the administration of criminal justice system. The general public perception of the concept of law and justice is synonymous with crime and criminal process. The significance of the subject affects the generality of the populace encompassing divergent opinions of lawyers, legal scholars, the politicians, government officials, organized labour, the private sectors, the sociologists, the academia, the police, and the officials of the prison, religious leaders and the citizenry.

The imperative of appraising the validity or constitutionality of death penalty in Nigeria in view of the right to life guaranteed by the constitution and the provision of Section 319 Criminal Code, which prescribes death sentence for murder case. There will be the need to consider the proprietary of retaining or abolishing the death penalty as dignifying punishment for capital crimes. The contending issues of will bring to focus an examination of the fundamental question as to whether "Right to life" as provided under S. 33(1) 1999 Constitution has in any way outlawed the death penalty. To consider whether death penalty *per se* amounts to torture, inhuman and degrading treatment under Section 34(1)(a) of the 1999 Constitution and, therefore intrinsically unconstitutional and whether or not this constitutes a majority or minority view in Nigeria *vis-à-vis* the pattern and trends of decided cases in foreign jurisdictions. That whether the condemned person's confinement on the death row for a prolonged length of time amounts to cruel, inhuman and degrading treatment and as such can be said to be contrary to Section 31(1) as of the 1979 Constitution and S. 34(1) of the 1999 Constitution thereby warranting the questioning of the validity of the punishment and substituting the same with life imprisonment.

In the same vein whether the carrying out of the death sentence by hanging or otherwise is barbaric and whether the undue delay in the execution of the death sentence coupled with the deplorable conditions under which the prisoners awaiting execution were confined and the mode or manner of execution amounts to inhuman and degrading treatment. In addition whether in cases involving death row phenomenon it will be just for the court having found the situations to be disheartening and deplorable to declare the death penalty as a form of punishment that is unconstitutional, null and void in the circumstances. It will also not out of place to determine whether it is persuasive for the Nigerian Courts to adopt the prevailing movements in many foreign countries in enforcing peoples' rights that death penalty and practice of death-row phenomenon infringe on human rights of prisoners in view of notable decisions from Trinidad and Tobago, Jamaica, South Africa, Zimbabwe, America and Canada to mention a few.

Bearing in mind that the prevalence of death-row phenomenon in virtually all jurisdictions where death penalty exists such as America, Britain and Nigeria supports the cardinal principle of criminal justice that capital offences being heinous crimes, the punishment highest known to law must be cautiously implemented, as the post-conviction periods have served and continue to serve as an important mechanism in correcting constitutional errors that occur during the trial and appeal processes.

In the alternative whether such condemned persons cannot complain of undue delay in the execution of the death sentence to warrant its commutation to life imprisonments, as the right of appeal is a constitutional right open to condemned persons. In the final analysis the aggregate of divergent public opinions on the acceptability or rejection of death penalty as suitable punishment for capital crimes in modern times.

Snapshots of the study on Death Penalty

Nigerians have been engaged in the debate over the morality and effectiveness of the death penalty, as well as issues of evaluating its application. Most executions in this country are conducted without public awareness, except very few members of the society like the close relations of the victim who want to be assured that "justice" has been done, relatives of the convicts who may be monitoring the plight of the condemned and the public hangman, officials of the prison where the convict is kept and probably selected media men. Crime records have not been constant in Nigerian history. Official statistics on capital crimes are not published regularly in Nigeria unlike Britain and America. However the Nigerian Police keep statistical data on the number of crimes committed, the type of crimes, certain characteristics such as age and sex of convicted offenders. The figures of criminals sentenced to death are scattered in various court registries, ministries of justice at state levels all over the country, though these records are not accurate and reliable. More often, the media report many of these convictions under headlines especially for those sensational/politically motivated murder cases and inside of newspapers for those less prominent murder cases.

For purpose of legal scholarship, we cannot rely completely on media reports because of their peculiarities, while official reports in the gazettes do not necessarily reflect the totality of capital crimes that have taken place in the country at a particular period. The fact that crimes that have been officially recorded and those that were committed are two different issues; this is because before a crime can be recorded several factors must be present and these have serious implications as to whether the incident will appear in an official statistics or not. For example, the victim, the police or someone else must be aware that a crime has happened, if the police have not discovered it, someone must report it and the police must accept that the law has been violated.[32a]

[32a]Olatunbosun, A; Public Attitudes Towards Reporting Crimes in Nigeria in Nigerian Law and Practice Journal Vol. 2, No. 2 1998 (Council of Legal Education, NLS).

2

RECENT DEVELOPMENT ON DEATH PENALTY

Heated public debate centers on questions of deterrence, public safety, sentencing equity and the execution of innocents, among others but to the generality of the citizens the arguments opposing the death penalty are not all convincing. It is usually called, simply, the "chair" and at one time, was in constant use at New York's legendary sing Prison. But, no executions have occurred in New York since 1963, a time when support for capital punishment was eroding across the country. The state's capital punishment statute as declared unconstitutional in 1977. In this year, and in each of the following 17 years, democratic governors vetoed legislation to restore the death penalty. Yet in 1994, with the coming of republican Governor George Pataki, an agreement was quickly reached with legislative leaders on a law to revive the death penalty for several categories of murder, which included about ten types of homicides[65]. The signing of the law also replaced electrocution with lethal injection. New York's stance on capital punishment reflects an ongoing, nationwide trend. More than thirty others states have reinstated the death penalty since the early 1970's, with many others still considering the matter. Opinion surveys show strong support for the death penalty in all states of the country and among virtually all population groups. A Gallup Poll taken in 1994 reported that eighty percent of the population favoured the death sentence for persons convicted of murder. About forty percent advocating the death penalty for homicide said that they wanted revenge, "an eye for an eye." Roughly thirteen percent of the advocates cited its alleged deterrent effect. Yet, law enforcement officials throughout the country

---

[65]See Hugo Arlam Bedau, ed., "The Death Penalty in America, Oxford University Press, 1982. Walter F. Berns, for Capital Punishment: Crime and the Morality of the Death Penalty, New York, Basic Books, 1979.

do not consider the death penalty as an effective deterrent. In a national poll in 1995 of 386 police chiefs and sheriffs, the death penalty was ranked as the least cost-effective way of reducing violent crime. For convicted murderers who have been on death row for years, congress and the Supreme Court could turn the death penalty into a reality. A bill approved by the house in early February of 1995 would curb the ability of inmates to file habeas corpus petitions, in which they seek federal review of their convictions in state courts on grounds that their constitutional rights have been violated. As the courts, lawmakers and the public continue the capital punishment debate; one of the key questions being asked is whether habeas corpus reform will speed the pace of executions. Supporters of the House-passed bill limiting habeas corpus appeals by prisoners say the measure would save taxpayers money. Paul Kamenar, executive legal director of the Washington Legal Foundation, a pro-death-penalty group says the habeas corpus bill "will go a long way toward eliminating inordinate delays in carrying out the death penalty. On the other hand, Leigh Dingerson, Executive Director of the National Coalition to Abolish the Death Penalty, questions whether limiting habeas corpus appeals will have much impact[66]. "It is hard to tell what the effect will be because every case going through the appeals process is different. It is not as if there are 2800 uniform cases that can all be expedited the minute some legal barriers are lifted." She continues, "The pace of executions may increase slightly, but we are not going to see floodgates opening. The question of whether innocent people actually are convicted and executed is endlessly debated. Discussion of the issue can revolve around a study published in 1987 by Hugo Adam Bedau and Michael L. Radelet. These two named 350 persons which they said had probably been wrongly convicted of potentially capital crimes in the U.S. between 1900 and 1987. Most were either pardoned or had their convictions overturned because of new evidence. But, the authors say that twenty-three people were executed in error. Once these people are executed, there is really not much that can be done about it. Many people often wonder if the death penalty deters people from committing capital crimes. If you were to round up some 3,000 people who are under death sentence in this country and execute them all today and the act shown on television, would the streets be any safer tomorrow? Executions satisfy the public's demand that murderers suffer

[66]Ernest Van den Haag, John Phillips Conrad, The Death Penalty: A Debate, New York: Plenum, 1983. For a bibliography on the subject, See U. Leone, International Bibliography on 'Capital Punishment' (1987) Revue Internationale de droit Penal 823.

punishment commensurate with their offences. A 1985 study shows that the death penalty deters more potential homicides than earlier studies suggested. Yet, some experts argue that the death penalty actually encourages homicide in some circumstances. It is said that the threat of capital punishment raises the stakes of getting caught[67]. Author Michael Kronerwetter wrote,

> Anyone already subject to the death penalty has little to lose by killing again and again. The potential sentence cannot be made worse than it already is. This makes criminals who already face death for a previous crime more likely to kill in order to avoid being captured . . . to silence any witnesses against them[68].

Many psychiatrists also speculate that homicide may occasionally serve as a roundabout route to suicide. It was concluded that Gary Mark Gilmore committed two-execution style murders in Utah because he knew that he would face the firing squad[69].

Another main issue at large in capital punishment is whether or not mentally retarded defendants should be executed. Although death penalty opponents have had little success in recent years, they have made progress in protecting mentally retarded defendants. A popular case was that of Rickey Ray Rector, whose brain damage was so severe that he planned to eat his desert after his execution. There are about ten states now that ban the execution of the mentally retarded, as do the 1988 and 1994 anti-crime bills passed by Congress. There were many early abolition efforts against capital punishment. Opponents of it condemn the penalty as inhumane. By the mid-1960's, the death penalty seemed fated for extinction. Just seven executions were conducted in 1965, one in 1966, and two in 1967.

---

[67]See William C. Bailey, Ruth D. Peterson, "Murder and Capital Punishment: A Monthly Time-Series Analysis of Execution Publicity" (1989) 54 American Sociological Rev. 722. See also Louis Filler, "Movements to Abolish the Death Penalty in the United States" (1952) 284 Annals of the American Academy of Political and Social Science 124.

[68]See Albert Camus, Arthur Koestler eds. Reflexions sur la Peine Capitale, Paris: Pluriel, 1979. Hugo Adam Bedau, "Objections to the Death Penalty from the Moral Point of View" (1972) 58 Revue International de droit penal 557.

[69]See the commentaries of Voice of America Reports of 13th of March 2003.

The Rationale and Principle of Punishment

It is no longer unfashionable to begin law books with definitions. This is because of the difficulty frequently encountered in defining the subject-matter of a particular branch of the law; and this predicament is no more greatly felt than in criminal law. Anyebe[70] has described this as flirting with definitions. According to him, what law is has occupied the attention of other disciplines more than it has attracted the infinite disputation o f lawyers themselves. But in defining what law is, members of the legal profession have behaved like the proverbial needle, which undertakes tailoring for all and sundry but itself remains perpetually naked. However a research on crimes, which does not tell its readers what a crime is allows it to proceed with its own preconceived ideas of what is a crime. But there is a popular meaning of crime, which is different from, and narrower than, the legal meaning.[71] For example, a social scientist will consider the treatise complete in case he tinkered with a definition of law.[72]

Not that the lawyers have not attempted the definition of law, i.e. the creator of their trade, they have. But in the attempt to do so, they have remained as divided as pigeons suddenly invaded at midnight by a cat. The result has been confusion which students of jurisprudence have found lucrative in collecting and collating to qualify them as eminent jurists. In the process they partitioned themselves into various cubicles called schools: Austinian School, Justinian School, ad nauseam. As to what is the legal meaning of crime, the audience is entitled to know what it is. An attempt to define a crime at a glance encounters a difficulty in the sense that a true definition must contain all the ingredients

---

[70]Anyebe; A. P ,Customary Law: The War Without Arms (Fourth Dimension Publishers, 1985) at p. 3.

[71]Snyder: Criminal Justice – Text and Cases (1958) p. 1. Hart, (Jnr): "The Aims of the Criminal Law" 23 and Contemporary Problems, p. 402. Hull: Studies in Jurisprudence and Criminal Theory (1958) 200. R. Garofalo: Criminology (1914), p. 59, defining crime as a violation of the prevalent sentiments of pity and probity. Thomes and Znaniecki: The Polish Peasant in Europe and America (1927) Vol. II. pp. 1753-1755, defining crime from the standpoint of social psychology as an action, which is antagonistic to the solidarity of that group which the individual considers as his own.

[72]See e.g. Prof. Armstrong: West African Inquest (Oxford University Press 1968) p. 5; Prof. Paul Bohannan *op. cit.* at p. 57. See Prof. E. E. O. Alemika, 'Philosophies and Strategies of Crime Prevention and Crime Control: An Overview, paper presented at the Dialogue on National Crime Prevention Strategy organized by National Consultative Committee in Justice Sector Region and Access to Justice Team, Abuja, 2003.

of the definition. But true reflection will show that this is impossible. While a lawmaker has the powers to make an act or omission as a crime or that an act or omission not a crime, such does not change in nature in any respect other than in terms of legal classification., For example, suicide was a crime in England until 3 August 1961, when, by the Suicide Act 1961, it became perfectly lawful to kill oneself. Also, Homosexuals acts committed in private by male persons who have attained the age of 21 were offences until 27 July 1967, when, by the sexual offences Act 1967, such acts became permissible. Thus, the nature of the acts in question, their morality or immorality and their consequences do not change overnight, but their legal nature does. Ijalaye has rightly canvassed this view in this way:

> We now live in a world where many countries have now legalized homosexuality. That is why we now speak of "Gay Liberation - i.e. the freeing of homosexuals from social disadvantages and prejudices" The world has even conceded "Gay Rights - i.e. the rights of homosexuals to equal treatment with heterosexuals.[73]

Many other countries like Germany, Denmark, and America have not only legalized homosexual acts, but have also permitted marriages between persons of the same sex.

A working definition of a crime contains all its observable characteristics that are precisely the same before as after the statute comes into force. One of these is that it must be a public wrong. So that when an act consists in wrongdoing that directly and in serious degree threatens the security or well-being of society it is a crime.[74] This explains why when acts have been made crimes either by judicial decision or by legislation and yet it does not necessarily accurately represent the present state of affairs.

In furtherance of the relationship between morality and law, Smith & Hogan argued that

[73]The Nigerian Law of Rape in the Context of Global Development, (2004) Ibadan Bar Journal Vol. 3, No. 1 at p. 10.

[74]Pound, 'Towards a Better Criminal Law", 21 A.B.A.J. 499 at p. 503. See Maime, Ancient Law Chapter X, Fortes & Evans. Pritchard: African Political Systems (1940) pp. 11-14. Plucknett, T.F.T. Edward I and the Criminal Law (1960) Ch. 3. Hall, theft, Law and Society (1952) Chs. 1 & 2. Michael and Adler, Crime, Law and Society (1933) pp. 353-357.

> if punishment is assessed in accordance with the degree of moral blameworthiness, it seems to follow that it is imposed because of the moral blameworthiness.[75]

Holmes, while criticizing the concept of punishment quoted Hegel, said:

> There is a mystic bond between wrong and mathematical form that wrong being the negation of right, punishment is the negation of that negation, or retribution. Thus the punishment must be equal, in sense or proportionate to the crime, because its only function is to destroy it. Others, without this logical apparatus, are constant to rely upon a felt necessity that suffering should follow wrongdoing.[76]

Definition of Crime

Like most germane legal concepts, the word 'crime' is devoid of a universally accepted meaning. In popular or ordinary usage, the word 'crime' simply connotes any antisocial behaviour, whereas in legal parlance, it is a conduct punishable by law Hence Earl Jowitt defines crime as follows: "an act or default which tends to the prejudice of the community and is forbidden by law on pain of punishment inflicted at the instance of the state"[77]. This is not to say that there is a real difference between the lay conception of crime and the lawyers understanding of the word. According to Justice Karibi-Whyte[78], the only noticeable difference is one between what the law ought to describe as crime and what it actually so designates, namely, the 'ought' and 'is' of the law.

"Crime is not an entity in fact but an entity in law; it is not action but infraction" (*il delitto non e un ente di fatto rua un ente guiridico, e una infrazione e non un' asione).*[79]

The formulation of a satisfactory and universally accepted definition of the word crime has been and still is one of the most difficult tasks for writers in criminal law. Glanville Williams has described the effort as one of the thorny

---

[75](1996) (8th ed) London, Butterworth's Edinghbough, Dublin).

[76]Holmes: The Common Law at pg. 48.

[77]Dictionary of English Law, 1959 at page 557.

[78]Groundwork of Nigerian Criminal Law (1986) (NLP Ltd., Lagos) at p. 22.

[79]See Carrara; Modern Approach to Criminal Law.

intellectual problems of the law. This difficulty probably stems out of the fact that the concept is in itself complex and the word itself elusive. There has however been a different attempt made to give a definition to the word. In the Criminal Code and Penal Code, the word offence instead of the word crime has been used. Section 2 of the Criminal code defines offence as "acts or omissions, which render the person doing the act or making the omission liable to punishment under this code."

According to Blackstone,[80] a crime, or misdemeanour is an act committed or omitted in violation of a public law. This definition merely points towards the identification of conduct as criminal. The definition also places crime and misdemeanor as synonymous though they are not, as the former encompasses the latter. In his own contribution to the definition of crime, Clark[81] like Blackstone equals 'crime' with public wrongs and suggested that crimes are best defined in general, by the procedure with which that procedure is employed. According to him, 'it is beyond doubt, the belief of a community, or its authorities, as to the degree and extent of that tendency which leads to the special treatment of certain conduct as criminal." Clark's definition mainly rests on procedure.

At about the same period when Clark wrote, Sir Fitzjames Stephens[82] after indicating that there is a clear difference between the popular and legal meaning of crime, defined crime in its strict legal connotation as "an act or omission punished by law." To him, the popular or moral conception adds to this, the notion of moral guilt of specially deep and degrading kind. He pointed out that by the word 'criminal', people in general; understand not only a person who is liable to be punished, but a person who ought to be punished because he has done something at once wicked and obviously injurious in a high degree to the commonest interest of society.

The fault in Stephens's definition lies in its inadequacy. Halsbury[83] defined crime as "... an unlawful act or default which is an offence against the public, and renders the person guilty of the act or default liable to legal punishment"[8]. This definition is merely a description of the circumstances whereby conduct would lead to legal punishment. It does not really tell us what crime is. Professor

[80]Commentaries on the Law of England, 4 Vols, Oxford 1967.

[81]Criminal Law

[82]History of the Criminal Law of England.

[83]Laws of England.

Kenny[84] criticized the definition firstly on the grounds that publicness as an essential requirement of crime was derived from Roman law and that in Roman law it was derived from a mistaken view of Roman legal history. He further pointed out that injury to the community is not an essential attribute of crime since there was a great deal of conduct not prohibited by the criminal law even though they were highly injurious to the community. Brett[85] has rejected this criticism as misconceived. He argues that if taken in a negative sense it could be seen that what the definition indicates is that conduct, which is not injurious to the public is not criminal.

Kenny after a careful analysis and criticisms of different definitions and rejecting all of them then defined crime as ". . . wrongs whose sanction is punitive and is in no way remissible by any private person, but remissible by the Crown alone if remissible at all."[86]

Glanville Williams,[87] referring to Kenny's definition has said "... an attempt to define crime in terms of one item of procedure only is mistaken . . . . this test tells you whether an act is a crime only if you already know whether the sanction is remissible by the Crown. Almost always, however, the latter has to be deduced from the former, instead of vice versa."

Adopting a slightly different approach, Stephens defined crime as "an act of omission in respect of which legal punishment may be inflicted on the person who is in default either by acting or omitting to act." Stephen himself admitted that the definition is too wide for practical purposes.

Sir Carleton Allen[88] proffered a definition which was different from the earlier ones, but made no improvements on those attempts. He argued that it is not enough that crime is a punishable wrong, but why is it punishable? To him crime is crime because it consists in wrong doing which directly and in a serious degree threatens the security and the well being of society and because it is not safe to leave it repressible only by compensation of the party injured. This definition too is not devoid of criticisms in that, the fact that behaviour is punished or that action was taken in a certain manner does not really explain the characteristics of the behaviour.

---

[84]Criminal Law.

[85]An Inquiry into Criminal Guilt.

[86]*Op. cit.*

[87]*Op. cit.*

[88]"The Nature of a Crime" 13J of Comp. Lat (3rd Ser.) p.1

Okonkwo and Naish[89] defined crime as those breaches of the law resulting in special accusatorial procedure controlled by the state, and liable to sanction over and above compensation and costs.

From the foregoing it is apposite to state that there is no unanimously accepted definition of the word 'crime' as most definitions proffered simply describe 'crime' and most of the jurists have confused the idea of description with that of definition.

The Description and the Nature of Criminal Behaviour

Having said that there is no single definition of the word "Crime" that would satisfy all shades of opinion due to the obvious fact that there are as many definitions of "Crime" as there are persons who have one dealing or the other with morality, crime, criminal law and the criminal process. These people include the criminal law teacher, the criminologist, the penologist, the sociologist, the anthropologist, the judge, the police, the practitioner of criminal law and even the clergy, the believer and atheist.

Attempts at a working definition of criminal law have been faced with problems of acceptability. The learned authors Smith and Hogan warned us in their book[90] of the frustration and futility attendant with an exercise to define the subject matter of any particular branch of the law. The magnitude of this frustration is even more manifest and pronounced in attempts to define 'Crime'. Hence, Adeyemi has pointed out that:

> "Even though criminal law has been in operation in human communities for several centuries, yet lawyers have so far never agreed on any satisfactory definition of the word crime."[91]

In spite of the fact that there is no universally acceptable definition of "crime" yet several learned authors and jurists, Cross and Jones[92], Mr. Justice

[89]Criminal Law in Nigeria, (2nd ed. London, Sweet & Maxwell) (1980) at p. 18.
[90]*Criminal Law London* (1996) 8th ed. (Butterworths London, Edinburgh, Dublin).
[91]"The Criminal Law Process as a Selection Instrument for the Administration of Criminal Justice" in *Nigerian Criminal Process* (ed) Adeyemi, A.A. (1977) at p. 28.
[92]*Introduction to Criminal Law* (1988) (11th ed.) (Butterworths, London).

Litledate[93], Stephen[94], L.B. Curzon[95], Terrence Morris[96], Okonkwo and Naish[97], Mr. Justice Fakayode[98] to mention a few have put forward working definitions. The scope of what should be the framework of any attempt at defining "Crime" given by Lord Atkin as far back as 1931 still remains applicable today:

> The domain of criminal jurisprudence can only be ascertained by examining what acts at any particular period are declared by the state to be crimes, and the only common nature they will be found to possess is that they are prohibited by the state and that those who commit them are punished.[99]

The applicable primary laws in Nigeria are Criminal Code and Penal Code for the Southern and Northern states respectively. Section 2 of the Criminal Code (CC) defines offences as:

> "Acts or omissions, which render the person doing the act or making the omission liable to punishment under this code."[100]

This statutory definition fails among others to indicate those criteria or peculiar characteristics, which must determine the inclusion of any particular act or omission in the list of each prohibition contained in the code. Thus, it has been suggested that an *apriori* approach to the definition of crime and crime behaviour should be adopted. The idea behind this is that it is not enough for the state out of its own whims and caprices, to simply declare what is criminal behaviour. Rather, what amounts to criminal behaviour should be properly outlined for the benefit of the society in general. Apparently, the weakness of this definition under the criminal justice system has been taken

---

[93]See *Mann v. Owen* (1829) 9 B & C, 602.

[94]A general view of the Criminal Law of England (1883).

[95]Criminal Law (1984) (4th ed.) (London MacDonald & Evans.

[96]"The Social Toleration of Crime in *The Changing Concepts of Crime and Its Treatments* (1966) H. Klare (ed.) at p. 16-18.

[97]*Criminal Law in Nigeria* (1980) (2nd Ed.) (London Sweet & Maxwell at p. 21.

[98]*The Nigerian Criminal Code Companion,* (1977) (Benin-Ethiope Publishing Corporation).

[99]*Proprietary Articles Trade Association v. A.G. for Canada* (1931) A.C. 310, at 324. See also *Aoko v.. Fagbemi* (1961) 1 All NLR 400.

[100]Note that both criminal and Penal Codes use the term "offence" as against "crime". Also the courts normally use both terms indiscriminately and interchangeably.

care of under the constitution. Section 36 of the Constitution of The Federal Republic of Nigeria, 1999 provides:

> ". . . a person shall not be convicted of a criminal offence unless that offence is defined and the penalty thereof is prescribed in a written law . . . "

By virtue of this provision, it will be illegal and unconstitutional for any organ of the state, out of its own volition, to prosecute or convict a person for an offence that is not written in our statute book:

Definition in Terms of Procedure

Apart from defining "Crime" in terms of its contents or substance as done above, it may be viewed in terms of procedure, so that the meaning will manifest itself in that respect. Thus, crime can be distinguished from a "civil" wrong based on the procedures adopted in the approaches applicable to both. Generally, the mode of a criminal trial under common law systems is accusatorial or adversarial in nature, and results in a finding of guilt or innocence. The prosecution of crimes is usually undertaken and controlled in most cases, by the state and at public expense. The argument for this practice is that crime is a public wrong while civil proceeding redresses private wrongs.[101] It has been further argued that many crimes do harm to the community, or parts of it, especially such offences as murder, rape, arson, treason or riot. But this public character of crime is not an infallible test for distinguishing it from civil wrongs as this is without prejudice to the right of individuals to undertake private prosecution.[102] Though individuals can undertake private prosecution, they are, however not free to waive prosecution or conviction thereof. The right to exercise such power of waiver is strictly at the instance of the state by entering a "*nolle prosequi*"[103] or grant of pardon by the state.[104] Unlike the system

[101]See Okonkwo & Naish *op. cit.* at p. 22.

[102]See SS 342, 343 CPA.

[103]See *State v. Ilori* (1983) 2 SC 155, *Akilu v. Fawehinmi* 1989 3 NWLR (Pt. 112) 685 at 738. See Sections 160, 191, 1979 Nigerian Constitution Sections 174, 211 of 1999 Nigerian Constitution, and SS 75 and 284 CPA.

[104]See 160, 190 of the 1979 Nigerian Constitution, Section 175, 212 of the 1999 Nigerian Constitution.

applicable in some civil law countries where the jurisprudential network of laws, rules and procedures are characterized by opposing parties contending against each other for a result favourable to themselves. In such system, the judge acts as an independent party. Essentially, the legislative authority in a community creates crimes, be it despotic, oligarchic or democratic in nature, in response to certain needs for the protection of both the government and citizens. Thus, criminal liability is imposed on conduct felt to be against the general interests of society, although it may be related to conduct felt to be against the interests of particular groups e.g. power elite – military rulers, in fact some criminologists see criminal law mainly in this light, however this may be considered an extreme view. The function of criminal law includes the need to preserve public order and decency, protecting the citizen from what is offensive and injurious as well as providing sufficient safeguards against the exploitation and corruption of the most vulnerable members of society (e.g. the young, the weak in mind or body; the inexperienced). As such, if millions of people in Nigeria have to live together, their lives will be more pleasant and peaceful if some measures are taken to prevent people from killing or physically attacking others, walking into their houses and taking away – valuables. These types of behaviour are anti-social and must be controlled. But it is not the function of criminal law to interfere in the private lives of citizens or to seek to enforce any particular pattern of behaviour. It has been propounded that there must remain a realm of private morality and immorality, which is not a business of the law. One school of thought is of the view that public morality is essential for the stability and continuance of society and that to permit private acts of gross immorality is to undermine the foundations of that society.[105] Another school of thought is of the opposing view that society ought to be able to tolerate acts, which are harmful only to the individual who commits them, however outrageous they may appear to the rest of the community.[106]

There is a perennial controversy on how to distinguish between acts that are criminal and those that are merely immoral. While it is true that many if not most acts, which are regarded as immoral, are also illegal, yet the spheres of crime and morals do no more than intersect. Thus, there is not always agreement on what kind of conduct should be considered criminal for

[105]See *Wolfenden Committee on Homosexual Offences and Prostitution Report in Britain* (1957) (Cmnd. 247).

[106]See also Devlin "The Enforcement of Morals" (1959 Maccabean Lecture). Hart, The Listener (July 1959): Rostwo (1960) CLJ 174; Hart, *Law, Liberty and Morality* (1963) Harry Camp Lectures.

example, smoking in public places is considered anti-social by many, along with eating smelly fast food on public transport, or putting on too much perfume or after shave lotion and except of course, smoking which can even harm others who passively inhale the smoke. Yet none of these is a crime and very few people would wish them to be. On the other hand, there are types of behaviour, which may affect nobody, but the people involved – smoking cannabis, failing to wear a seat belt, or helmet by a cyclist hooting of a car horn can, in some situations, can harm other people in the sense of constituting a nuisance are examples – which are nevertheless criminal acts.

Apparently, it is in the light of the foregoing complexity in the analysis on morality and criminality that the learned authors, Okonkwo and Naish have remarked thus:

> The real difficulty about trying to discover some substantive, as opposed to procedural, hallmark of crime, is that the criminal law is so varied in content – a variability due to the fact that any human conduct, however noble or outrageous, can be categorized as criminal simply being forbidden on pain of punishment by the legislative power in any particular community . . . . And conduct which is seriously criminal when committed within man's immediate community may not be regarded as such when committed against an alien outsider.[107]

This author agrees with the opinion of Okonkwo and Naish that the content of criminal law may vary not only from age to age, and country to country, it may also vary within the same country at the same period in history. Perhaps this explains why slave trade 200 years ago was a recognized activity but now it is a serious international crime which violates the rule of *jus cogens*; so also are the cases of twin-killing, and some cultural practices such as the *Osu* caste system among the Igbo people of Eastern Nigeria. It is respectfully submitted that the types of conduct, which are considered criminal, vary from society to society. Under the English legal system, e.g. homosexuality was once a crime, it is no longer so. Until a couple of years ago, it was not a crime for a man to rape his wife. A husband can now rape his wife in some countries. Similarly, homosexuality has been given legal and social status in America. Former President Bill Clinton appointed James Hormel, a gay, as ambassador to Luxembourg after series of

[107] *Op. cit.*, p 21.

opposition lasting 20 months. Furthermore, the clamour for Gay Rights has been a high profile theme to the Democrats as campaigning programme. Also the former Vice-President, Al-Gore, visited a Gay and lesbian Centre during a campaign visit to California[108]. Also under rules of Private International Law for example, a marriage between a widower and his decreased wife's sister in Denmark was held legal under Danish Law but treated as illegal in England being a union which is contrary to God's law on the ground of incest.[109]

In Nigeria, there are two systems of criminal law, and such types of conduct as adultery and drinking alcohol are offences only in the Northern State but they are not offences in the Southern States. In certain situations, the same conduct may be criminal when committed by one person and legal when committed by another (e.g. marriage by a man to another woman during the lifetime of his spouse[110]. That is why bigamy is a crime even in a predominantly polygynous society as it is a question of choice on the form of marriage by the parties concerned. This position is reinforced by the golden principle that law is an instrument for social change in a given society, thus as general attitudes change over time, so do attitudes to the kind of behaviour, we label as criminal. This should be the objective of lawmakers in every democratic society. It is no gainsaying that a democratic law need not necessarily be out of touch with the needs of the community; regrettably, the criminal code, which was enacted by the colonialist for us, appears to continue to command fairly widespread acceptance in Southern Nigeria. In the words of Okonkwo & Naish:

> "It is clear that society attitude underlying criminal law is in a constant process of change. Certain crimes (e.g. the stringent law of sedition which has been found to be of continuing use after 1960) may therefore become obsolete, though not formally abolished."[111]

The learned authors further adduced reason why 'crime' is punished. They said that it is punished because it was thought to be a serious threat to society at the time when the legislation on the subject matter was passed. According to them, the crime of "Promoting Native war" might now reasonably be

---

[108]See *The Guardian,* Thursday July 1, 1999.

[109]See *Brook v. Brook* (1861) 9 H.C.C. 193.

[110]The relevant question is, should bigamy be a crime? – CF the dilemma of Reed J. in passing sentence, in *R. v. Princewell* (1963) N.R.N.L.R. 54. See also Okonkwo, "Bigamy in a Polygamous Society (Nigeria) 1976 1 Nig. J.R. 76.

[111]*Op. cit.* 24.

considered more appropriate to a colonial era than to an era of independence. They argued that this is a situation where public opinion might be in advance of the law. With due respect to the learned authors, this argument is valid in the sense that before the attainment of independence status in 1960, the agitations of our nationalists then were accompanied with the use of force in few extreme situations by some allied militant groups to press home their demands for a sovereign nation, and these were regarded by the colonial government then as activities to 'promote native war'.

However, in recent times situations similar to that period emerged with agitations for "equality, fairness and justice" by the youths in Niger-Delta Area leading to the formation of different militant groups among the Ijaws in the oil producing areas and more recently the *Oodua People's Congress* (OPC) in the Yoruba speaking areas of the country. These developments can be likened to the positions that were operating during the colonial era. Therefore, the argument moves in a circle as the operative word of the provision of section 42 of the criminal code can be amended to read "promoting ethnic interest by war." Nevertheless, the emergence of these groups was as a result of loss of confidence in the police and other law enforcement agents to curb incidents of crime in our society. Accordingly, it is not always sufficient that in a democracy, that the majority agree that conduct prohibited by the law should in fact be punished – the prohibition of alcohol in the United States between 1919 and 1933 is a classic example of the unwanted crime which was abolished as a result of the role of the highly organized and vocal minority pressure group that could not be ignored.

Whatever the legal machinery used for making a certain type of conduct criminal, the subject must be considered from three different perspectives:

> the attitude of the legislature when it creates offences (behind which usually stands public opinion); the attitude of the administration which enforces the law; and of the courts which interpret it.

It is therefore desirable that criminal law must be kept in step with public opinion especially in the administration of the law by the law-enforcing agencies. It is one thing for parliament to forbid a conduct, but is quite another thing to enforce that prohibition. The police and the state counsel wield a considerable discretion in the prosecution of crimes, and in the course of exercising this power the fact that a particular crime is obsolete, or is not in accord with general opinion or is difficult to enforce may at times influence them against enforcement. This actual position of things has been pointed out and rightly too, by Ijalaye that some provisions of our criminal code and other statutes on criminal law have gathered dust over the years and need to be detached and thrown into the dustbin.[112]

It is crystal clear from the above-expositions that the problem as to what constitutes a crime will ever remain as unsettled and controversial as we have tried to analyse here. The focus of this work is not to dwell on the relationship between criminal law and morality. The separation of law and morals is a favourite subject for further academic research involving intriguing questions that are likely to emanate from this highly philosophical topic.[113] The truth of the matter is that the link between morality and criminal law is very strong, and in everyday use, the word 'crime' with the exception of a few criminal offences, carries undertones of immorality, of sin and of wrong doing. This writer therefore shares the view expressed that the ultimate justification of law is to serve moral ends.[114] Morality must be the basis of criminal law. Thus, the position should be that the criminality or otherwise of an act should depend upon the degree of its anti-sociality, which invariably must be viewed with reference to the accepted rules of morality of the community in question. In other words, at any time in any society, there will be some kinds of behaviour about which there is dispute. For example, smoking cannabis is a crime and some people argue that it should not be, while abortion (within certain rules) is not a crime, for instance, where the live of the mother is in danger, although some believe it should be. It is important therefore, to realize that there is no absolute definition of criminal behaviour; the word "criminal" is no more than a label attached to different

---

[112]See "The Sociological School of Jurisprudence and the Nigerian Legal Order" published in Nigeria and Challenge of Knowledge Essays in Honour of Jonathan Olusesan Dipeolu (1992) where the learned Professor cited the following laws: Laws of Bigamy, Section 370c.c. Bush Burning Ondo State Edict No. 4 of 1989; Slaughtering of Animals - Public Health Act. Cap. 165 (1958) Laws of the Federation of Nigeria; Burial in Houses S.246 CC; The Land Use Decree (now Act) 1978; The Principle of Federal Character: "The Constitution of the Federal Republic of Nigeria, 1979: Lynching: Mob Justice versus Right to Life Under the Nigerian Constitution 1979.

[113]See the following: Stoljar "More Thinking on Law and Morals" (1961) 14 Current Legal Problems, 140; Joseph Omoregbe, Ethics - A Systematic and Historical Study, p. 37-41; Lord Atkin's dictum in *Proprietary Articles Trade Association v. A.G. Canada* (1937) AC 300 at 324. See also Mike A.A. Ozekhome, Criminal Law; Problems of Definition and Interaction with Morality. "The Advocate". (Special Edition of International Journal of the Law Students' Society, University of Ife, Nigeria, vol. 8, page 72 at 75-80.

[114]See Morris Ginsberg, 'On Justice in Society', (1965) at p. 218 quoted by Adeyemi *op. cit.*, p. 30.

types of behaviour at different times in different societies.[115]

Consequently, crime, particularly the commission of it, is what any society of human beings detests most vehemently. It often destabilizes the psyche of the society. When a crime is committed, it stings the larger society, which favour adequate sanction in the interest of justice. It is not justice or quest for it for the lawyers alone, or the parties alone; it is justice for all the people. The courts, the police and the advocates have very crucial roles to play in the dispensation of justice. The role of each is distinct from the other. And it is when each side leaves no stone untouched in the discharge of its responsibility that justice to all can be ensured.

Causation of Crimes

Presumably, if we know why crimes are committed we can do one or two things; eliminating all causes of crimes and/or by reducing all conducive factors to its barest minimum. Lord Denning,[116] in his view said that in order that an action should be punished, it must be morally blame-worthy, and must be a sin, while Stephen J.[117] stated that it is desirable that criminals should be hated. Nevertheless, there are several factors responsible for the causation of crimes ranging from personal reasons to societal factors. As regards personal factors, it ranges from hereditary influence to habitual influences, while societal factors range from peer group influences to socio-economic factors in the country. Adeyemi has given explanations to cover demographic shift involving urban/rural migration inflation rates, unemployment, per capital income level, school wastages, intervention and impact of civil war, socio-political/economic problems, decline in public morality, atomization of the family, parental deprivation resulting from broken homes and socio-cultural factors etc. as criminogenic factors for the explanations of the nature, pattern and trends of crime and criminality in our society[118].

---

[115]See Cathenne Elliott and Frances Quinn, *Criminal Law,* (1996) (Longman London & New York) 1996.

[116]*R. v. C.O.P.* (1953) Cmd. 8732 p. 18.

[117]*A general view of the Criminal Law of England.*

[118]Op.cit.

Types of Crimes

Traditionally, crimes are divided into two forms; felonies and misdemeanours. Writers usually draw a line of distinction between outrageously callous conducts such as murder, armed robbery, manslaughter, rape, assault occasioning harm etc. which are often referred to as "*Mala in se*". In other words, these offences are usually termed as Choate crimes. On the other hand, simple offences are termed innocuous crimes; at times they are technical offences, which are not morally and universally condemnable.

Advancement in technology has further expanded the forms of crimes in our society. Thus, the problem of lumping together statistically and, even, criminological incomparable offences need to be readdressed, as some of these offences do not behave similarly in pattern and trends. There are changes in classification of these offences now, apparently due to emergence of new dimensions into the commission of these offences. For obvious reasons, it would be right to say that categories of crimes are never closed.

The study on types of criminals is a bye-product of efforts of criminologists and penologists notable in this field were Cesare de Beccaria, Jeremy Bentham and Cesare Lombroso. There is hardly any topic more fascinating and thought provoking than development made in the area of criminological thoughts. Several eminent jurists, learned authors, sociologists, philosophers and medical experts produced several literatures with different ideas in different countries. Two renowned schools of thought; the Utilitarian/classical School led by Jeremy Bentham and the Positive School led by Cesare Lombroso have contributed immensely to the study of criminals. The Utilitarian school anchored its view on the doctrine of 'Pleasure and Pain' i.e. the greatest possible happiness of the greatest number. According to them, the case of crime is social and not necessarily biological. According to them, there are certain types of physical irregularities or stigmata regarded as being characteristic of the criminal. That criminals are born, not made and that they conform to certain physical characteristics which make them (criminals), look different and easily distinguishable from ordinary human beings. They further argue that there is a connection between crime and human physique to the anatomy of the skull and the brain and other parts of the body.[119] Prominent features of the criminal are characterized by certain malformation of the skeleton and the skull such as 'oversized brain', 'a receding forehead' high-cheek bones,

[119]See Lombroso, *Crime: Its causes and remedies.* (1913) (Boston) W. Norwood East. *Medical Aspects of Crime,* (1936) (London). Ch. 7.

squatting eyes, bushy and prominent eye-brows, a twisted nose, big ears etc.[120] This belief is strongly reflected in popular writings and several well-known figures in great works of world literature such as Homer's Thersites or Shakespeare's Richard III or in part also in Julius Caesar:

> "Let me have men about me that are fat,
> sleek-headed men and such as sleep o'nights;
> Yond Cassius has a lean and hungry look,
> He thinks too much; such men are dangerous."[121]

Furthermore, an English judge had once remarked thus:

> "The fat does not write anonymous letters. It is the lean bodies that sit at writing tables and bony fingers that dip pens in vitriol and build up bomb-shells for harmless postmen to deliver."[122]

Lombroso finally postulated the following categories of criminals:

(1) The born criminal: derived from birth and in most cases hereditary from his parents and often have little resistance to criminal stimuli and high degree of propensity to commit crime.
(2) The insane criminal: affected by a clinically diagnosis mental disease of psychoses.[123]
(3) The passional criminal: the criminal through passion either chronic mental state or through emotion and in most cases such a criminal is nervously excitable.
(4) The occasional criminal constitutes the majority of lawbreakers, a bye product of family and social problems.[124]
(5) The habitual criminal: a product of the social environmental caused by abandonment by his family.[125]

---

[120]M.F. Ashley Montagu, 'The Biologist looks at crime', Ann Amer. Acad. Polit. Soc. Sci., vol. 217, Sept. 1941.
[121]See Manniheim, *Comparative Criminology* (1970), (vol. 1) (London Routledge and Kegan Paul, Third Impression) p. 212-217.
[122]Hermann Mannheim *Ibid.* p. 212, *The Times* 11th October, 1935.
[123]William Healy, *Mental Conflicts and Misconduct,* (1936), Boston p. 321.
[124]Charles Gorung, *The English Convert,* H.M.S.O.; (1943) London, pp. 200-1.
[125]Norval Morris, *The Habitual Criminal,* (1957) (London) pp. 310-354.

Aims of Punishment

Punishment is the act of a legitimate authority depriving an offender of a good of which he is no longer worthy. Why punish? Four purposes traditionally justify any punishment, not just capital punishment. They include protection from the criminal, deterrence, rehabilitation and retributive justice. The first three purposes are widely accepted. Almost everyone agrees that society must be able to defend itself against convicted murderers, rapists, thieves and the like. The protection of the common good justifies removing criminals from situations in which they pose a threat. That such punishment deters others who may be tempted to act criminally likewise helps preserve and protect the tranquility of society. Criminals serving their sentences should also be provided, or may even be forced to take advantage of, opportunities for rehabilitation so that they may re-enter society as productive citizens.

According to H.L.A. Hart,[126] the definition of punishment must include the following:

(i) It must involve pain or other consequences normally considered unpleasant.
(ii) It must be for an offence against legal rules.
(iii) It must be of an actual or supposed offender for his offence.
(iv) It must be intentionally administered by human beings other than the offender.
(v) It must be imposed and administered by an authority constituted by a legal system against which the offence is committed.

In calling this the standard or central case of punishment one shall relegate to the position of sub-standard or secondary cases the following among many other possibilities:

(a) Punishments for breaches of legal rules imposed or administered otherwise than by officials (decentralized sanctions).
(b) Punishments for breaches of non-legal rules or orders (punishments in a family or school).
(c) Vicarious or collective punishment of some member of a

[126]Punishment and Responsibility (Essay in the Philosophy of Law (Clarendon Press, Oxford 1968) at pp. 4-8.

social group for actions done by others without the former's authorization, encouragement, control or permission.

(d) Punishment of persons (otherwise than under (c)) who neither are in fact nor supposed to be offenders.

The chief importance of listing these sub-standard cases is to prevent the use of what one can call the 'definitional stop' in discussions of punishment. This is an abuse of definition especially tempting when use is made of conditions (ii) and (iii) of the standard case in arguing against the utilitarian claim that the practice of punishment is justified by the beneficial consequences resulting from the observance of the laws which it secures. Here the stock 'retributive' argument[127] is: If this is the justification of punishment, why not apply it, when it pays to do so, to those innocent of any crime, chosen at random, or to the wife and children of the offender? And here the wrong reply is: That, by definition, would not be 'punishment' and it is the justification of punishment, which is in issue.[128] Not only will this definitional stop fail to satisfy the advocate of 'retribution', it would prevent us from investigating the very thing which modern skepticism most calls in question: namely the rational and moral status of our preference for a system of punishment under which measures painful to individuals are to be taken against them only when they have committed an offence. Why do we prefer this to other forms of social hygiene which we might employ to prevent anti-social behaviour and which we do employ in special circumstances, sometimes with reluctance? No account of punishment can afford to dismiss this question with a definition.

The nature of an offence

Before we consider any question of justification we must identify a preliminary question to which the answer is so simple that the question may not appear worth asking; yet it is clear that some curious 'theories' of punishment gain their only plausibility from ignoring it, and others from

[127]A.C. Ewing, The Morality of Punishment, D.J.B. Hawkins, Punishment and Moral Responsibility (The King's Good Servant, p. 92), J.D. Mabbott, 'Punishment', Mind (1939), p. 152.

[128]Mr. Benn seemed to succumb at times to the temptation to give 'The short answer to the critics of utilitarian theories of punishment – that they are theories of punishment not of any sort of technique involving suffering' (*op. cit.*, p. 332).

confusing it with other questions. This question is: Why are certain kinds of action forbidden by law and so made crimes or offences? The answer is: To announce to society that these actions are not to be done and to secure that fewer of them are done. These are the common immediate aims of making any conduct a criminal offence and until we have laws made with these primary aims we shall lack the notion of a 'crime' and so of a 'criminal'. Without recourse to the simple idea that the criminal law sets up, in its rules, standards of behaviour to encourage certain types of conduct and discourage others we cannot distinguish a punishment in the form of a fine from a tax on a course of conduct.[129] This indeed is one grave objection to those theories of law, which in the interests of simplicity or uniformity obscures the distinction between primary laws setting standards for behaviour and secondary laws specifying what officials must or may do when they are broken. Such theories insist that all legal rules are 'really' directions to officials to exact 'sanctions' under certain conditions, e.g. if people kill.[130] Yet only if we keep alive the distinction (which such theories thus obscure) between the primary objective of the law in encouraging or discouraging certain kinds of behaviour, and its merely ancillary sanction or remedial steps, can we give sense to the notion of a crime or offence.

It is important however to stress the fact that in thus identifying the immediate aims of the criminal law we have not reached the stage of justification. There are indeed many forms of undesirable behaviour which it would be foolish (become ineffective or too costly) to attempt to inhibit by use of the law and some of these may be better left to educators, trades unions, churches, marriage guidance councils or other non-legal agencies. Conversely there are some forms of conduct, which we believe cannot be effectively inhibited without use of the law. But it is only too plain that in fact the law may make activities criminal, which it is morally important to promote and the suppressing of these may be quite unjustifiable. Yet confusion between the simple immediate aim of any criminal legislation and

---

[129]This generally clear distinction may be blurred. Taxes may be imposed to discourage the activities taxed though the law does not announce this as it does when it makes them criminal. Conversely fines payable for some criminal offences because of a depreciation of currency become so small that they are cheerfully paid and offences are frequent. They are then felt to be mere taxes because the sense is lost that the rule is meant to be taken seriously as a standard of behaviour.

[130]Cf. Kelsen, General theory of Law and State (1945), pp. 30-33, 33-34, 143-4. 'Law is the primary norm, which stipulates the sanction . . .' (*ibid.* 61).

the justification of punishment seems to be the most charitable explanation of the claim that punishment is *justified* as an 'emphatic denunciation by the community of a crime'. Lord Denning's dictum that this is the ultimate justification of punishment[131] can be saved from Mr. Benn's criticism, noted above, only if it is treated as a blurred statement of the truth that the aim not of punishment, but of criminal legislation is indeed to denounce certain types of conduct as something not to be practiced. Conversely the immediate aim of criminal legislation cannot be any of the things which are usually mentioned as justifying punishment: for until it is settled what conduct is to be legally denounced and discouraged we have not settled from what we are to *deter* people, or who are to be considered *criminals* from whom we are to exact *retribution*, or on whom we are to wreak *vengeance*, or whom we are to *reform*.

Even those who look upon human law as a mere instrument for enforcing 'morality as such' (itself conceived as the law of God or Nature) and who at the stage of justifying punishment wish to appeal not to socially beneficial consequences but simply to the intrinsic value of inflicting suffering on wrongdoers who have disturbed by their offence the moral order, would not deny that the aim of criminal legislation is to set up types of behaviour (in this case conformity with a pre-existing moral law) as legal standards of behaviour and to secure conformity with them. No doubt in all communities certain moral offences, e.g. killing, will always be selected for suppression as crimes and it is conceivable that this may be done not to protect human beings from being killed but to save the potential murderer from sin; but it would be paradoxical to look upon the law as designed not to discourage murder at all (even conceived as sin rather than harm) but simply to extract the penalty from the murderer.

The Theory of Retribution

This is the oldest theory of punishment, which states that criminals deserve to suffer for their crimes. It is a process of "looking back" at the circumstances of the crime committed, and deciding what punishment the accused deserves for his conduct, having regard to his responsibility for the crime. It has been associated with the development and maintenance of religious creeds and

[131]In evidence to the Royal Commission on Capital Punishment, Cmd. 8932. para. 53 (1953). *Supra*, P. 2, n. 3.

dates back to the Mosaic Law – *lex Tailionis* – "an eye for an eye and a tooth for a tooth".

The theory implies moralistic philosophy i.e. that a crime is a moral wrong. It is imperative that a criminal should be punished with a penalty proportionate to the offence committed. Apparently, it is from this aspect that the theory is also known as fair deserts. Perhaps, the theory still owes much of its cultural support to the great religions, which equate crime with sin and call for its repression. This explains Lord Denning's view that ever since the time of King Henry; for an act to be punishable, it must be morally blameworthy and it must be a sin.[132] This approach to punishment involves the wreaking of vengeance and infliction of pain by society, on behalf of itself or the injured individual, on the wickedness of the offenders.

Salmond succinctly put the public feelings in this way:

> We have too much forgotten that the mental attitudes which best becomes us when fitting justice is done upon the evil doer is, not pity, but solemn exultation.[133]

It contains also the idea that he who kills must be killed and that a more wicked man should suffer more severe pain. Thus, the offender by undergoing punishment is offered a chance to expiate his wickedness to relive his conscience, and to 'pay' for what he has done.

Retributive justice is often misunderstood as simple vengeance. Vengeance arises from anger or hatred and typically punishes until that emotion is satisfied. In fact, religions teach that retributive justice is punishment's primary purpose. For example, the Catechism of the Catholic Church says:

> Punishment has the primary aim of redressing the disorder introduced by the offence. When it is willingly accepted by the guilty party, it assumes the value of expiation.[134]

On the part of the state, it can only justly punish those who have committed a crime, not others no matter what good purposes that might serve. Thus punishment of any kind may only be justly administered to the guilty and never to the innocent. John Paul II further buttresses this position when he writes:

---

[132]The RT. Hon.Sir Alfred Denning, The Changing Law,(London Stevens& Sons Ltd. 1953 p.10

[133]On Jurisprudence (11th) quoted by Glanville Williams at p. 101.

[134]See The Vatican Lecture series

> Not even a murderer loses his personal dignity, and God himself pledges to guarantee them.[135]

Aside theological point of view, the application of retributive justice recognizes and reaffirms the humanity of the person punished. It only puts on trial and punish human beings because only human beings enjoy freedom in such a way that they may be held responsible for their actions. Retributive justice demands that there must be a proportion between crime and punishment. The most serious crimes merit most serious punishment, and inconsequential offences merit inconsequential punishments. Retribution emphasizes proportionality, as it will be unjust to give a man who stole a loaf of bread life imprisonment, even if this will greatly deter others from stealing bread, in other words, punishment must not legitimately exceed proportionality. It must be proportionate to the crime committed.

Although crime and punishment must be proportionate, they can never perfectly proportionate save perhaps on financial matters. Perhaps, the most forceful judicial statement of the retributive attitude to punishment is that of Stephen, J.:

> I am . . . of opinion that this close alliance between criminal law and moral sentiment is in all way healthy and advantageous to the community. I think it highly desirable that criminals should be hated, that the punishments inflicted upon them should be so contrived as to give expression to that hatred, and to justify it so far as the provision of means for expressing and gratifying a healthy and natural sentiment can justify and encourage it.[136]

He went on to say further that:

> Punishment is justified because it provides an orderly and socially accepted outlet for the revenge emotion just as marriage provides a socially accepted outlet for sexual appetite.[137]

The views expressed above clearly demonstrated the reasons why some people feel that revenge is the necessary remedy for a crime committed.

---

[135] *Ibid.*

[136] 2 H.C.L. 81-82 (Smith and Hogan) *op. cit.*.

[137] *Ibid.*

The second aspect of the retribution theory is that the punishment must fit the crime or the level of harm done. This is best demonstrated in attempt cases. Though, failure to complete the offence by no means necessarily shows that the offender is less dangerous, he may have been unlucky. His detection may have been the reason of abandonment and he may have even wished to postpone the commission of the offence. Yet failure to complete the commission is a mitigating factor in determining the nature of punishment to be awarded for the attempted crime. Punishments for attempt cases are usually lesser than the punishment for the completed crime. For example, under the English judicial system, rape is punishable with life imprisonment while attempted rape carries seven years imprisonment. This means that the punishment is tailored to the level of harm done.[138] Under the Nigerian Criminal Code, S. 357 provided a life imprisonment for a rapist while an attempted rape carries a fourteen years imprisonment with or without whipping as provided for in S. 359. These provisions are in line with the view earlier expressed that the aim of punishment is that it should fit the crime committed. Significantly, the mental element necessary for the crime of rape is the same for attempted rape, yet the statutory punishment for each differs.

Similarly, under the provisions of S. 319 (1) of the Criminal Code murder is punishable with a death sentence; however attempted murder carries a life imprisonment sentence as provided for in S. 320 of the Criminal Code. The above aptly reinforces the view that the punishment must fit the crime. A dangerous driving that attracts two years jail term if no death occurs would attract a five years imprisonment if death occurs, even though the driver drove the same way and with the same state of mind.[139]

In the Streatfield Committee Report[140] in England, the concept of let the punishment fit the crime was described as follows:

> The primary objective was to fix a sentence proportionate to the offender's culpability, and the system has been loosely discussed as the 'tariff system'.

---

[138]See Smith and Hogan, *op. cit.*

[139]*Ibid.*, p. 9.

[140]Page 257 of the Report Quoted by KETTH DEVLIN – Sentencing offenders in Magistrates Court – Sweet and Maxwell 1970 p. 5.

The twin approach of the retributive theory may be justified on the principle of self-protection. Apart from any question as to its moral character, there is also the argument that the offenders are dangerous to the society and ought to be prevented to gratify the feelings of hatred, revenge or resentment.[141] But whatever might be the justification, the revenge theory has found its ways into the penal status of the Nigerian Laws.

Retribution in Legislation

As seen with the provisions of Sections 357 and 359 of the Criminal Code, relating to the offence of rape and its punishment, the Criminal Code and the Penal Code are replete with legislation that depict the retributive nature of the punishment that readily comes to mind is the provision of S. 319(1) of the Criminal Code that says: Subject to the provisions of this section any person who commits the offence of murder shall be sentenced to death.[142] Also S. 208 of the Criminal Code provides that any person who directs or controls or presides at any trial by ordeal and if such trial results in the death of another, the punishment for the person who presides over the trial is the punishment of death.[143] Three other offences punishable with death were adopted by the Penal code. S. 159 provides that giving false evidence, which results in the conviction and execution of an innocent person, is punishable with death. Similarly, abetting the suicide of a minor or a mentally abnormal person is punishable with death[144] and finally S. 229 provides that attempting to commit culpable homicide by a person already serving a life sentence carries the death penalty.

Retributivism in Sentencing

The retributive attitude provided for under the Criminal Code as well as the Penal Code finds expression in the judicial attitudes towards sentencing of

[141](1874) See generally Stephen James at pages 161-162.

[142]See also S. 221 of the Penal Code.

[143]Penal Code extends liability of death penalty of anyone who was present at such a trial.

[144]S. 227 of the Penal Code.

offenders. According to Allan Milner.[145]

> It is the badness of the offenders, which is being punished, and the worse he behaves the more severely will he be punished. Working within the limit laid down by legislation, the judge will pass a sentence which he believes adequately reflects the gravity of the offence in the eyes of the community.

The attitude of the trial Judge in passing the sentence of death might at times be excessive even to a person who is of unsound mind. And this attitude is not limited to Nigeria only, it is found in other jurisdiction all over the world. In *R. v. Mitchess*[146] where the appellant had thrown bleach into the eyes of pursuers attempting to apprehend him, the court, upholding a sentence of ten years imprisonment, observed that it was "a horrible offence" and that the sentence had to mark public repulsion. This attitude may underline the attitude of the Supreme Court in the case of Peter *Abu v. The State*[147] where the appeal against the sentence of death was dismissed by the court on the fact stated. The facts being that the accused on the night of 8 March 1994 had a dispute with his wife. The wife, the deceased was a Christian while the husband, the appellant, was a Moslem. The dispute arose over the desire of the wife to continue the attendance of Church. The dispute grew violent; the accused picked a hatchet, attacked and killed his wife. The accused thereafter attempted suicide by hanging when he was rescued and arrested. The trial court found him guilty and sentenced him to death. Witnesses testified that the accused was found rolling on the ground and screaming with cable rope tied round his neck. The defence suggested that the accused was of unsound mind but this was rejected both by the trial court and the Supreme Court. The sentence of death was therefore affirmed. This is a clear case of retributive sentence. The question is that who gained from the death of both the wife and the husband? Is it the society or the judicial personnel? It is our view that the only aim of this sentence is to revenge the murder of the wife by the husband without considering the effect such punishment would have on the family, the children and the entire society where the accused and his wife lived.

---

[145]The Nigerian Penal system – Sweet and Maxwell 1972, p. 959.

[146][1965] Crim. L.R. 292, 319.

[147](1976) 5 S.C. 21.

Retributivism in sentencing was carried to a radical height in the Kenyan case of *Rex v. Kumwaka Wa Mulumbi*[148] where Sir Charles Grifflin C.J. affirmed the sentences of death of sixty (60) accused persons on the charge of killing a woman believed to have been a witch. Seventy people were found guilty of the offence of murder. Ten were juveniles and were ordered to be detained at the Governor's pleasure while the remaining sixty were sentenced to death. The court found that there was malice aforethought within the Kenya Penal Code and that self-defence was not a tenable plea.

On the facts of the case, it was apparent that there was belief in witchcraft in the society. Yet the court sentenced sixty people to death over the death of a "witch", because according to Charles Griffin C.J. "For Courts to adopt any other attitude . . . would be to encourage the belief that an aggrieved party may take the law into his own hand . . ." Certainly there is the element of revenge in this case. Soyinka writing on Africa's perception of who is a 'witch' states:

> A child's concept of what a woman is, is bound up with the image of his or her mother, sisters, aunts etc. When that child encounters for the first time, an unusually hairy woman; something that he or she has never encountered before, such a child looks instinctively for a category that will explain the difference, and if that difference is one that has inspired fear, opts instinctively for a pejorative category. Thus, for the child, a word that may come to mind immediately within his limited vocabulary is – witch.[149]

Furthermore, the eminent Nobel Laurel stated that, ordinarily, the child's definition of woman might be that of a domesticated social being. The day that child encounters a woman living by herself, either within the village or in a hamlet just outside, he dips into that bag of referential and comes up with the word, "witch".[150]

[148](1932) 14 K.L.R. 137.

[149]Cults: A People in 'Denial' Interventions III (2005) (Book Craft Ltd.) in a subtitle, Descent of Barbarism and the End of the Collegial' first delivered in August 2003 at the Obafemi Awolowo University, Ile-Ife Law Students Week in honour of retired judge of the Supreme Court, Justice Kayode Eso at pg. 47.

[150]*Ibid. p. 48.* See also Chukkol, K.S. "Witchcraft and the Criminal Law in Nigeria" (1981) 2 The Attorney 23; Aremu, L.O. "Criminal Responsibility for Homicide in Nigeria and Supernatural Beliefs (1980) International Comparative Law Quarterly 113; Ojo, J.D. "The Place of Supernatural Powers in the Criminal Law" (1977), Nigerian Behavioural Sciences Journal.

According to Soyinka, rarely would such a child think of 'hermit' homeless woman' 'student of nature', 'widow', 'abandoned mother' or simply, a different woman.

This African child's perception has been described by Soyinka as:

> Consequence of subtle to overt brainwashing from adult conversation direct warnings or observation – we know that children left on their own, exhibit a natural openness of mind to the world.[151]

Analysing the inapt description of a witch, Soyinka further said:

> Now this strange woman may be no more than a victim of circumstances or else a victim of choice. She may even be slightly mentally affected or deformed "Before you know it she becomes target practice for children's missiles. They throw rubbish on her doorstep and even drop refuse in her water pot.[152]

In a bid to show that the concept of witch is universal, Prof. Soyinka referred to Arthur Miller's dramatization of the notorious Salem witch-hunt of the United States to buttress the point that society may even move to commit judicial murder as a result of such hysteria. In the words of Soyinka,

> The citizens of a puritamie settlement called Salem set up, by default, some kind of Inquisitional Court in which the final, damning word on who were witches and who were not, lay with children. A society of hard-boiled pioneer stock, fleeing a phobia of difference in a female slave, threw itself under the murderous protection of a church ministry and lost the very freedom it had set out to defend. Those settlers became accessories to judicial murder – but also potential victims themselves.[153]

In his write up, Soyinka rhetorically asked the question, Are witches real? And he swiftly answered, "I do not know. I have never seen them". He however

---

[151] *Ibid.* p. 48.
[152] *Ibid.* p. 48.
[153] *Ibid.* p. 49.

narrated an eyewitness account of a situation where a woman narrowly missed death through his personal intervention in the street of Lagos. He said:

I know however that, five centuries after the history of the witches of Salem in the late eighties of this immediate past century, I did rescue a woman in Palm Groove Estate, Lagos, on an otherwise quiet Sunday morning. She was about to be stoned to death by a crowd that had somehow decided that she was a witch. I took her to hospital and had her looked after. Enquiries that I made later indicated that she was only a destitute whose mind had become temporarily unhinged.[154]

In that scenario, men, women, children pursued the woman, pelting her with stones as she staggered from the road into a ditch and out again. In spite of interposition of his body between the lynch mob and the crowd, it took the arrival of two armed police to make the lynch mob finally disperse.

In summary, Soyinka described this typical example of a mass hysteria whose foundation will be found in phobia. The wages of sin may be death; they are also, all too often – murder.[155]Similarly, in the case of *R. v. Dudley and Stephens*[156] two accused were indicted for the murder of a boy on the high seas. They have been cast away in the storm in an open boat. After twenty days, and having exhausted the food they had, they killed and fed upon the little boy with them who was weak and at the point of death. They lived on his carcass for few days before they were rescued. It was found as a fact that the boy might have died had they not killed him but this was no defence to a charge of murder. The two accused were found guilty of murder and they were sentenced to death.[157] Lord Coleridge, C.J. stated:

> We are often compelled to set up standards we cannot reach ourselves and to lay down rules, which we could not ourselves satisfy. But a man has no right to declare temptation to be an excuse though he might himself have yielded to it, nor allow compassion for the criminal to change or weaken in any manner that legal definition of crime.

This case again shows the level the judicial system often goes to satisfy the 'eye for an eye' and 'tooth for a tooth' urges in punishment. Little consideration is often given to the society and people for whom the law is made.

---

[154]*Ibid.* p. 49.

[155]*Ibid.* p. 49.

[156](1884) 14 Q.B.D. 273.

[157]The sentences was later committed by government prerogative to 6 months.

Criticism of Retributive Theory

The basic weaknesses of this theory have often been exposed. "The foremost is obvious that there is no natural and self-evident relationship between a scale of the seriousness of offences and one of the severities of punishments".[158] Retributive punishment is described as savage, barbaric and backward looking. To punish just for the purpose of punishment is crude retaliation. The theory is said to be a moral paradox. It is full of moral contradictions. For example, how far, can the eye for an eye theory be pushed without it resulting in absurdity? On this an eye for an eye theory, Mr. Justice Akinola Aguda (retired) said:

> It has been argued that according to the teachings of the Bible, capital punishment is justifiable on the philosophy of "an eye for an eye" and "a tooth for a tooth", a philosophy propounded by Moses thousands of years before the greatest religious teachers of the world . . . a member of the British parliament was reported during the debate on capital punishment in 1948 as saying that he received the following letter from a voter in his constituency . . . "its our creed that it's an eye for an eye and a tooth for a tooth, and we are going against our own religious by doing away with something that has been taught to us for donkey's year". This voter and others like him do not seem to consider what Ezekiel said . . . " As I live saith the Lord God, I have no pleasure in the death of the wicked, buy let the wicked turn from his way and live. [159]

From different perspectives one might look at the revenge theory of punishment. It is apparent that it is both anachronistic and indeed barbaric.

Deterrence

The utilitarian aim of punishment have Jeremy Bentham as the patron – Saint Bentham believed, as Seneca puts it that law in punishing wrong

[158]Alan Milner – The Nigerian penal system *op. cit.*, p. 9 at 64.

[159]Being the text of a talk given to the Ibadan Branch of the Nigerian Bar Association on January 24, 1964 on the topic: Capital Punishment: Should it be Abolished" – Select Law Lectures and papers. By Mr. Justice Akinola Aguda – Associated Publishers (Nig.) Ltd., Ibadan 1971 p. 219.

aims at three ends, either it may correct him whom it punishes, or that his punishment may render other men better, or that by bad men being put out of the way, the rest may live without fear.[160] This position is supported by Hobbes who stated that punishment should be inflicted for the correction of the offender on the direction of others.[161]The utilitarian believes that some Hedonistic Calculus governs man and pain and pleasure are the springs of human action. When a man perceives pain as the consequence of an act, he is acted upon with a certain force to withdraw from the commission of the act. But if the apparent magnitude or value of the pain he expects to be the result of his act be greater than the apparent value of pleasure he expects to be the consequence of the act, he will be absolutely prevented from performing it and the mischief, which would have ensued, is by that means prevented.[162] This school therefore propounded that the lawmakers should weigh the scale of pain and pleasure. Once the scale of pain is heavier than pleasure, people will refrain from committing crime. Bentham says the only aim of punishment is to satisfy the people. Any law that provides pleasure to the greatest number of people is good law. The deterrence theory takes two forms. They are special deterrence and general deference. Deference has the most potent principle of punishment. Special deterrence is that punishment should make the criminal not to engage in such criminal act again. For example, an executed armed robber is forever deterred from committing the same offence again. In *State v. Okechukwu* Nkemena J., stated: This type of offence is very common nowadays and a deterrent sentence is called for in this case. Ignorant persons should not be allowed to experiment with lives of others[163]. The Judge then imposed a sentence of nine years in a case of manslaughter by a medical quack. A nine years jail term would definitely deter the accused from committing the same offence until he returns from the prison. The second aspect is the general deterrence. People in general or intending criminals should be deterred by the type of punishment awarded to the criminal for his act.

[160]See Bentham – Principles of Penal Law p.17.

[161]See Soji Omole – Application of the Theories behind Criminal Punishment. The Advocate (Special Edition) Vol. 8 p. 64 for general discussion of this topic.

[162]*Ibid.*

[163](1965) 9 E.N.L.R. 91 at 94.

Deterrence in Legislation

Side by side with the attitude of retribution has developed the attitude, which assumes that crime can be prevented and reduced by the threat of severe penal measures. A potential sentence is specified in each piece of penal legislation, not merely to give notice of what penalty is considered justly proportional to the offence, but also a visible threat to the potential offender that he will be liable to a penalty of this severity if he offends. It is perhaps because this deterrent function is so obvious that it is only expressly mentioned in one piece of legislation. Section 387 of the Criminal Procedure Act requires the court to consider "the prevalence of crime within its jurisdiction" in deciding whether to order corporal punishment.

In times of social stress, when law breaking is hard to control, the deterrent threat is the common expedient. The death penalty (S. 319 cc) and other Corporal Punishment in particular have produced more reliance of the deterrent value of punishment than any other measures. Sometimes the legislature recognizes the prevalence of a particular offence and increases the penalty to increase the general deterrence; thus in 1985, Decree 20 was passed by the Military Administration of General Buhari in Nigeria that provided death sentence for drug pushers.[164] The purpose was to serve as a general deterrence to the would-be cocaine pushers. Recently, special tribunals were set up to try higher institution students' accused of being members of secret cult. The punishment ranges from rustication by the Universities or jail terms for those found guilty by the Courts of law.

Deterrence in Punishment

Legislators' faith in deterrence normally arises at a distance from the actual crimes and the criminals who commit them. The judges are in closer contact with the offences and current in the trends of criminal behaviour. Thus the court in *R. v. Olagbaye* stated that

> this court is of the opinion that having regards to the prevalence of this particular crime the sentences passed are inadequate. [165]

[164]Three condemned men were publicly executed – Ojuolape, Ogedengbe and Lawal before the Decree was repealed.

[165](1936) 3 W.A.C.A. 81.

In 1958 Salmon J. sentenced to four years imprisonment each of nine youths convicted of assaults and wounding offences on coloured men; their appeal were dismissed by the court of Criminal Appeal. These young men had no previous convictions and it is probable that, if their offence had not been committed in a period of race riots, which greatly disturbed the public, they would have been much more leniently dealt with.[166] In *Rex v. Atman Singh* s/o *Chanda Singh.*[167] Appellant, an elderly Sikh, pleaded guilty to the unlawfully wounding his wife. She had gone off to Nairobi to live with another man. The appellant brought her back to Mombassa, and then cut off her nose and ears. He was sentenced to seven years with hard labour and appealed the sentence. His appeal was dismissed and the seven years sentence was confirmed. The court stated that

> We do not consider that the sentence is excessive. When one considers that one of the most important objects of punishments is deterrence, our view is that a lesser sentence might be misunderstood. If there still exist amongst the Sikh or any other Indian Community a custom of disfiguring deserting or unfaithful wives in the hideouts and barbarous fashion exemplified in this case, then the demand for a heavy sentence for such acts should be all the more necessary. It is possible that if the case had come before any of us for trial, that the accused might have received an even heavier sentence.[168]

The rationale for the sentence in this case is self-explicit from this pronouncement of the court. However, Justice Olatawura O. (as he then was) applied the deterrent theory of punishment in a positive way in the case of *The State v. Ibadan Awusapo*[169] The accused, on the 10th day of August, 1973 came home from school to collect his school fees. His father had gone to the farm, and in his absence the accused took his father's gun and started to play with it. In the process he pulled the trigger. The gun went off and killed his brother who was standing by the door of their hut. The trial Judge found the accused

---

[166]See Smith and Hogan Criminal Law 3rd Edition page 18. Hunt (1958) *The Times*, November, 26.

[167](Kenya 1942) 9 E.A.C.A. 69.

[168]*Ibid.*

[169](1986) 1 ODSWMLR 64 at 66-67.

guilty of negligent act causing harm. The court said:

> The fact that the deceased died as a result of the act of the accused will be enough burdens for the accused to carry for quite some time if not all the time. While punishments are inflicted to be a deterrent to others the effect the punishment will have on the accused is also to be taken into consideration. The accused, who at the time of the offence was in a school, has by this act lost the opportunity, of a secondary school education. This loss by itself is a life punishment. In the circumstances of this tragic case, I will not send the accused to jail. He is cautioned and discharged[170].

Obviously, the non-prevalence of this type of crime committed is one of the reasons that the accused was only cautioned and discharged. If it were a prevalence offence in the area, a heavier punishment would have been imposed to serve as a deterrent to the people in the communities around. Indeed the prevalence of crime in the area is one of the facts in which the former Western State High Court[171] rules required trial courts to provide information, in their record of proceedings.[172]

Criticism of Deterrence Theory

The utilitarian theory of criminal punishment is said to have drawn the greatest flak from contemporary writers.[173] Many criticisms have been made against the moral dilemma involved in using human beings as a means to an end. In the first place, there is no accepted data to confirm the assertion that deterrent punishment helps to reduce the rate of crime. Special and general deterrent may not work in a situation where we have recidivist. In any case it is argued that it is against the law of God to punish merely to deter others.

The other criticism against this theory is that the Benthamite model is imperfect psychologically. Criminals in most cases do not calculate pain and pleasure before they act. Before committing a criminal act, many criminals

[170] *Ibid.*

[171] Now Ondo, Ogun, Oyo and Osun States.

[172] See Alan Milner *op. cit.*

[173] Dr. Vukor-Quarshies *op., cit.*

acted from reasons other than for pain and pleasure. A criminal who committed a crime of passion does not consider the pain/pleasure options before acting. In *Commonwealth v. Ritter*[174] Stern J., says:

> Where a murder is committed under the impulse of some frenzy or strong passion or where it results from a mind weakened by long brooding over a social entanglement or by alcoholism or the like such a person is not likely to be deterred by the death penalty imposed on those who commit similar offences.

Apart from the above, the deterrent philosophy has also been criticized on the ground that the philosophy is intellectualistic, individualistic, voluntarilistic as well as positivistic.[175] The assumption that an individual can calculate and arrive at a reasonable answer before committing any crime is intellectualistic. The intelligence level of individual differs; therefore the thinking faculty of individual is not likely to be the same with the others. The Benthamite presumption of calculating of the pain and pleasure level of an act suffers patently from this intellectualistic point of view. Apart from the above, the deterrent philosophy has also been criticized on the ground that the philosophy is intellectualistic, individualistic, voluntaristic as well as positivistic.[176] Similarly, Bentham and his followers concentrated on the individual in the society. The school believes that once an individual in society is understood, then all others in the society are understood. No account of societal causes of crime is taken. Because human beings are regarded as the same all over the world, pain and pleasure are made the yardstick. This is individualistic. This theory is also attacked as being voluntaristic in that the protagonists of the deterrence theory assumed that everybody who commits an offence acts on free will and out of his free choice. But some commit crime because they cannot help themselves. In this connection, Dr. Akinola Aguda[177] said:

> Barring the cases of obviously insane persons who commit murder, 1,241 out of 3,046, guilty of murder in England between 1900 and 1948 were declared insane. We are told by Kate Friend-lander . . .

[174]13 D.C. 285. Reported in Kidish & Paulson.

[175]Dr. Vukor-quarshie *op., cit.*

[176]Dr. Vukor-quarshie: Notes on Criminal Law, University of Ife.

[177]Dr. Akinola Agunda: *op., cit.*, pages 231-232.

> that we are wrong in assuming that either the law-abiding citizen or the delinquent is able to alter at will his basic attitude towards the community. The actions of normal and still more obviously of the neurotic persons are based upon unconscious tendencies accumulated from experiences from early childhood . . . . And one day, a man who has his aggressive urge repressed in (this) way in infancy, may have an opportunity of an outburst resulting in murder from which nothing in this world could have deterred him, not even the gallows . . . .[178]

The deterrence school of punishment never considered this fact of life.

Finally, the Deterrence School is criticized as being positivistic in that the School typified by Bentham and his followers assume that they know all the causes of crime in the society. They believe in the self-imposed hypothesis of natural conception. That is, crime is the nature of man. That man is hedonistic. They are totally confident that they know the causes of crime. But in reality, causes of crimes vary from one society to another and there is no universally accepted determinant. Despite the above criticism of the Bentham Deterrence School, it can be safely concluded that the effect of the theory is great in the modern penal system. But this reliance can be changed once the judicial personnel actually appreciate the incompleteness that typified this theory. Perhaps other theories might come to play a greater role in the sentencing stage at a trial.

Restraint Theory

This is sometimes referred to as the prophylaxis theory, the objective here is simply to detain the offender and by so doing physically to prevent him from repeating offences. The theory sets out to remove the criminal from society and put him where he can do no harm. Its success depends upon the powers of the courts to impose adequate sentences and upon the ability of the institutions themselves to prevent escape. This theory often finds expression in constant traffic violator who may have his licence to drive withdrawn from him. Restrain is a policy of last resort, to which the community turns only if it cannot achieve its objectives by more constructive means.[179]

---

[178]Keith Devlini – *Op. cit.*, p. 9 at 10.

[179]Alan Milner *op. cit.*, p. 83.

Restraint in Legislation and Sentencing

The death penalty has obvious claims to being the most effective measure of restraint though its supporters do not often use this ground as justification.[180] Imprisonment to recidivist may be justified as long as the offender is effectively confined to prison he is prevented from repeating his offences.

Local authorities have extensive powers to require people to leave the area over which they have jurisdiction.[181] In Oyo State for example, a magistrate has power to require any person who is likely to commit a breach of the peace or disturb public tranquility to enter into recognizance up to twelve months to maintain peace[182] or the Magistrate may ask for security for good behaviour for suspected persons[183] or even security for a good behaviour for habitual offenders.[184] Simple prevention lies at the root of disqualification and forfeiture; the hotel owner whose liquor licence is removed, the professional forbidden to practice his profession or the increment of the term of imprisonment of a convicted criminal on appeal. Thus in *R. v. Cooks*[185] a sentence of five years' preventive detention on a man aged 43 charged with shop lifting and with nineteen previous convictions of a similar nature, was upheld on the ground that he was "making nuisance of himself". Similarly in *R. v. Cave*[186] an appeal against a sentence of six years imprisonment by a man who had pleaded guilty to four charges of indecent assault on boys aged nine to eleven, where eleven others offences were taken into consideration, was dismissed on the basis that it was too great a risk to allow him to remain at liberty. This is precisely the rationale of the court in the case of *R. v. Adebesin & Ors.*[187] Accused persons were sentenced to concurrent sentences of ten years with hard labour and eight years respectively, for burglary, stealing and robbery. On appeal, the sentences were enhanced thus "the accused were members of an armed gang committing burglary and robbery, moreover the first accused had previously been convicted of wounding and attempted shooting. For the protection of the public they should be sent to prison for even longer terms than those imposed

[180] *Ibid.*

[181] Local Government Authority Law (1983 Law Cap. 77) S. 48 (N).

[182] S. 35(1) C.P.L. Cap. 31 Laws of Oyo State.

[183] S. 36 C.P.L. Cap. 32 Laws of Oyo State.

[184] S. 37 (a) – (f) C.P.L. Cap. 31 Laws of Oyo State.

[185] [1965] Crim. L.R. 123.

[186] [1965] Criminal L.R. 448.

[187] 6 W.A.C.A. 197 (1940).

by the trial Judge." The sentence of the first accused was thereby increased to fifteen years while the second accused sentence was increased to twelve years".

The Criticism of Restraint Theory

The effectiveness of the restraint theory lies in the immediate disability created for the offender. A persistent traffic violator may drive without a licence after a lapse of time, but initially his dangerousness is curtailed. Whenever the prohibited offence or activity can be performed without detection, the theory has failed. The death penalty is obviously always preventive; those killed for cocaine offences in 1985 in Nigeria never had the opportunity to commit the offence again. Imprisonment too, as long as it is not defeated by escape is a form of restraint, for it effectively cuts off the offender from his criminal opportunities in the outside world. And those who entered into security for good behaviour, as long as they respect the order of the court, will be cautious in not committing further crime within the period in question. However, the weaknesses of restraint theory of punishment lie in the fact that prevention of crime cannot be accepted as the main criterion of acceptability. No community would tolerate death penalty for all offenders; be it cocaine pushers, coup plotters,[188] no matter how effective this theory may be. In the process of balancing the different objectives of the law, prevention of future law breaking may be a valid consideration but to allow it to predominate would be dangerous[189] and unacceptable to the society.

Rehabilitation or Reform Theory

This is the School that is gaining more and more ground today. This School advocates that instead of concentrating on the criminal, lawmakers should identify the causes of crime and eliminate them. Their rallying cry is "let punishment fit the criminal, not the crime." The objective is to encourage the offender to abstain from criminal behaviour in the future by providing

---

[188]In Nigeria, both the execution of cocaine pushers in 1985 and the execution of coup plotters were preceded with passionate plea of mercy from the majority of the citizens and International Community.

[189]See Alan Milner *op., cit.*

him for example, with social support in the form of probation, or a second chance in the form of an absolute or conditional discharge.[190] Alan Milner[191] called this the social readjustment theory. This theory postulates that by training the criminal or reforming him, he is better suited for a role in society. The placement of convicts on probation and corrective training epitomize the object of this theory.[192] Okonkwo and Naish argued that many of the rehabilitative of reformative methods or punishment are not punishment at all, since the aim is not to punish an offender by imposing some unpleasantries upon him, but rather to prevent him from offending again by transforming his attitude so that he himself will voluntarily refrain from offending again. The individualization of treatment is the essence of rehabilitation theory.[193] At times the court will have little to do where the social readjustment has taken place independently. This is implicitly recognized by the frequent use of the caution and discharge option or the binding over to keep the peace and have good behaviour and absolute and conditional discharge.[194] These latter powers are specifically to be exercised when the court considers that "it is expedient to inflict punishment or to make a probation order."[195] One aspect of the application of this principle is the provision of law that allows a complainant to withdraw his complaint against an accused during the trial of a criminal case, but before the final order is made.[196] Bairamian J., in *Basma v. R.*[197] while binding over appellant for twelve months to keep the peace said:

> We think the appellant behaved badly and we tell him so emphatically; but in the circumstances imprisonment was not in our view the right order to make. He is a young person without any previous record; his offence was a misdemeanour and the person he assaulted was his sister, he has made it up with her and her husband and paid ample compensation .... In such a case the court

[190]Keith Devlin *op. cit.*

[191]Alan Milner *op. cit.*

[192]Soji Omole *op. cit.*

[193]Okonkwo and Naish Criminal Law in Nigeria (2nd Edition) (Sweet & Maxwell) p. 9 at 33.

[194]See e.g. *State v. Ibadan Awujapo* (1986) 1 ODSMLR 64, *op. cit.*

[195]Probation of offenders Law (1963) Law Cap. 107. See also Section 435(1) of the C.P.L. Cap. 31 Laws of Oyo State 1978.

[196]Section 284 C.P.L. Cap. 31 Laws of Oyo State, 1978. This is similarly contained in the same section of the Laws of Ogun, Ondo, Osun and many states of the Federal Republic of Nigeria.

[197](1959) 16 W.A.C.A. at 96.

> does well to promote reconciliation and may stretch leniency to the utmost for the sake of promoting amity between persons who are closely connected."[198]

The process of concentrating effort on the improvement of the individual delinquent is a relatively modern development. According to Alan Milner, within the sphere of the English influenced law, it owes much to few particular facts. The first is the growth of a frustrating awareness that other approaches to the handling of criminal problems have not been effective. The Federal Minister of Internal Affairs in Nigeria, in introducing the Prison Bill in the Parliament in 1960 is recorded as saying:[199]

> My view is that offenders should be punished. But that is not the end of the matter. It is a very expensive business just to go on punishing people – expensive to the Government and expensive to society. Let me put it this way. The satisfaction which society might get from punishing an offender is bought at the price of making that offender into a confirmed criminal . . . All we can do is punish him again, and again after that repetition. This is a very wasteful and expensive business. It just does not make sense.

The second is the historical influence of religion. The wish to reclaim lost souls to bring about a moral improvement through contemplation and the acceptance of religious teaching has certainly underlain many penal changes.

Furthermore, the development and refinement of the study of human and social psychology in the nineteenth and twentieth centuries gave impetus to the view that crime and other deviant behaviour may best be explained in terms of personal and social conflicts. This is coupled within the growing conviction that society can best be served by attempting constructive measures with offenders.[200]

---

[198]House of Rep. Deb. (1960-61 Session) Vol. 2155 (Fed.). See Alan Milner *op., cit.*, p. 77 footnote 39.

199These points are listed by Alan Milner.

[200]S.17 of the Children and Young Persons Act Cap. 32 Vol. 1 of 1958 L.F.N. Part III provides for probation and parole for juveniles.

Limitations of Rehabilitation Theory

Rehabilitation theory also has some limitations that may discourage its being endeared to everyone in the society. Okonkwo and Naish pointed out that it is often regarded as exposing the community to risk, in that an offender is left at large. Thus only people who may not constitute great danger to the public usually benefit from its application. These are the juveniles.[201]

The other limitation is the question posed that where is the government supposed to find funds for training convicts? Similarly, the question is often asked that how do you reform a criminal? And is reformation the duty and scope of Criminal Law? In the case of Nigeria, a trend has developed. All the institutions that are supposed to reform criminals are not so functional. The optimism of Okonkwo and Naish that "certain types of institution with rehabilitation rather than deterrence in mind have been, or are in the process of being established in the country", has not materialized. The authors had Borstal training institutions for young offenders in mind. But there is no such institution in Nigeria today. The prison system is more of an institution of training hardened criminals rather than reforming them. The conditions of the prisons are just not conducive for any reformative process. As a result there is hardly a Utopia in reformative theory as far as Nigeria is concerned.

In the light of the foregoing analysis on the theories of punishment, it is imperative to make a case study of a decision where the bare bones of the theories were given flesh and blood in application. This is the judgment of Stern, J.[202] in the case of, *Commonwealth v. Ritter.*[203] Stern, J. Defendant, a married man for several years maintained a cordial relationship with the deceased, a woman married to another man. Defendant had a history of alcohol addiction and was given to fits of frenzy. Following a heated exchange between himself and the deceased over his accusation that deceased was chasing him off after exhausting his money and ruing his marriage, defendant shot and killed her and attempted, un-successfully, to kill himself. Defendant pleaded guilty to an indictment on a charge of murder, which under Pennsylvania law warranted a conviction of second-degree murder unless the court should find affirmatively

[201]*Op. cit., cit.,* at p. 36.

[202](As he then was) He later became the Chief Justice of the Pennsylvania Supreme Court.

[203]The fact and extract of this case is given by KADISH AND PAULSEN. Because of the importance of this case and the exhaustive examination of the theory of punishment, the whole judgment is produced.

that the presence of premeditation and deliberation warranted a conviction of first degree murder and capital punishment. These are the essential facts and from a consideration of them the court had no hesitation in arriving at the conclusion, as it does, that the murder of Mrs. Kennard by the defendant was wilful, deliberate and premeditated and constitutes murder of the first degree. The real question for the determination of the court was as to the penalty to be inflicted. The applicable law provides:

> That every person convicted of the crime of murder of the first degree shall be sentenced to suffer death in the manner provided by law, or to undergo imprisonment for life, at the discretion of the jury trying the case, which shall fix the penalty by its verdict . . . In cases of pleas of guilty, the court where it determines the crime to be murder of the first degree shall at its discretion, impose sentence of death or imprisonment of life . . .[204]

What then should be the punishment inflicted upon the defendant in this particular case? What consideration should weigh in the matter? It must be assumed that the discretion given by the act is to be exercised by the jury or by the court, as the case may be, on some rational basis, and not in an arbitrary, capricious or whimsical manner. The Law, however, furnishes no precedents upon which any theory of determination of the question is to be sought. Indeed, it is obvious that the problem is not one of law at all, but only of penology. Generally speaking, there have been advanced four theories as the basis upon which society should act in imposing penalties upon those who violate its laws. These are: (1) to bring about the reformation of the evil doer; (2) to effect retribution of revenge upon him; (3) to restrain him physically, so as to make it impossible for him to commit further crime; and (4) to deter others from similarly violating the law.

Let us briefly consider these in order:

> 1. As far as the principle of reformation is concerned, however important it may be in the general run of cases, it is obviously has little or no application to such a case as the present. Whichever be the penalty here inflicted, the defendant will not again be in contact with one's relation to the community and

[204]The Act of May 14, 1925.

not primarily with his inward moral development, and the spiritual regeneration of defendant is not, in such a case as this, a dominant fact . . .

2. The second theory, which has been urged as a basis for the imposition of penalties, is that of retribution. This may be regarded as the doctrine of legal revenge, or punishment merely for the sake of punishment. It is to pay back the wrongdoer for his wrongdoing, to make him suffer by way of retaliation even if no benefit results thereby to himself or to others. This theory of punishments looks to the past and not the future, and rests solely upon the foundation of vindictive justice. It is this idea of punishment that generally prevails. Historically, it may be said that the origin of all legal punishments had its root in the natural impulse of revenge. At first this instinct was gratified by retaliatory measures on the part of the individual who suffered by the crime committed, or, in the case of murder, by his relatives. Later, the State took away the right of retaliation from individuals, and its own assumption of the function of revenge really constituted the beginning of Criminal Law. The entire course, however, of the refinement and humanizing of society has been in the direction of dispelling from penology any such theory. Indeed, even in classical times moralists and philosophers rejected the idea entirely. Plato puts into the mouth of protagoras the word: "No one punishes those who have been guilty of injustice solely because they have committed injustice, unless indeed he punishes in a brutal and unreasonable manner when any one makes use of his reason in inflicting punishment, he punishes, not on account of the fault that is past, for no one can bring it about that what has been done may not have been done, but on account of a fault come, in order at the person punished may not again commit the fault and that his punishment may restrain from similar acts those persons who witness the punishment."[205]

Seneca taught that the law, in punishing wrong, aims at three ends: 'Either that it may correct him whom it punishes, or that it may correct him whom it punishes, or that his punishment may

[205]The Laws, Book VIII London Harmondsworth, 1970

render other men better, or that, by bad men being put out of the way, the rest may live without fear."[206]

In later days, Beccaria expressed the purpose of punishment as follows: "The end of punishment is simply to prevent the criminal from doing further injury to society and to prevent others from committing the like offence".[207]Hobbes said "We are forbidden to inflict punishment with any other design than for correction for the offender, or direction of others."[208]

3. Rejecting, therefore, the theory of retribution as a proper basis upon which to impose the penalty of law, we come to the third principle which has been advocated, namely, the restraint of the wrong-doer in order to make it impossible for him to commit further crime. Here we arrive not only at a justifiable basis for action but at one which is vital to the protection of society. To permit a man of dangerous criminal tendencies to be in a position where he can give indulgence to such propensities would be a folly which no community should suffer itself to commit, any more that it should allow a wild animal to range at will in the city streets. If therefore, there is danger that a defendant may again commit crime. Society should restrain his liberty until such danger be past, and, in cases similar to the present, if reasonably necessary for that purpose to terminate his life. Admittedly, restraint by imprisonment can never be as wholly effectual as execution, and there are, from time to time, cases where imprisonment may not be sufficient for the protection of society. It is on this ground that it is pertinent to take testimony in regard to the history of a defendant and of the circumstances attending his commission of crime. If his record shows that he is of a dangerous type, or that he habitually commits grave crimes, or that he has a homicidal tendency, or that he is hopelessly depraved, or that he has a savage nature, or that he has committed murder under circumstances of such atrocity and inhuman brutality as to make his continued existence one of likely danger to society, then, it is submitted that the sentence of death is both justifiable and advisable. The community may not

[206]See The Collected Works of J.S. Mill, ed. J.M. Robson et. al, 21 Vols (\Toronto) (1963-84).

[207]Essays on Crime and Punishment (1963) Indian Polis Books Merril Inc.

[208]The Leviathan ed. C.B. Macpherson, Baltimore, 1968.

> be safe with such a man imprisonment, he may again commit murder within the prison walls, or may escape and again make innocent victims his prey, or may even, by cunning simulation of repentance, obtain a pardon from governmental authorities.

In evaluating the record of the present case from this point of view in order to determine whether the defendant's continuation in life would be a lurking menace to society. One finds nothing in the evidence, which would lead to that conclusion. The murder, which he committed, was the result of many years of entanglement – a terrible tragedy, it is true, but one, which was not the result of any, blood thirstiness or lust for crime. This record is that of a drunkard, with a resulting tendency toward quarrelsome, but, outside of the present case, he cannot fairly be characterized as a man of uncontrollable violence or of homicidal tendency or having any general enmity to the laws of society. As far as the necessity of his own restraint is concerned, one would conclude, therefore, that, by his incarceration in prison for the reminder of his life, society would be sufficiently protected from any further depredations of his part.

4. This brings us to the final and what must be fairly regarded as one of the most important objectives of punishment, namely, the elegant of deterrence the theory which regards the penalty as being not an end in itself but the means of attaining an end, namely, the frightening of others who might be tempted to imitate the criminal. From this angle a penalty is a cautionary measure, aimed at the prevention of further crime in the community. There has been much controversy and an enormous amount of literature on the subject as to whether the death penalty does or does not act as a deterrent. As stated before, the law of Pennsylvania retains the death penalty as an optional alternative. The real question is not as to whether the death penalty is in general a deterrent but as to the particular kinds of murder cases in which execution would or would not be most likely to effect deterrence. It becomes a problem of determining the basis upon which to make such classification.

To sum up, therefore, it is submitted that in case where a tribunal is called upon to determine the penalty to be imposed upon a murderer, the two elements which should be taken into consideration are those of restraint and deterrence, the death penalty being imposed when called for by either of these factors; that the consideration of restraint may demand such penalty when the murderer has a record of crimes of violence, or a homicidal tendency, or commits a murder under such circumstances of calm and deliberate atrocity as to indicate a savage and hopelessly antisocial nature, that the consideration of deterrence may call for the death penalty when the crime results not from an emotional frenzy but from a deliberately and mentally plotted destruction of human life or a crime likely to involve it, as in the instances previously suggested; that otherwise the penalty of life imprisonment may be sufficient for the purpose of the protection of society; and that from a study and analysis of the testimony in the present case, including the history of the defendant and all the circumstances leading up to, attending and following the commission of the crime, an adequate and proper penalty is life imprisonment. Thus, it may be said that, perhaps, after all, the penalty of life imprisonment is not so much a substitute for capital punishment as a slower method of inflicting it.

One unique feature about this case lies in the ability of Stern, P.: The trial Judge to have exercised his discretion after examining the aims of punishment. He also displayed a deep-rooted knowledge of these theories of punishment. He could have stopped at the level when he was satisfied that the defendant committed the offence charged. He could even have awarded a life imprisonment (as he has the discretion to do under the Law) without necessarily giving a reason for so doing, but he went the extra mile and gave a well researched judgment that endeared not only the lawyers but also the entire member of the society to this judgment.

In Nigeria, our judges are hereby admonished to follow this pattern of sentencing wherever cases of such highest punishments known to law i.e. murder, treason, sedition, armed robbery and coup d'etat are brought before them for determination. Going through reported cases of capital crimes, one discovers that many of our judges do not devote much time to consider applicable theory of punishment. What will better serve the plight of the accused person. In most instances there is no record showing that some trial judges do consider the theories of punishment what they are pre-occupied with are to determine whether the quality of evidence adduced by the prosecution establishes the offence charged beyond reasonable doubt to warrant conviction or if the quality of evidence is deficient/insufficient to discharge the accused person with or without being acquitted.

Application of the theories behind criminal punishment

There is perhaps no area of substantive criminal law that has been so neglected as the theories behind criminal punishment. [209] More often than

[209]Soji Omole, *op. cit.*

not judgment is delivered without any analysis of the rationale and criteria on which punishment is imposed. Very few judges bother to spell out the factors guiding them in punishing convicts.[210] However this branch of the law is a very important one, with due regard to the wide discretion given to the courts in imposing punishment made by the legislature. In every society there have existed from time immemorial various notions as to the rationale for imposing sanction on deviants. For instance, in most African societies punishment by (requirement or) sacrifices was to "palliate the gods" or otherwise retributive.[211] In the modern day, people still have their own notions of justice and punishment and this influences the courts.[212] The case of *Anthony Enahoro v The Queen*[213] illustrates this point. Here the appellant was the 2nd Vice-President of the Action Group a political party. He was convicted on various counts of treason and treasonable felony and had his sentence reduced, for the sentence passed by the lower court was in excess of that of leading participant in the crimes. Of all the various theories behind criminal punishment, it is important to examine particularly their applications to case – laws and their various merits and demerits so as to provide a platform for assessing their relevance in the administration of criminal justice systems.

There are various modes of classification of the objects of criminal punishment as applied by different authors as they suit their context. However, there is consensus that there can be a broad classification into utilitarian and non-utilitarian Schools. The other categories fall under these two heads. Retribution, which is the non-utilitarian classification to be considered, has its origin in various pre-medieval codes.[214] It is essentially a backward looking object of punishment, which has as its corner stone that punishment should be commensurate to the offence committed.[215] An exemplification of its operation is capital punishment for murder. The judicial application is illustrated in the case of *R. v. Kumwaka Mulumbi*[216] in which the conviction of sixty appellants for the killing of a witch, who was supposed to have cast a spell on the wife of the first accused and refused to remove it, was upheld. The

[210] Some think it belongs to the field of penology.

[211] See *Infra*.

[212] See *R. v. Agwuna* (1949) 12 W.A.C.A. 456 ("A man who already had convictions for similar offences before he committed the second one does not deserve to be treated with leniency").

[213] Anthony *Enahoro v. The Queen* (1965) N.M.L.R. 265 at 283.

[214] The Babylonian Code, Hamurabi's Code etc.

[215] Okonkwo & Nash, *op. cit.* at p. 28.

[216] (1932) K.L.R. 137.

"witch" was beaten to death with thin sticks carried by the accused. Sir Charles Griffith C.J. (as he then was) found as fact that the accused knew that the government forbade the killing of witches and they felt no remorse for their action and he therefore upheld the sentence of death on all of them.[217] This apparently is ridiculous but it is illustrative of the fact that retributive justice in action for punishment for grave crimes should adequately reflect the revulsion felt by the greater number of citizens for them. The objects of punishment should not be considered as deterrent, reformative, preventive or nothing else. The ultimate justification for punishment is the emphatic denunciation by the community of the crime.[218]

Retribution, which may be likened to vengeance of vendetta, is considered to be a real thing that cannot be ignored until humanity is raised to higher echelons yet unattained in the long ages of struggle and ascent.

The object of punishment had been the most accepted until recent times and the judicial attitude is forcefully stated by Stephen J. in Holmes,[219] . . . I, think it is highly desirable that criminals should be hated, that the punishment inflicted on them should be so contrived as to give expression to that hatred to justify it so far as the provision of means for expressing and gratifying a healthy and natural sentiment can justify and encourage it."

In the light of modern philosophy and knowledge, one is tempted to ask whether it is right to wrought pain and inflict vengeance for the purpose of punishment in the name of "letting of steam" by members of society? Has the offender been given a chance to expiate his wickedness?

Whatever position might be taken, it is clear that retribution as a forward-looking objective is fast fading out an object of criminal punishment. It should be borne in mind that a community, which is too ready to forgive the wrongdoers, may end up condoning the crime.[220] Deterrence is one of the most judicially favoured objects of punishment.[221] It is forward looking with an eye on future results. It aims primarily at the prevention of future crimes. There

---

[217]See also *R. v. Atma Singh* c/o Chanda Singh 9 E.A.C.A. 69 (1) *R. v. Ugo Chima* 10 W.A.C.A. 223.

[218]Denning L.J., in *R. v. C.O.P.* (1953) Cmd. 8732 p. 18.

[219]Cardozo J. "Selected Writings" p. 378.

[220]Goddhart, English Law and the moral law 93 (1953) "Without a sense of retribution we may lose our sense of wrong. Retribution in punishment is an expression of the community's disapproval of crime and if this retribution is not given recognition then the disapproval may also disappear"

[221]It is under the utilitarian School.

are two kinds of deterrence (i) Special deterrence (ii) General deterrence. In the first category, punishment is meted out to the particular offender in the hope that he will be dissuaded from committing future crimes. In General deterrence, the society is put into consideration and the assumption is that by the punishment of the offender, others would be deterred from committing like offences. In *State v. Okechukwu*[222] an offence was committed involving a quack Medical Doctor, and Nkemena J. (as he then was) in delivering judgment, said: "This type of offence is very common nowadays and a deterrent sentence is called for in this case". Further illustration of deterrent punishment is provided by the judgment of Salmon J. (as he then was) who in 1958 sentenced to four years imprisonment each of nine youths convicted for assault and wounding offences on coloured men at a time of race riots.[223] This penalty would otherwise have been too heavy.

Deterrent punishment is not an end in itself but a means of bringing an end. It is appropriate for meticulously planned offences such as highway robbery and burglaries, but at times it is imposed to show that necessity does not carry a privilege. In the case of *R. v. Dudley and Stephens.*[224] Deterrence was obviously at work there. Deterrence has its own demerits.[225] Is it fair that a man should be used to dear others? The theory as a whole rests upon unproved assumptions on human bchaviour. How many people have been deterred from committing crimes? As stated by Judge Joseph N. Ulman of Supreme Bench of Maryland, U.S.A. "So far as is known nobody has devised nor even attempted to devise any material method of testing its validity, certainly not in any measurable or quantitative manner, it is so subjective a faction that it is almost impossible to conceive of any method by which to test it. Yet it would seem to be one of those social realities, which is real becausc thc 'common sense' of society tells us that it is real and the sentencing Judge cannot afford to over look it.[226]

[222]*Op. cit.*

[223]See Smith & Hogan "Criminal Law" p. 13.

[224](1884) 14 Q.B.D. 273.

[225]See Asquith L.J. "The guilt of a man who committed a crime when it happens to be on the increase is no greater than that of another man who commits the same crime when it is on the wane. The truth is that in such cases the Judge is not administering strict justice but choosing the lesser of two practical evils. He decides that a moderate injustice to the criminal is a lesser evil than the consequence to the Public of a further rise to crime wave" The Listner XLIII at page 821.

[226]"The trial Judge's dilemma – A Judge's view.

The judgment of the appellate court in *R. v. Adebesin*[227] introduces us to the theory of punishment known as restraint or disablement, which is also in the Utilitarian School of punishment. This was an appeal from he conviction of two men for armed robbery and burglary. In a similar case, *R. v. Jhunu*[228] Appellants were members of an unarmed gang of men who bugled a house by force and were sentenced to three years' imprisonment with hard labour, their sentences were held inadequate in that the higher court was of the opinion that the public must be protected against burglary of this nature carried out by gangs, by the imposition of more severe penalties.

This object of punishment is the most logical, for the best way to protect the society is by keeping away the criminal so that he is unable to commit any more crimes. As Edmund Davies J. stated, in the Great Train Robbery Case:[229]

> It will be an affront if you were to be at liberty in the near future to enjoy these ill-gotten gains. I propose to ensure that such an opportunity should be denied you for a very long time. The logic is that as roving wild animals should be put away, in a like manner the public should be protected from criminals.

Commonwealth v. Ritter[230] provides an illuminating departure from what is supposed to be the order of the day. Stern J. in delivering judgment carefully considered the various theories of criminal punishment and then decided to apply restraint as an object of punishment and imposed a sentence of life imprisonment. Reform or rehabilitation is the last but by no means the least of the theories to be considered. It has as its rallying cry that punishment should fit the criminal not the crime. It is the latest in the Utilitarian School.

This theory postulates that by training the criminal or reforming him, he is better suited for a role in Society. The placement of convicts on probation[231] and corrective training[232] are epitomes of this object of criminal punishment.

Where is government supposed to find the funds of training convicts in the face of pressing social needs? Rehabilitation is no doubt an expensive

---

[227] *Op. cit.*

[228] 7. W.A.C.A.

[229] See Prof. Cross (1965) 81 L.Q.R. at p 218.

[230] (1940) 6 W.A.C.A. 197.

[231] See S. 438 C.C. and Part III of Children and Young Persons Act.

[232] *R. v. McCaughty* (1955) 2 All E.R. 927.

object of punishment. Where reform of the offender conflicts with deterrence, the principle of reformation will most likely give way. In *R. v. Stewarts*[233] a boy of 16 years' old had a three-year sentence imposed on him for robbery with violence, thereby robbing him of opportunity to continue his education without an option of disciplinary training. Okonkwo believes that there is an educative theory of criminal punishment and certain legislations are made of criminal punishment and certain legislations are made to effect this object.[234] On closer scrutiny, it is submitted that this is no more than a variant of the deterrence object of punishment and it is therefore false to create any categorization as education theory. In recapitulation, it is conceded that all the objects of criminal punishment have their positive aspect and Messrs Smith and Hogan have rightly observed that Deterrence and Reformation are now in vogue. It is submitted however that the identification of crime and its punishment with moral blame-worthiness must not be shoved aside and thus punishment should always be commensurate to the offence committed. In opposition to the philosophy of the utilitarianism, man should still be punished solely for the sake of his offence. As stated by no less an authority than the legend of law, Lord Denning M.R. "In order that an act should be punishable, it must be morally blameworthy, it must be a sin."[235]

[233](1961) Criminal L.R. 844.

[234]"The changing Law" Lord Denning.

[235]"The changing Law" Lord Denning.

3

DEATH PENALTY AND HUMAN RIGHTS

It is imperative to examine the concept of human rights, the constitutionality of right to life, the death row phenomenon and other related subject-matters vis-à-vis the practice of death penalty in Nigeria. In this regard it will be expedient to further make use of various descriptive analysis on the subject, relevant constitutional provisions of foreign jurisdictions and decided cases in Nigeria as well as foreign jurisdiction with a view to evaluating the propriety or otherwise of the administration of death penalty in the country.

What Are Human Rights?

Human rights are difficult to define. They are better explained as those fundamental and inalienable rights, which are essential for life as a human being. The law of nature has bestowed on mankind certain inalienable rights, which have been recognized and protected in all the Constitutions of the world including Nigeria. Thus, all human rights are universal, indivisible and interdependent and interrelated.[236] Though many states regard human rights as falling within domestic jurisdiction and not a matter to be tackled by international law, nevertheless human rights is a subject of contemporary international law and the efforts to regulate human rights at the international

[236]See The Vienna Declaration of Human Rights and Programme of Action, June 25, 1993 which identified particularly vulnerable groups of individuals as being women, minorities, children, refugees, indigenous people, prisoners and persons with disabilities. See also Rebecca M. M. Wallace, International Law, 3rd Edition 1997 at p. 205.

level have gained momentum after World War II. It is in the realization of this global awareness that the Universal Declaration of Human Rights was adopted by the United Nations General Assembly in 1948; also it is the same global awareness that prompted Nigeria to ratify the African Charter on Human and Peoples' Rights[237] to enable us move with the rest of the human race in the observance, implementation and enforcement of these rights. Before the current civilian dispensation, precisely under late Gen. Abacha regime, Nigeria witnessed unprecedented records of human rights violation such as extra-judicial killing, torture, harassment and ill treatment of citizens.[238] The Abubakar Regime ushered in some positive and significant developments in the observance of human rights.[239] The preceding civilian administrations have set up mechanisms and various ways of improving human rights situation. The judiciary is expected to actively show its readiness to complement the efforts of the Executive by an inspiring judicial approach to enforce the observance of human rights where appropriate and feasible.[240] The enforcement of human rights is a tribute to the rule of law being the first principle of democracy as exemplified in the doctrine of separation of powers, which is antithetical to autocracy. It is worthy of note that the rule of law may sometimes be given some form of recognition under autocratic governance, but the rule of law in such circumstances is constantly under stress, which invariably affects the functioning of the judiciary. Yet under that state of affairs, the judiciary must strive to excel in considering cases of abuse of human rights in order to do what is feasible to redress such abuse.

Condemned Persons and their Fundamental Rights

If a person condemned to death by a court of competent jurisdiction complains under Chapter IV of the Constitution of the Federal Republic of Nigeria, 1999, that any of the provisions of this chapter has been breached in regard to him, is he entitled to enforce these rights? And if he is so entitled,

[237]See African Charter on Human and Peoples' Rights (Ratification and Enforcement) Act Cap. 16 Vol. 1 LFN 1990, where Nigeria adopted the African Charter on Human and Peoples' Rights as part of her Municipal Law.

[238]See Nigeria Human Rights Report, September 1998 published by Constitutional Rights Project; Chapter 2 pp. 13-46.

[239]*Op. cit.*, Chapter 1, p. 1.

[240]See *Ogugu v. The State* (1994) 9 NWLR pt. 366 p. 47.

to which of the provisions, before which court can he seek redress? These issues and other related ones will be examined in this paper with a view to determining whether or not a condemned person automatically forfeits his fundamental rights as soon as he is convicted and sentenced to death. This chapter also evaluates the manner of execution of condemned prisoners by hanging in Nigeria vis-à-vis the evolving and dynamic international clamour in other jurisdictions that the death penalty has come to be regarded in contemporary human rights jurisprudence as a violation of the right not to be subjected to torture, inhuman and degrading punishment with particular searchlight on the inevitable long wait between the imposition of the death sentence and the actual infliction of death, usually referred to as the "death-row phenomenon" as a crucial factor in the characterization of the death penalty as a destructive, cruel and degrading "treatment in the evolving standards of civilization."

Novel cases of human rights claims may arise in regard to the condemned prisoners in difficult situations like that of complaints of torture, inhuman and degrading treatment, the judiciary should be able to cope with the situations and circumstances of the time and prevailing operational conditions, but not on the mere reflection behind dim light, and sighting the shortened form of their silhouette readily conclude that they had a diminutive stature which makes it too impossible for them to attempt the job of solving human rights abuse of an unusual type.[241]Under such circumstances, the court is expected to determine whether the cause of action brought by the condemned prisoner has merit or not depending on the strength of the case. The Court of Appeal Lagos Division extensively considered the rights or otherwise of a condemned person in the case of *Peter Nemi v. Attorney-General of Lagos State & Anor.*,[242] the appellant and four other persons were convicted of conspiracy to commit armed robbery and sentenced to death on February 28, 1986 after he had been in custody since he was arrested on September, 1982. The Court of Appeal dismissed his appeal on March 29, 1990 and by the Supreme Court on October 14, 1994. The appellant then applied *ex parte* in an action filed in the Federal High Court, Lagos on January 17, 1995 and was granted leave to enforce his fundamental right based on the following reliefs:

---

[241]Per Olomojobi J., Federal High Court of Lagos in *Peter Nemi v. Attorney-General of Lagos State & Anor.* (unreported).

[242]CA/L/221/95 delivered on Wednesday, July 3, 1996 reported in the Guardian July 30 1996.

(i) declaration that the prison confinement of the Applicant under sentence of death since February 28, 1986 (a period of eight years) constitutes an infringement of Applicant's fundamental rights against torture, inhuman and degrading treatment protected by section 31(1)(a) of the Constitution of Federal Republic of Nigeria, 1979; and

(ii) an order directing that the sentence of death on the applicant be quashed and/or commuted to such term of imprisonment as this honourable court may direct.

During the hearing of motion on Notice, the defendants/respondents raised a preliminary objection on the grounds that:

(a) the appellant had no legal capacity to institute the action;
(b) the court lacked the jurisdiction to entertain it; and
(c) the application was incompetent in law.

The learned trial judge, Olomojobi, J., upheld the objection and held that the court was not competent to adjudicate on the action.

The appellant raised only one issue for determination at the Court of Appeal Lagos:

> Whether in the circumstance of this case, the Federal High Court is precluded from assuming jurisdiction to entertain the Appellant's application to enforce his fundamental rights.

The Court of Appeal held *inter alia* that it is open to a condemned person to seek redress by virtue of Section 42 of the 1979 Constitution (Section 46 of the 1999 Constitution) in a High Court in the State where the breach took place.

The Rights of Appeal

A condemned person that has been sentenced to death by a High Court is entitled to exercise his right of appeal up to the Supreme Court even if the Court of Appeal affirms the sentence.

S. 24(1) of the 1999 Constitution provides:

> An appeal shall lie from decisions of the Federal High Court or a High Court to the Court of Appeal as of right in the following cases –
> (a) final decisions in any civil or criminal proceedings before the Federal High Court or a High Court sitting at first instance.
> (b) ....
> (c) decisions in any civil or criminal proceedings on questions as to the interpretation or application of this Constitution;
> (d) decisions in any civil or criminal proceedings on questions as to whether any of the provisions of Chapter IV of this Constitution has been, is being or is likely to be, contravened in relation to any person;
> (e) decisions in any criminal proceedings in which the Federal High Court or a High Court has imposed a sentence of death.

The Supreme Court has appellate jurisdiction in all the above stated instances from decisions of the Court of Appeal by virtue of Section 233 of the Constitution. In the course of exercising his Constitutional right, a condemned prisoner must not be rushed or stampeded into invoking his right of judicial process because of the irredeemable consequences of administration of death sentence. Similarly, the administrative procedure contained in the implementation of judicial pronouncement of death sentence by the Executive arm serves as an avenue to correct certain fundamental anomalies, mistakes or errors of Constitutional dimensions, which did not emerge or could not have been ascertained during the length of trial and appeals.[243] This factual dimension justifies the need for retaining the ample system of judicial review (in capital offences), and underscores the danger of 'tinkering with the machinery of death'.[244] The significance of this principle is vividly revealed in the case of *Baruwa v. The State;*[245] where the appellant and another were arrested and charged for murder in January 1982 and sentenced to death on June 24, 1985. The appellant appealed against his sentence. The process of appeal took 11 years after he was sentenced (and 14 years from

---

[243]For example in America it has been reported that over the past twenty-three years, a large number of persons awaiting execution on death row have ultimately been set free because they were proven to be innocent. See The Report of International Commission of Jurists Administration of the Death Penalty in the United Statess, June 1996 at p. 64.

[244]The Report of International Commission of Jurists etc. *op. cit.*

[245]1999 NWLR.

the date of his arrest), delivering the judgment of the Court of Appeal, Justice Uwaifo held that the evidence adduced at the trial was grossly insufficient, tendentious, suspicious and contradictory. The Learned Justice further held that the finding of guilty by the High Court was perverse and speculative; the appellant was discharged and acquitted. The pathetic aspects of this case are of two folds: it was established that the appellant only played the role of "good Samaritan" by reporting to the Police that an unknown man was lying dead or dying unattended to in a public place, this eventually earned him his long incarceration and agony. More disturbing is the fact that the other person charged along with Baruwa and sentenced to death at the High Court died in custody before the processing of appeal having undergone harrowing experience of prolonged incarceration in prison yard faced with the reality of a pending death sentence.

The Sanctity of Rights of Appeal

The rights of appeal open to a condemned person is fundamental and must be honoured in all ramifications, the appellant cannot be blamed for taking part in the judicial process of appeal even if the exercise of this right constitutes a delay in the process as it is made compulsory. The Respondent cannot apply that a suit brought by the appellant should be struck out or dismissed *in limine*. The Supreme Court has held in a number of cases that a condemned man is entitled under the Constitution to appeal against his sentence up to the Supreme Court and cannot blame the authority for allowing him to exercise his Constitutional rights through the judicial process of appeal even though he spends long period of years to undertake this right.[246] For instance, in the case of *Peter Nnemi v The State*[247] from the time of arrest (1982) up to the time the Supreme Court delivered its judgment in 1994; a period of 12 years has passed. Similarly, in the case of *Baruwa v. The State,*[248] the appellant was arrested in 1982 and sentenced to death in 1985 and an appeal to Court of Appeal judgment was delivered in 1996, a period of 14 years when he was discharged and acquitted. The notion that all accused should receive fair and

[246] *Peter Nemi v. Attorney General Lagos State* [1996] 6 NWLR 42. *Effiom v. The State* [1995] 1 N.W.L.R. (Pt. 373) 507, *Kalu v. The State* [1998] 12 SCNJ 1, *Okoro v. The State* [1998] 12 SCNJ 84.
[247] *Op. cit.*
[248] *Ibid.*

equal prosecutorial treatment by the State is an aspect of the rule of law. The Supreme Court reiterated this principle in *Nofiu Bello v. The State,*[249] where the appellant who was sentenced to death on a charge of armed robbery by a High Court of Oyo State was executed while his appeal was pending in court. The Supreme Court condemned this action and stated poignantly that the Attorney's General office demands greater personal responsibility in the performance of public duties and must ensure that all avenues of appeal have been exhausted before advising the Governor to confirm the execution. The court then awarded damages for the dependants of the appellant.

The Prerogative of Mercy

A condemned person may apply in person or through someone on his behalf or the prison authorities may forward his prison report for purposes of periodical review to the President or Governor of a State for clemency. An application of this nature must be accompanied with relevant particulars and testimonials from reputable persons testifying to the conduct of the condemned person. This application must be rooted through the office of the Attorney General[250] of the Federation or of the State as the case may be. According to Wade and Phillips,[251] Prerogative of Mercy is the only means of reviewing judicially the judgment of a criminal court of final jurisdiction as a veritable means of rectifying any injustice through the grant of pardon. Before this application is considered, the judgment must be final and not subject to an appeal to a higher court. The Attorney General is empowered to render legal opinion on such an application of prerogative of mercy in case of death sentence by either suggesting to the Advisory Council and the Chief Executive a recommendation of commutation of sentence from death to life imprisonment or refusing such an application.

[249][1980] 8-11 SC. 130.

[250]See The Report of Mr. Tunji Oni, the then Solicitor-General and Permanent Secretary, Ministry of Justice Oyo State presented to officers of the Ministry of Justice following the public reaction to the role of the Ministry in the execution of Nafiu Bello while his appeal was pending.

[251]Constitutional Law, 6th Edition, p. 303.

Criminal Procedure Act

A trial court itself can refer a case to the President or the Governor where the condemned person has been found to be of unsound mind and ordered that the convict be kept in custody during the Governor's pleasure.[252] The office of the Governor upon the receipt of this report sends the file to the Attorney General's office to prepare appropriate warrant based on the directions of the judge.

Robbery and Fire-arms Act

After a conviction under the Robbery and Firearms (Special Provisions) Act 1990 is made the Chairman of the tribunal refers the sentence to the Governor for consideration, section 1(3) states:

> The sentence of death imposed under this section may be executed by hanging the offender by the neck till he be dead or by causing him to suffer death by firing squad as the Governor may direct.[253]

Under Military regimes in Nigeria, the decision of this Tribunal was not subject to appeal i.e. the accused convicted is denied a right of appeal. But under the present dispensation, condemned persons are entitled to exercise their Constitutional rights of appeal up to the Supreme Court. Due to the fact that ours is a crime infested society, attention is naturally focused on the punitive element of criminal law necessitating the setting apart of designated places called "prisons" for the confinement of offenders, the undesirable elements convicted of crimes. Unlike the awaiting trial persons, convicts enjoy relative care and attention of the prison authorities in terms of feeding and accommodation as it is the responsibility of the state to cater for them being recognized entities by law, while they exist the prison authorities must take them into consideration in their plans.[254] It is pertinent at this juncture to ask

---

[252]See Section 401 Criminal Procedure Act.

[253]Death sentence by hanging is the manner recognized under the Criminal Code and Procedure, however death sentence by firing squad was introduced by the Military Regime of Gen. Gowon as a deterrent penalty for the members of public who may wish to venture into armed robbery.

[254]See Adeniyi Olatubosun, "The Plight of Awaiting Trial Persons Under The Criminal Justice System In Nigeria" in Topical Issues in Nigeria Law, essays in Honour of Justice N. O. Adekola Ed. Laoye & Akintayo, Zenith Publishers 2000 at p. 123.

the following questions: Can it be rightly said that a condemned person has no right to life, cannot enforce any fundamental rights and is therefore as good as dead? Does it mean that a condemned prisoner can be lawfully starved to death by the prison authorities? Can he be lawfully punished, by a slow and systemic elimination of his limbs one after another, until he is dead? Would any of these amounts to inhuman treatment or torture? Is a condemned prisoner not a person or an individual? In answering these questions, they must be thoroughly examined from every angle and determined in an action complaining of their breach; when breached, they are to be redressed in all circumstances as appropriate.

Right to Life

Section 33(1) of the Constitution provides:

> Every person has a right to life, and no one shall be deprived intentionally of his life, save in execution of the sentence of a court in respect of a criminal offence of which he has been found guilty in Nigeria.

This section guarantees and protects the right to life. But it also recognizes deprivation of right to life so long as it is pursuant to the execution of the sentence of a court in a criminal offence of which the accused has been found guilty in Nigeria. Thus Section 33 (1) of the Constitution permits death penalty so long as it is inflicted pursuant to the sentence of a court of law in Nigeria in a criminal offence. Therefore, the imposition or execution of the death sentence in Nigeria is not subjected to any form of arbitrary, discriminatory or selective exercise of discretion on the part of any court or any other quarters whatever. The death penalty in Nigeria can by no stretch of the imagination be said to be invalid or unconstitutional.[255] Apart from the provisions of Section 33(1), there are also provisions of Sections 233(2)(d) and 241(1)(e) of the Constitution which recognize the death penalty as a form of sentence.

---

[255]Per Iguh J.S.C. in *Kalu v. The State (supra)* further observed, "If the framers of the Constitution had wanted to abolish the death penalty they would have done so expressly. That abolition or retention of death penalty is a matter for the legislature to decide and it is not for the court to wade into judicial legislation.

Furthermore death penalty is provided for by our criminal laws for example under Section 319 of the Criminal Code:

> Subject to the provisions of this Section any person who commits the offence of murder shall be sentenced to death.

It is therefore crystal clear from the provisions of the Constitution that right to life is qualified and as such death penalty under such circumstance is Constitutional, permissible and valid. It can therefore be rightly said that Section 33(1) of the Constitution is free from any ambiguity whatever. It cannot be derogated from. By the first part of this section, the Constitution, in plain language, recognizes and protects the right to life. But by its subsequent part, or proviso is a qualifying clause which permits life to be taken in execution of the sentence of a court in respect of a criminal offence of which the accused has been found guilty.

Right to Dignity of Human Person

Section 34(1) states:

> Every individual is entitled to respect for the dignity of his person, and accordingly –
> (a) no person shall be subjected to torture or to inhuman or degrading treatment.

Under the administration of criminal justice system when a person is sentenced to death the question of bail for him pending execution is impossible; he must be kept in custody for the final day. The condemned person is kept at a designated prison yard for a period of time before his execution is carried out.

This waiting period is known as the Death-row phenomenon. In Nigeria, death-row prisoners spend on average five to 10 years. Of all the rights guaranteed under Chapter IV of the 1999 Constitution, Section 34 appears to be the only right which confers unqualified right on a condemned person to seek redress in a High Court through Section 46 of the Constitution if he feels his fundamental right under Section 34(1) has been breached in regard to him. Thus, if after death sentence has passed and the accused is in prison custody and anything arises which injures his person, such will be a cause of action under fundamental rights. In such a case the death sentence stands, but a new cause of action has arisen which can be separately enforced and remedied.

The Supreme Court has been called upon in cases of *Peter Nemi v. The State;*[256] *Effiom v. The State;*[257] *Kalu v. The State*[258] in recent times to determine:

> (i) the validity or Constitutionality of death penalty in Nigeria;
> (ii) whether long period of time for which a condemned prisoner has been awaiting his execution constitute torture, inhuman and degrading treatment to warrant his execution to be committed to terms of imprisonment.

It should be noted that learned counsel for the appellants in these cases, especially Olisa Agbakoba (now SAN) argued strongly and vehemently too that the issue raised in the appeal is novel and has not been determined in this country therefore it is not an issue to be brushed aside without first giving it a very serious and full consideration by examining the issue within the context of our Constitutional provisions and in conjunction with the relevant provisions of the African Charter on Human and Peoples' Rights. The Supreme Court admitted that "a very far-reaching Constitutional question has been raised in the appeal"[259] as a result of which it empanelled a full court of seven justices, invited eminent counsel nationwide and Attorney-Generals of all the States and the Federation as *amici curia* in addition to briefs filed by all counsel for the appellants and the states concerned.

After listening to arguments on all sides for and against issues raised in the appeal, the Supreme Court held *inter alia* that:

> The confinement of the appellant under sentence of death for prolonged length of time from the date of his conviction is regrettable, it does not amount to torture, inhuman and degrading treatment.

[256] *op. cit.*
[257] *op. cit.*
[258] *op. cit.*
[259] Per Bello C.J.N. (as he then was).

Although the Supreme Court of Nigeria had the opportunities to consider the position of foreign jurisdictions through decided cases cited such as *Abott v. A.G. of Trinidad and Tobago*;[260] *Riley v. A.G. of Jamaica*;[261] and *Bell v. D.P.P. of Jamaica*[262] where the Privy Council took the hard and tortuous journey through the cases to reach a landmark decision on a provision in the Jamaican Constitution similar to Section 34(1)(a) of our Constitution particularly in the case of *Pratt v. A.G. for Jamaica*[263] to hold that prolonged custody of a condemned person from the date his conviction is affirmed by the highest Court of the land constitutes an infringement on human right of the prisoner in regard to his dignity to warrant either commutation of his death sentence to terms of imprisonment or release as the case may be. Nevertheless the conclusion of our Supreme Court to the effect that the undue delay in the execution of the death sentence, coupled with the deplorable conditions under which the prisoners awaiting execution were confined which gave rise to inhuman and degrading treatment complained of by the condemned person are not issues to be addressed by the courts but by the legislature is with due respect untenable and invalid. It is not acceptable to hold that novel cases of human rights claims arising from indeterminable and unascertainable years of anticipatory execution cannot be remedied by the apex court of the land through its judicial pronouncement to solve human rights abuse of an unusual type of this nature. In contemporary society, it is the duty of the judiciary to accept the challenge to confront and examine the novel aspect of human rights as daunting as the stress being undergone by the condemned prisoners in the circumstances.[264] It should be pointed out that the right not to be subjected to torture, inhuman or degrading treatment under Section 34(1)(a) of the 1999 Constitution is a non-derogable right, i.e., one of the rights that may not be derogated from by legislation. Those specific rights in respect of which the Constitution permits derogation by legislation are set out in Section 45(1) and (2) of the Constitution.

---

[260][1979] 1 W.L.R. 1342.

[261][1983] A.C. 719 (P.C.

[262](1985) 2 All E.R. 585.

[263](1993) 4 All E.R. 769.

[264]**See** *Catholic Commission for Justice and Peace in Zimbabwe v. A.G.* No. S.C. 73/1993 unreported delivered on June 24, 1993 now [1993] (4) S.A. 239 (ZSC), where the Supreme Court of Zimbabwe in its original jurisdiction under Section 24 of their Constitution entertained a similar case.

Section 45(1) and (2) provides as follows:

> Nothing in sections 37, 38, 39, 40 and 41 of this Constitution shall invalidate any law that is reasonably justifiable in a democratic society –
> (a) in the interest of defence, public safety, public order, public morality or public health; or
> (b) for the purpose of protecting the rights and freedom of other persons;
> (2) An act of the National Assembly shall not be invalidated by reason only that it provides for the taking, during periods of emergency or measures that derogate from the provisions of sections 33 or 35 of this Constitution . . . .

It is therefore submitted that a condemned person cannot seek redress on specific rights namely: right to private and family life; right to freedom of thought, conscience and religion; right to freedom of expression and the press; right to peaceful assembly and association and right to freedom of movement by virtue of the fact that having tried and found guilty of a capital offence, the condemned person is restricted from enjoying these inalienable rights by operation of law. However, a condemned person is reasonably entitled to his "safety" and welfare within the prison's regulations on the conditions of convicts in prison even though he is awaiting his execution. Thus while the condemned person is in the custody of the state, the state has a responsibility to ensure that he is not put in undue dangers of his health and safety. Therefore, if the state of health of a condemned person demands treatment on special drugs, it must be provided by the state and where these were not available and the prisoner wants to have access to this special drugs at his own expenses[265] the prison authorities should oblige him to enjoy such necessary goods provided the administration of the said drugs is carried out under the supervision or in the presence of medical doctor/physician in charge of the prison yards where the applicant is detained or hospitalized as the case may be. This arrangement

[265]See Adeniyi Olatubosun, "Constraints in the Administration of Criminal Justice in Nigeria" M.Phil thesis submitted to Obafemi Awolowo University, 2002. See also CA/L/141/96 reported in *The Guardian*, July 16, 1996.

is to ensure that the responsibility of the state to secure the prisoner's safety is in no way compromised.[266]

Manner of Execution

A condemned prisoner is a person or an individual accordingly ending his life must be done in accordance to the due process of law. Under the Criminal Procedure Act, the manner of carrying out the sentence of death is by hanging. Therefore, in a case pertaining to the death row phenomenon, the appellant is entitled to allege that the execution by hanging is barbaric or otherwise and can even complain that the undue delay in the execution of the death sentence coupled with the deplorable conditions under which the prisoners awaiting execution were confined warrant commutation of his death sentence to life imprisonment. It is trite law that death sentence is a reality and Constitutional in Nigeria as a penalty for heinous crimes. At post-conviction stage, the offender can no longer rely on the presumption of innocence, as there is an overriding presumption of guilt making the sentence of death as properly imposed. The due process of law is to ensure punishment only of the guilty and not of the innocent so as to ensure that those convicted of capital offence have been properly so convicted. It is the opinion of this writer that by operation of law murder being a heinous crime, the punishment highest known to law the principle of criminal jurisprudence demands that t must be cautiously implemented. Perhaps, it is in consonance with this cardinal principle of law that post-conviction periods of condemned prisoners (death-row phenomenon) serve as an important mechanism in correcting Constitutional errors that is likely to occur during the trial and appeal process, for example, it was the denial of late Ken Sarowiwa and others the opportunity of death-row period before the process of their execution was carried out during late General Abacha Regime that led to universal condemnation of the Federal Military Government's action and the suspension of Nigeria from Committee of Commonwealth Nations.

It should be pointed out that learned counsel for the appellant in *Kalu v. The State* vehemently attacked the process of execution of death sentence in

[266]See Hon. Justice Obaseki, J.S.C. "Causes of Congestion in Prisons and Proposals for Solution" Law Development and Administration in Nigeria 1990 published by the Federal Ministry of Justice, Law Review Series 1990 pp. 289-320.

Nigeria. He made a copious reference to an article written by Professor Chris Barnard that:

> The man's spinal cord will rupture at the point where it enters the skull, electro-chemical discharges will send his limbs flailing in a grotesque dance, eyes and tongue will start from the facial apertures under the assault of the rope and his bowels and bladder may simultaneously void themselves to soil the legs and drip on the floor...[267]

The South African Constitutional Court in the case of The State v. Makwanyane has quoted the above-stated description,[268] where O'Regan J. commented on the above description as follows: Thus frank description of the execution process leaves little doubt that it is one which is destructive of human dignity. No doubt, this manner of execution is gory and sordid, it is better imagined than experienced, the task of a hangman is most daunting and should be exercised with great caution. It is most disturbing to note that despite the fact that the Supreme Court of Nigeria conceded the point that the process of execution is sordid, the apex Court ruled that they were not concerned with the manner of carrying out the death sentence, but the sentence itself. The learned justices of the Supreme Court further held that anything else beyond the passing of the sentence is not the subject of appeal and that whatever process employed is not relevant. The Supreme Court further stated that the foreign decisions cited on the point though strongly persuasive appear academic. With due respect, this view is unacceptable under contemporary standards of decency in view of the enormity of pain being inflicted in course of carrying out this process. The mental agony inherent in this exercise is simply beyond question, harrowing and horrific and as such it is impermissibly cruel. Much as the victim, of a murderous assault was entitled to life, so also is the murderer liable to death for his deed. The victims of murder are entitled to their fundamental rights; the condemned persons are entitled to their human rights, same right to life. It remains uncontroverted that our Constitution recognizes death sentence and that manifests in the provision "save in execution of the sentence of a court" in section 33(1) above quoted. The sentence of death is fully recognized and approved by the Constitution

---

[267]Rand Daily Mail of June 12, 1978.

[268][1995] (6) B.C.L.R. 665 (CC); [1995] S.A.C.L.R. LEXIS 218.

vide the provisions of Section 233(2)(d), 241(1)(e). Similarly section 319(1) of the Criminal Code under which a condemned person was tried and convicted only provided for the death penalty for the offence charged and not the sentence. Penalty in this context is not synonymous with sentence and the two must not be confused. The provision for the death sentence is prescribed under Section 367(1) & (2) of the Criminal Procedure Law – it reads:

> (1) The punishment of death is inflicted by hanging the offender by neck till he be dead.
> (2) Sentence of death shall be pronounced in the following form – The sentence of the court upon you is that you be hanged by the neck until you be dead and may the Lord have mercy on your soul.

Contrary to the argument that death sentence (by hanging) is barbaric and sordid; it still wears human face in the sense that its pronouncement acknowledges divine grace. The end result of capital punishment by hanging is intrinsically the same with death penalty by administering injection[269] prevalent in the United States of America – the resultant effect of both methods is death. It is therefore our opinion that having regard to the historical and cultural backgrounds of our society, the generally held norms values, aspirations and local conditions that the death penalty is a necessary and acceptable form of punishment for heinous crimes. Shorn of procedural abuses, it helps to preserve equilibrium in the society by providing a measured and appropriate response to barbarous criminal acts that threaten the moral foundation and bastion of the Nigerian society. However, so long as capital punishment remains valid under the Nigerian legal system the state must accept the responsibility of ensuring that execution follows as swiftly as practicable after sentence, allowing a reasonable time for appeal and consideration of reprieve by the executive. A situation whereby a condemned prisoner is kept in the death row for over 13 years or more in anticipation of his execution is to say the least cruel, inhuman and degrading treatment. Except we reconsider the proprietary of retaining death penalty as a dignifying form of punishment,[270]

[269]Recently in America, the Oklahoma City bomber Timothy McVeigh was executed by lethal injection on Monday June 11, 2001 at the Federal Prison in Terri Haute, United Statess. He became the first prisoner executed by the U.S. government in 38 years reported in *The Punch*, Tuesday June 12, 2001.

[270]See the address delivered by Governor Lam. Adesina of Oyo State on Wednesday 27th June 2001 at House of Chiefs, Secretariat Ibadan during the swearing-in of 7 new judges in Oyo State.

our judiciary will continue to be disturbed by the distressing spectacle of cases pertaining to death-row phenomenon arising from the long sojourns of condemned prisoners on death-row.

Awaiting Trial Persons and Human Rights

Unlike the convicts who enjoy relative care and attention of the prison authorities in terms of feeding and accommodation, awaiting trial persons are not adequately catered for. Nevertheless, many prisons in the country are overflowing with the swelling ranks of awaiting trial persons. This phenomenon has become a source of worry for the government and the general public. Several causes account for prison congestions with the underlying penal policy of the Nigerian legal system. The source of supply of awaiting trial persons are many as they are usually brought to the prisons by various law enforcement agencies, while they are not direct "properties" of the prison officers, yet the "donors" do not provide adequately for their welfare. Invariably the prison authorities have to expend money, energy, human and material resources protecting these detainees than convicts.

The plight of detainees has become worrisome for judges, legal practitioners, human rights organizations and the public in recent times.[271] They have been advocating for quick dispensation of justice to avert a situation where those detained may not return alive. Apparently moved by the pathetic situation of detainees at the Ikoyi Prisons, the then Chairman of Human Rights Commission, Hon. Justice Nwokedi remarked;

> The situation is too bad, it is heart rending, it is unimaginable for somebody to have spent 10 years without trial. We have to get in touch with the State's Attorney General to either prosecute them or free them".

Also, Hon. Justice Obaseki analysed the degree of congestion in Lagos State graphically as follows:

[271]See Adeniyi Olatubosun, "The Plight of Awaiting Trial Persons under the Criminal Justice System in Nigeria" in Topical Issues to Nigerian Law, Essays in honour of Hon. Justice N. O. Adekola (2000) Zenith Publishers.

> Ikoyi prison, Lagos has accommodation for only 800 persons. In December, 1985, there were 2,091 inmates, 1,499 were unconvicted persons of the 2,367 inmates. 1,975 were unconvicted persons awaiting trial. Kirikiri Prison has accommodation for 1,765 inmates. But by the 9th June, 1987 there were 3,713 inmates residents. Of this number, 1,583 were unconvicted persons awaiting trial, 214 condemned prisoners awaiting execution and 139 detained...[272]

The above exposition indicates that the prison yards have ceased to be deterrent and reformative homes for the treatment of offenders. As a follow-up to this study, the present writer has undertaken field surveys in some selected prisons in Nigeria, the findings will be analysed later in this work. The summary of the state of living in the Nigerian prisons depicts a degenerated environment breeding horrors of prison of life such as sleeping on bare floor and poor hygienic conditions. The inhuman treatment of conforming inmates and non-segregation of prisoners, and detainees breed criminality and moral degeneration. The retired Chief Judge of Lagos State, Hon. Justice Samuel Ilori evaluated the magnitude of danger, the situation portends in this way;

> Detainees had a lot of security implication to the large society as they pose a threat to the society while awaiting trial if they could break jail. The citizenry would also be in danger if an escaped detainee were a dangerous criminal. We want quick proper trial for detainees instead of keeping them there for years, let the law take its proper course.

The swelling ranks of awaiting trial persons in the Nigerian prisons have lowered the standard of penal system compared with the standard laid down by the International Human Rights organization. The fundamental human rights enshrined in the Constitution of the Federal Republic of Nigeria, 1999 should be honoured in the administration of criminal justice system by transforming the inhuman environment in the prison yards to humane environment for the prisoners and the awaiting trial persons in order to achieve our collective aspirations towards speedy and functional administration of criminal justice process. The Court of Appeal reiterated this point in the case of *Chief Gani Fawehinmi v. Gen. Sani Abacha & Ors.* that the state has a responsibility to

---

[272]See *The Guardian*, June 1996.

ensure that a person who is in custody is not put in undue dangers to his health and safety.

The trends now prevailing in advanced countries tilt towards reducing dependency on punitive measures in contemporary criminal justice system, Nigeria cannot afford to lag behind. Perhaps, the position of the participants at the Harare Conference on the need for African countries to give serious concern to alternatives to imprisonment is apposite:

> The more traditionally accepted measures of restitution, compensation and fines be adopted in the main penal measures in place of imprisonment, particularly as African cannot appreciate a treatment like imprisonment which, if it benefits at all, is benefiting only the government in total disregard of the victim and the African need to maintain social equilibrium.[273]

Some eminent jurists have made several suggestions in standard works on reforms of the Nigerian prison system, which this writer associates with as practical solution in resolving the problem of prison congestions and the plights of those awaiting trial persons that are yet to acquire legal status of occupancy in the prison yards.

The Constitutionality of Death Penalty

The Nigerian Constitution is the supreme law of the land. Every other law must subsume itself to the confines of the Constitution and any law whatsoever that runs contrary to the provisions of the Constitution shall be declared null and void and of no effect to the extent of its incompatibility.

The Supreme Court of Nigeria was called upon in the following cases: *Ade Ogugu and Others v. The State,*[274] *Nemi v. Attorney General of Lagos State,*[275] *Azeez Okoro v. The State,*[276] *Kalu v. The State* to determine the validity or Constitutionality of death penalty as a form of punishment to the capital

---

[273]See The Second Seminar for Heads of Penitentiary Administrator in African Countries Report, Harare, Zimbabwe, 29 February – 5 March 1988.

[274](1934] 94 NWLR (Pt. 366). 1

[275][1996] 6 NWLR 42.

[276][1998] 12 SCNJ 84.

offence of murder as presented under Section 319(1) of the Criminal Code[277] and the question whether the provisions of the said S. 319(1) CC are not contrary to and inconsistent with Section (1)(a) of the Constitution of the Federal Republic of Nigeria, 1979. In view of the Constitutional importance of the question raised in the appeal and the far reaching effect, the decision of the Supreme Court would have on the Nigerian criminal jurisprudence, a number of senior and eminent learned counsel were invited by the court as *amici curiae* to address the court on the questions raised. Following this invitation many legal practitioners filed very useful, pungent and thought provoking briefs of argument. The eminent lawyers filed comprehensive, stimulating and clearly impressive briefs and their arguments and oral submissions were scholarly presented. TheLearned counsel for the appellant, Olisa Agbakoba in his opening submission pointed out that there is no reported local decision of any of the superior courts of record in which the validity of death sentence was either canvassed or raised. He urged the Supreme Court to seek guidance from the decisions of the courts of other common law jurisdictions on such or similar matters. He further submitted that where a Constitutional or statutory provision in respect of fundamental human rights permits requires for judicial interpretation, the courts are entitled to seek guidance from international human rights norms and to universally accepted sources of moral standards as aids to such interpretation. The acceptable views on the Constitutionality of the death penalty as a mode of punishment were considered. The appellant placed heavy reliance on the jurisprudence of other countries, notably, South Africa, Tanzania, Canada, Hungary and the U.S.A. By the contemporary human right standards and values now prevailing in these countries the operative death penalty in Nigeria runs contrary to the intendment of the Constitution which guarantees right to life and right to dignity of person and that the present mode of execution amounts to torture, inhuman or degrading treatment. He cited many authorities and decisions from other jurisdictions, particularly, the Supreme Courts of USA, Zimbabwe, Namibia and Privy Council of U.K. in respect of appeals from the courts of Appeal of Trinidad and Tobago, Jamaica and the Commonwealth of the Bahamas. In these decisions,[278] the Constitutionality of the death penalty

[277]Laws of Lagos State of Nigeria, 1973.

[278]See *Weems v. U.S.* 217 US 349; *Williams Henry Furman v. State of Georgia* 408 US 288 at 263-264; *Catholic Commission for Justice & Peace, Zimbabwe v. A.G. of Zimbabwe & Others* (1993) (4) S.A. 239 (ZSC); *The State v. Makwanyane & Another* (1995) (6) BCLR 665 (CC) *Lincoln Anthony Guerra v. Cipriani Baptiste & Others* (1996) 1 AC 397 (PC)

as a form of sentence for the capital offence of murder came directly into question, having regard to the various Constitutional provisions in issue in the countries concerned. The consensus of judicial opinion in all these cases is that the substantive contents of specific human rights guarantees must be left open ended to enable them accommodate evolving standards of civilization., It is as a result of this "evolving and dynamic" process that the death penalty has come to be regarded in contemporary human rights jurisprudence as a violation of the right not to be subjected to torture, inhuman and degrading punishment for murder."

In *Earl Pratt & Anor. v. Attorney-General of Jamaica,* the applicants were convicted of murder in January, 1979 and sentenced to death. At the conclusion of their appellate remedies, their convictions and sentence were affirmed. Thereafter, they filed a fresh application in the Supreme Court of Jamaica claiming breach of their fundamental human right for having been subjected to inhuman and degrading treatment following the prolonged delay between their sentence and the proposed date of their execution. The proceedings in issue were commenced in the Supreme Court of Jamaica, a court of first instance. The fundamental right issue was not raised or determined in a Court of appellate jurisdiction. It was initiated and determined by a court of original jurisdiction, and prosecuted up to the highest appellate court, the Judicial Committee of the Privy Council in the United Kingdom.[279] Similar procedure was also followed in the case of *Catholic Commission for Justice and Peace in Zimbabwe v. Attorney-General Zimbabwe & Others.* In this case, the prisoner had been tried and convicted for murder and sentenced to death. Having unsuccessfully exhausted their appellate remedies, fresh proceedings by way of application were filed on their behalf seeking for an order to prevent their execution.[280]

In *Mbushuu & Anor v. The Republic,*[281] the Tanzania Court of Appeal held that although the death penalty is a form of "cruel, inhuman and degrading treatment", it affirmed that it was nonetheless Constitutionally permissible, having regard to the *qualified* nature of the right to life as entrenched in the Tanzanian Constitution. The right to life in their Constitution was neither absolute nor unqualified. In the Zimbabwean Supreme Court case of *Catholic Commission for Justice and Peace, in Zimbabwe v. Attorney-General, Zimbabwe*

[279] [1994] 2 A.C. 1.

[280] [1993] (4) S.A. 239 (ZSC).

[281] (Criminal Appeal No. 142) of 1994, 30th January, 1995.

and Other,[282] which Gubbay, CJ delivered the lead judgment which adopted the position that the right to life was qualified and upheld the Constitutional validity of the death penalty in Zimbabwe. The learned Chief Justice said:

> It was not sought, nor could it reasonably be, to overturn the death sentences on the ground that they were unlawfully imposed. The judgments of this court dismissing the appeals of the condemned prisoners cannot be disturbed. They are final. And the Constitutionality of the death penalty, *per se*, as well as the mode of its execution by hanging, are also not susceptible of attack.

However, the Constitutional Court of South Africa in *The State v. Makwanyane & Anor.* held that the death penalty violated the Constitutional protection of freedom from cruel, inhuman and degrading treatment under section 11(1) of the South African Constitution and was, in consequence, invalid and unconstitutional. The court held *inter alia*,

> The unqualified right to life vested in every person by section 9 of our Constitution is another factor crucially relevant to the question whether the death sentence is cruel, inhuman or degrading punishment within the meaning of Section 11(2) of our Constitution. In this respect our Constitution differs materially from the Constitutions of the United States and India. It also differs materially from the European Convention and the International Covenant civil and Political Rights.[283]

An equally vital reason why the death penalty was declared unconstitutional was on account of the arbitrary, discriminatory and selective nature of its exercise at all material times in South Africa. The court further remarked,

> . . . These differences still exist, which means that the law governing the imposition of the death sentence in South Africa is not uniform. The greatest disparity is in the Eastern Cape Province. A person who commits murder and is brought to trial in that part of the province which was formerly Ciskei, cannot be sentenced

---

[282][1993] (41) SA 239.

[283]*Ibid.*, pp. 49-50.

> to death, whilst a person who commits murder and is brought to trial in another part of the same province, can be sentenced to death. There is no rational reason for this distinction, which is the result of history, and we asked for argument to be addressed to us on the question of whether this difference has a bearing on the Constitutionality of Section 277(1)(a) of the Criminal Procedure Act.

Thus, a careful perusal of the various foreign authorities, which the appellants in Nigerian cases relied upon in urging the Supreme Court to proscribe death penalty, seems to have repeatedly pronounced the death penalty to be constitutionally valid. The views that death sentence is intrinsically unconstitutional seems to be a minority one. The operative clause is whether the right to life therein contained is qualified or unqualified. If qualified the death penalty was, in the main, held to be constitutional. If unqualified, however, the death penalty was, declared to be unconstitutional.

In particular, the South African Constitutional Court pronounced the death penalty unconstitutional on account of the fact that the right to life and also because of the arbitrary, selective and discriminatory nature of its exercise at all material times in South Africa. Further condemnation on the imposition of the death penalty for murder is that it is also incapable of correction in the event of an error and negated the essential context of the right to life. The elements of arbitrariness are also involved in the imposition of the death sentence. The judgment of the Ogoni Civil Disturbance Tribunal convicting and sentencing to death Mr. Ken Saro-Wiwa and eight other Ogoni is an example of a miscarriage of justice. The judgment had been roundly condemned throughout the world. It is important to point out that this condemnation is not on the merit of the judgment but against the whole trial as regards its unlawfulness and unfairness.[284] The judgment of the Tribunal is assaulted by errors of prejudicial and presumptive evaluation of evidence, faulty identification of ingredients of the offence and application of same to the fact before it. It assumed that guilt is corporate, i.e. membership or leadership of organizations and not individual participation. It wrongly found all those who contributed to the situations that led to the civil disturbance are without more, liable for procurement and counseling of resultant murder. The general consensus of opinions is that there was no fair trial at the Tribunal.

[284]Charge NO. OCDT/PH/1/95.

Extracts from the facts of the Case

The five accused persons were charged for the murder of Chief E.N. Kobani, Chief S.N. Orage, Mr. T.B. Orage and Mr. A.T. Badey. The four-count charge, with little deletion as to the name of the deceased read: "That you . . .on the 21st day of May 1994 at Giokoo in Gokana, Rivers State, murdered ... in that the 1st, 2nd and 3rd accused persons counseled and procured the 4th and 5th accused person in company of others, some of whom are at large, to inflict grievous harm on the participants of the Council of Chiefs meeting at Giokoo whereby the said ... was killed contrary to section 220 of the Criminal Code.

From the charge it is very clear that the accused persons were charged for the offence of murder as defined under the Criminal Code not the Decree No. 2 1987. The decree merely incorporated the offence of murder in its item 13. This insight will be very instructive later in the critique, Mr. Ken Saro Wiwa, Ledum Mitee, Dr. Kiobel, John Kpuinen and Berabom Bera are 1st, 2nd, 3rd, 4th and 5th accused persons respectively in the first trial.

Improper Appraisal of Evidence

The prime duty of a judge trying a criminal case (without a jury as in our jurisdiction) is to hear evidence of witnesses, credit or discredit each piece of evidence, and make findings of facts that are coherently and logically deducible from the evidence before him. The responsibility to assess and credit evidence led before it is inescapable by a court or tribunal notwithstanding whether there is evidence in rebuttal or not. It is certainly not the law that once an accused person, pursuant to his Constitutional right elects not to give evidence, all evidence led against him becomes automatically credible and reliable for conviction. This will be pervasive. It will rewrite the presumption of innocence. But the Tribunal stated, in great violence to principle of law, that "The truth is that any unchallenged evidence is presumed admitted". This is perverse.

Wholesale Acceptance of Evidence of Prosecution Witnesses

The Prosecution, called nineteen witnesses to prove its case, in charge No OCDT/PH/1/95 involving Ken Saro-Wiwa and four others. A total of 25 documents were admitted as exhibits. No where in its lengthy judgment did the Tribunal critically evaluate evidence of these witnesses notwithstanding that they were cross-examined by defense counsel. Exercise of judicial discretion to believe a witness testimony is not automatic. A tribunal or judge must actually evaluate the veracity of the story of a witness in terms of its internal consistence and coherence with evidence of other witnesses. It is a breach of judicial function to ascribe veracity to pieces of evidence that have been discredited during the cross-examination. For example it is on record that Alhaji Kobani told the court that he witnessed the killing of all the four deceased persons. But Chief F.A. Kpai (an eye witness of the murder) testified that Mr. S.N. Orage was killed elsewhere. The Tribunal also accepted in its entirety all the evidence of David Keenom as regards the accused persons, notwithstanding that under cross-examination he contradicted himself in several relevant points. The Tribunal believed wholly the evidence of Alhaji Kobani (PW3) that when Dr. Kiobel visited the shrine, he spoke with the youths who shouted "E sho-bey'" notwithstanding that during cross-examination, he was confronted with his extra-judicial statement where he clearly stated that Dr. Kiobel merely visited and left the shrine. It is significant that it was this evidence that formed the basis of the suspicion on which the Tribunal convicted Dr. Kiobel. While the court accepted wholesale the evidence of prosecution witness, it discredited for no reasons the evidence of defence witnesses. The only witness called by Dr. Kobel, the Gbenemene of Gokana, Chief Bagia was described as unreliable in his testimony solely because he slept in Dr. Kobel's house after the May 21 killing. This is not any reason to disbelieve the witness who was listed by prosecution and left out when it found out his testimony establishes Dr. Kiobel's innocence. If affiliation or affinity were ground to disbelieve a witness, then the court should not attach any value to testimonies of prosecution witnesses since almost all of them are either aggrieved relatives of the deceased or renegade MOSOP members. This double standard in wholesale believing evidence of prosecution witnesses and disbelieving that of the defence is contrary to the impartiality of a judicial tribunal and capable of miscarrying justice.

Hearsay, Opinions and Conjectures

In its evaluation of the evidence of witnesses who testified before it, the tribunal made no efforts to distinguish hearsay, opinion, and conjectures from admissible evidence. It relied indiscriminately on all the testimony of the prosecution witnesses. For example, David Keenom, PW 5 told the Tribunal that sometime after the 1st accused was released from detention, he instructed Mr. Goodluck Digbo to summon a meeting of National Youth Committee of Ogoni People (NYCOP). It was at such meeting that the instruction to kill the *vultures* was allegedly given. Under cross-examination, he admitted that the circular of the meeting was signed by Goodluck Digbo not the 1st accused but stated that he believed it was the first accused who instructed him. The Tribunal still relied on this opinion evidence and held that "on his release from detention, 1st accused instructed NYCOP's President to summon a meeting of NYCOP". Section 66 Evident Act[285] renders opinion evidence irrelevant and therefore inadmissible in any trial except in clearly stated circumstances. The Tribunal also relied on hearsay to make findings of guilt. It stated in its judgment that "3rd accused said that his car was damaged by MOSOP youths. Clement Ogaba, (PW.13) Superintendent of Police, IPO, said he saw one Mr. Iche who was said by 3rd accused to be his driver on the day of the incident. The driver told him they used car No. RVSG 30 and it was never damaged." It was the evidence of PW 13 and not the driver.

Nevertheless the Tribunal relied on it to find that Dr. Kiobel, 3rd accused was lying when he testified that his car was damaged by the irate mob. Most of the conclusions of the Tribunal were conjectures not supported by evidence from witnesses. In an attempt to fill in gaps in the evidence of prosecution witnesses, the Tribunal conjectured most perversely. It held:

> "There is no given or expressed reason why MOSOP and NYCOP supported a candidate i.e. 1st accused who did not enter as a candidate, or why rallies were arranged in Gokana for election campaigns which were illegal. In the absence of any valid explanation, we are left in no doubts that the purpose was to set off the events and consequential riot: which occasioned the murder of these leaders of Gokana."

However, the fact that the prosecution could not proffer valid explanation does not warrant the Tribunal to conjecture on what the reasons for the rallies were. Even if it is accepted that Ken-Wiwa was not a valid candidate for the election and MOSOP members deliberately organized rallies, in absence of

---

[285]Chapter 112 of the Laws of the Federation, 1990.

cogent evidence, it does not lead unequivocally to conclusion of set-up riots preparatory to murder. A court of law or judicial tribunal is not entitled to make inferences in absence of fact distilled from the filter of examination. In *Dumma v. State*[286] the Supreme Court deplored this attitude and held:

> "It is not the function of a trial judge by his own exercise and ingenuity to supply the evidence or carry out the mathematics of arriving at the answer which only evidence tested under cross-examination could supply".

The Tribunal after explaining that the 1st accused was not a candidate for the election and therefore ought not to campaign and that MOSOP and NYCOP supporters knew all these and still went ahead to organize the rallies, held:

> "We believe that these developments were anticipated by MOSOP and NYCOP. It was what they were waiting for, an excuse to put their secret plan in action. It was the riot too many."

How did the Tribunal come about this conclusion? There was no evidence that any of the accused persons apart from the 3rd accused person knew about the meeting. Al the witnesses testified positively that only designated leaders and Chief of Gokana were invited for the meeting. The Tribunal simply manufactured the conclusion irrespective of whether it is borne out by evidence before it or not.

Insufficiency of Evidence

The Tribunal relied on insufficient evidence to convict four of the accused persons for murder Three of them (Ken Saro-Wiwa, Ledum Mitee and Dr. Kiobel) were accused of procuring and counseling the two others (John Kpuinen and Berabom Bera) to commit murder. What is therefore required to find the first three guilty of procurement and counseling of murder is clear and credible evidence that 1st, 2nd and 3rd accused persons did actually at a certain time and venue procured the 4th and 5th accused person to kill. Nothing short of clear and credible evidence that the 4th and 5th accused persons actually

[286](1995) 8 NWLR (Pt. 415) 513 at p. 533

assaulted or was in a crowd that did assault the deceased where they clearly aided the assault can convict the 4th and 5th accused persons. Mere suspicion of their involvement or evidence of long standing feud or animosity against the deceased will not be enough to find them guilty of murder. Mere presence, no matter the circumstances cannot be enough to convict any of them of murder. The evidence against Mr. Ken Saro-Wiwa as summarized by the Tribunal is that he had disagreement with Late E.N. Kobani over the affairs of MOSOP, created NYCOP and convened meetings where he directed NYCOP officials to deal with the vultures. The evidence of procurement against him came from David Keenom and Limpa Gbaa. Keenom claimed that Ken Saro-Wiwa urged participants of a meeting he attended to deal with the vultures. Gbaa, testified that at a rally at Kpite, Tai, Ken Saro-Wiwa urged the crowd to deal with a vulture in the person of Chief Kobani who has collected forms for the Constitutional conference elections. Even if all these assertion are well founded, it needs to be proved by credible evidence that he procured particular persons to kill the deceased and these people actually killed the deceased. Even the evidence of Limpa Gbaa is not enough. It must be proved that it was those people counseled at a rally in Kpite-Tai who killed the deceased. If some other persons actually killed the deceased, the 1st accused person will not be criminally liable even if the evidence of procurement is accepted. The third accused Dr. Kiobel was charged for procuring and counseling the 4th and 5th accused to kill the deceased. Evidence sufficient to find him guilty of procurement must be such as directly shows that he actually and actively encouraged the 4th and 5th accused by positive act to kill the deceased. It is not proved beyond reasonable doubts in this respect to show that he was a serious member of MOSOP" or its steering committee member. The basis of culpability is not organization affiliation but individual participation. What did Dr. Kiobel do? The only evidence against him is that after the attack he drove into the shrine where some of the survivors took refuge with his car plates covered with leaves and conferred with the attackers who shouted *'E sho bey'* and then he drove away. He called a witness, H.R.H. J.P Bagia, the Gbenemena of Gokana who testified that the 3rd accused was threatened by the attackers when he tried to stop them from their act. Even if all the evidence against the 3rd accused was accepted, it could only amount to suspicion on his role and not establishment of guilt or proven participation in murder. None of these witnesses testified that the 3rd accused attended any of the meetings where the procurement allegedly took place. The general principle of criminal law is that suspicion, no matter how grave cannot take the place of legal proof. The

Supreme Court has he held that in the case of *Onafowokan v. The State*[287] that "a court of law can convict on one solitary credible evidence of a witness". He was not also present at the rally at Kpite-Tai where Mr. Limpa Gbaa said Ken Saro-Wiwa counseled that a vulture be dealt with. Where then is his involvement? The Tribunal seems to have lost sight of the fact that the deceased had been killed before the accused visited the scene of murder. He could not have procured the murder of the deceased by a posterior act. Acts that amount to counseling and procuring must precede the crime. The hasty manner in which the sentence of the Tribunal was carried out by the execution of the convicts within 30 days of the passing of the judgment without giving them the opportunity of exercising their rights of appeal to the Provisional Ruling Council and the resultant effects which became irredeemable made the trial the most tragic, horrific and wicked record of criminal justice system in Nigeria.

Death Row Phenomenon

The inevitable long wait between the imposition of the death sentence and the actual infliction of death, usually referred to as the death-row phenomenon makes characterization of the death penalty as a cruel, inhuman and degrading' treatment. Indeed, the decision in the U.S. case of *District Attorney for the Suffolk District v. Watson & Others*[288] poignantly debunked the proprietary of death penalty by the cursory remarks of Hennesey, C.J. thus:

> The death penalty is unacceptable under contemporary standards of decency in its unique and inherent capacity to inflict pain. The mental agony is, simply beyond question, a horror . . . we conclude . . . that the death penalty, with its full panoply of concomitant physical and mental tortures, is impermissibly cruel . . . when judged by contemporary standards of decency.
>
> The punishment of death for the offence of murder in Nigeria which is inflicted by hanging the offender by the neck till he be dead pursuant to the provisions of Section 367(1) Criminal Procedure has been described as sordid and destructive of human dignity[289].

[287](1987) 3 NWLR (Pt. 61) p. 552.

[288](1980) 381 Mass, 648 at 664 – 665.

[289]See Professor Chris Barnard's view *op. cit.*

Thus Barnard's comment has been more often quoted to describe this process of execution from the preponderance of foreign decisions on the death row phenomenon, Although, it was not the constitutionality of the death penalty as a form of punishment that was being challenged rather it was the alleged barbarity or otherwise of execution by hanging. The questions revolved around the undue delay in the execution of the death sentence and the deplorable conditions under which the prisoners awaiting execution were confined which gave rise to inhuman and degrading treatment. Perhaps, if the period of awaiting execution is reduced, the alleged traumatic experience of the convicts will be considerably tackled.

Frankly speaking, "the death row phenomenon" is a reality within the context of the Nigerian legal system. It is a form of due process ensuring ideals of criminal justice is attained. Recently, part of the findings of the National Study Group on Death Penalty revealed that about 500 Nigerians are on death row waiting for the hangman. The report further confirmed that many of those on death row had spent between 10 – 15 years awaiting their execution.

From the cases discussed above, Counsel has made copious arguments and legal reasoning on both sides on the proprietary or otherwise of death penalty. The appellants argued very strenuously that the death penalty necessarily inflicts both physical and mental pain on the victims and that this, *per se* amounts to torture, inhuman and degrading treatment. That the right not to be subjected to torture is a non-derogable right and that the death penalty which inescapably amounts to torture, inhuman and degrading treatment must, *ipso facto,* be unconstitutional.[290] The Supreme Court while appreciating the foreign decisions cited on the Constitutionality of death penalty as enriching, academic and interesting however observed that in all those cases, it was not the Constitutionality of the death penalty as a form of punishment that was being challenged. But rather the questions revolved around the undue delay in the execution of the death sentence, the deplorable conditions under which the prisoners awaiting execution were confined which gave rise to inhuman and degrading treatment and the mode or manner of execution. The Supreme Court further emphasized on the central question whether or not the death penalty in Nigeria should be abolished. The apex court indicated that arguments on death-row phenomenon or the alleged barbarity of execution

[290]See *The Saturday Punch*, October 23, 2004 at page 10. The Attorney General and Minister of Justice, Chief Akinlolu Olujinmi SAN constituted the group led by the Chairperson, Professor Oluyemisi Bamgbose.

by hanging may be proper basis for legislative abolition of the death penalty; the authority for any action abolishing the death penalty is not a matter for the law courts. Such repeal or revocation is within the exclusive jurisdiction of the legislature, except the process of law attacks such laws on grounds such as unconstitutionality, illegality or the like. The Supreme Court finally held that there is no provision in the Constitution of the Federal Republic of Nigeria, 1979 that renders the death penalty under section 319(1) of the Criminal Code of Lagos State unconstitutional. Instead, there are Sections 30(1), 213(2)(d) and 220(1)(e) which, in no mistaken terms recognize the death penalty.

On the Constitutionality of death sentence in any jurisdiction, what is germane is whether death penalty is a cruel, inhuman or degrading punishment within the context of the applicable Constitution. Thus, the decisions in foreign jurisdictions on death sentence would be apposite in Nigerian situation where the provisions of such Constitutions are similar to ours. But a cursory review of many of the foreign cases cited above, the view that the death sentence is unconstitutional is generally a minority view.

It is submitted that where the right to life is qualified like under the Nigerian Constitution, death penalty is to be held constitutionally valid. The same position operated in Tanzania, Zimbabwe, India, United States and the Caribbean countries. Therefore, it is not unconstitutional. The advocates of unconstitutionality of death penalty make heavy weight of arguments that the death-row period which a convicted person have been kept would have made him to go through mental anguish and torment and thereby exposed him to torture, inhuman and degrading treatment warranting commutation of his sentence from death to life imprisonment. It is submitted with respect that such viewpoints are sentiments and not legal reasoning. There is no provision of the statute along this position. Perhaps, it is only where the method of execution is so brutal or abhorrent or involves exorbitant or excessive pain that it can constitute torture, inhuman or degrading treatment. Even in such a situation, the proper person who is competent to say this is the condemned person being executed and who like suicide, the experience is personal and individualistic. Hanging *per se* which is applied in Nigeria has not been shown to fit this qualification. The abolition of the death penalty is a very weighty matter involving policy where decision should be a function of conscious and deliberate act of the highest policy formulating and law-making organ of the state, involving the opinion of the people in a referendum.

The empirical evidence against death penalty should not rest solely on ideological or intellectual reasons. Applying whatever canon of interpretation inspired by whatever humanitarian considerations to abolish death sentence without overwhelming support of the citizens may be counter-productive. The eventuality of self-help and revenge killing in the wake of dismay and disillusion likely to be aftermath of the revocation should not be under-estimated. It is respectfully submitted that the question regarding the Constitutionality of death penalty does not arise in Nigeria. The provision of the 1979 and the 1999 Constitutions cited above have shown beyond reasonable doubt that the legality of death penalty is guaranteed. Thus, the provisions of the Criminal Code and penal code on capital offences are within the purview of the Constitution and as such death penalty is lawful and valid under the criminal justice system in Nigeria.

Death Penalty and International Law

On a comparative analysis, for centuries no appreciable change has been made in the attitude towards death penalty. The study on the retention or abolition of death penalty in international law could not have been relevant years ago because its subject matter did not exist.[291] Crimes were then treated as subjects of municipal jurisdictions. All campaigns for the abolition of death penalty have gained international momentum in recent years. The trends began with a clamour for the limitation of the death penalty by excluding juveniles[292], pregnant women[293] and the elderly from its scope by restricting its application to an ever-shrinking list of serious crimes. Enhanced procedural safeguards were requested where the death penalty still obtained. The impact of international standard setting was evidenced by parallel developments in domestic laws of many countries.[294] Though its scope has been gradually restricted at international level, nevertheless its validity has never been completely or successfully impugned. International norms addressing the question of the death penalty are essentially a post second world war

[291]See (1) Protocol No. 6 to the Convention for the Protection of Human Rights and Fundamental Freedom Concerning the Abolition of the Death Penalty, ETS 114. (2) Second Optional Protocol of the International Convention on Civil and Protocol Rights aiming at the Abolition of the Death Penalty. (3) Additional Protocol to the American Convention on Human Rights to Abolition of the Death Penalty.

[292]See Section 368(3).

[293]See Section 368(1) & (2) CPA.

[294]*Ibid.*

phenomenon. The quest for abolition was promoted during the drafting of the Universal Declaration of Human Rights in 1948 as it found expression only implicitly in the recognition of what international human rights law described as the "right to Life". Even as at that time all but a handful of states maintained the death penalty and in the aftermath of a brutal struggle which had taken hundreds of millions of lives, few were contemplating its abolition. The idea of abolition gained momentum over the last two decades with the international law makers urging the limitation of the death penalty only to very serious crimes in countries where it is being retained excluding juveniles, pregnant women and the elderly from its scope. The international law makers while recognizing the principle of sovereignty of each country requested for enhanced procedural safeguards wherever death penalty still obtained. Eventually, three international instruments[295] were drafted that proclaimed the abolition of the death penalty. At present, about 49 countries have ratified these treaties and perhaps, the number is likely to grow rapidly. Four European states have pledged to ratify protocol No. 6 within 12 months as a condition for joining the council of Europe.

The events at international level in the past and very recently support this view point. For example, when Uruguay objected to the inclusion of the death penalty in the Charter of the Nuremberg Tribunal, it was accused of having Nazi sympathics. In 1946, a Norwegian court ruled that the death penalty was actually prescribed by international law and thus could be legitimately imposed despite the fact that it was *inapplicable* under the country's ordinary criminal law. The United Nations during the Korean War formally provided for imposition of the death penalty on prisoners of war for post-capture offences.

[295]See Law, Development and Administration in Nigeria, Vol. 1. Edited by Yemi Osinbajo & Awa U. Kalu (1990) Federal Ministry of Justice Law Review Series.

4

ALTERNATIVES TO DEATH SENTENCE

In the preceding chapters, we have emphasized that criminal process relied heavily on punishment as antidote for correcting antisocial conducts of offenders. The courts are so much concerned with the application of punishment within the context of the established theories in sentencing. The custodians of convicted prisoners also regard penal institutions as potent avenue to correct offenders and protect the public against those whose activities are offensive and injurious to the society. Empirical facts have shown that modern necessities demand a shift in the paradigm of aim of criminal justice from punitive philosophy to social philosophy of justice. For justice to be evenly distributed, all the stakeholders must have been touched in diverse ways by the end result of the courts' verdict. The efficacy of death sentence in the administration of criminal justice is on the decline in recent times, thereby making alternatives to death penalty imperatives towards attaining social cohesion and equilibrium.

Imprisonment

Advocates of abolition of death penalty have suggested that imprisonment serves a better alternative to death sentence. As it would be shown later, imprisonment stands to avoid elimination of human life in the course of punishment and it has been further argued that imprisonment serves as a form of correction in the treatment of offenders.

Compensation

The history of compensation to victims of crime is an ancient institution, which has had an established position in the realm of penology, and for a long period was almost inseparably attached to the institution of punishment.

This position may to some extent reflect the historical development from the primitive stage when criminal proceedings were largely left to the initiative of the victim and his family or tribe to the present stage when his power is, on the whole concentrated in the hands of the state.[296] The need to provide compensation for the victims was statutorily acknowledged in England as far back as the Forfeiture Act 1870, the Probation Act 1970, the Criminal Justice Act 1948, the Criminal Damage Act 1971, the Criminal Justice Act 1972 and the Criminal Courts Act 1973. This seems to be the total extent to which restitution is dealt with in England within the scope of criminal procedure. In all other respects it retains its civil character.

In Nigeria, the sentencing policy has so far had to rely heavily on the machinery of punishment, at the neglect of the victim's remedy. The provisions that exist, under the Criminal Procedure Act, (CPA) and the Criminal Procedure Code (CPC) are unsatisfactory.[297] For instance, conviction is a precondition for the award of compensation, which need not be the case. While, there is no definite procedure for quantifying the amount of compensation to be awarded and if the quantum of damages is to be awarded by the trial court, it is often determined without hearing from the victim as to the extent of the injuries suffered and other expenses incurred by the victim. Where the victim accepts the amount awarded, he is barred from taking any civil action for other collateral claims.[298] Under the English common law, (which applied in Nigeria) when the commission of a crime gives rise to a civil claim in favour of a private person, the principle of law is that the private person (i.e.

---

[296]See Dr. Stephen Schafer, *Restitution to Victims of Crime* (London Stevens & Sons Ltd. 1960) pp. 1-7. The historical antecedent was traced from the Middle Ages to the modern times. In support of this noble objective, reference should be made to International Conferences held in Stockholm in 1878, Rome in 1885, St. Petersburg in 1890, Christiana in 1891. At these Congresses, it was felt that modern laws were particularly weak on this point. For instance the Italian penologists Garofalo and Pierantoni dealt with the subject impressively to the effect that laws in different countries were harder on the victim than the offender. See also six valuable papers presented by Corvet, Flandin, Pascand, Poet, Prins and Zucker respectively. See also William Tallack, *Reparation to the Injured and the Rights of the Victim of Crime to Compensation* (London, 1990) pp. 6-7.

[297]Section 255 C.P.A. provides that compensation be paid to the prosecutor and not to the victim. Section 435(2) of the Act limits the amount of damage or compensation to a meager twenty naira in situations where although the charge against the offender is proved, the court does not proceed to conviction. See also sections 78 penal code, 357 and 365 criminal Procedure Code. These sections contain more elaborate provisions on restitution and compensation but in their application leave much room for improvement.

[298]See the Report of the National Committee on Remedies for Victims of Crime 23rd August, 1991.

he injured party) shall not be permitted to proceed with his action until the offender has been prosecuted or good excuse shown for non-prosecution. The rationale behind this legal concept was that a crime, which is a wrong against the state, and against the norms of society, should first be assuaged before the injury done to a private person could be redressed. In recent years, the scope of this legal concept was expanded and invariably private persons who suffered injuries during the commission of a crime were urged to be satisfied, in seeing that the offender was prosecuted and punished for the offence. Thus, it is clear that the emphasis of Nigerian Criminal Justice System is on the offender. Crimes, even those against the person, are viewed as offences against the state. From arrest to sentencing, the law is concerned mainly with the offender, although the trial initiated by the victim and relies on the victim's participation for is success, offers little direct relief to the victim. The system has been more punitive than restitutive and as such its operators have become insensitive to the victim's plight. The victim is largely left to seek redress in separate civil actions often involving costly proceedings.[299]

But the world has moved away from the standpoint. We now live in an age of intense criminality when brutal crimes, armed robberies, terrorism, bomb-blast, environmental pollution, assassination etc. are committed on a daily basis. For example, many advanced countries like the United Kingdom, the United States of America, Canada and Australia have evolved the progressive view that positive steps should be taken to give prompt and adequate compensation to victims of violent crimes.

Thus, it is rather a matter of great disappointment that the courts have not paid enough attention in criminal cases to the distress of the victim. An accused convicted is sentenced as of routine, while the victim and his dependants get nothing. A situation under which the victim becomes the Cinderella of the criminal trial no longer accords with the tripartite notion of social justice viz: justice to the accused, the society and the victim.[300] It is submitted that our country should embrace this new trend.

---

[299]The dichotomy between criminal and civil processes is derived from our adopted English common law.

[300]See Prof. Mool Singh, "Compensatory Justice in Criminal Law A Goal of Social Justice" 1991 Indian socio-legal Journal pp. 1-5. See also Edwin H. Sutherland, *Principles of Criminology* (4th Ed. Chicago 1947) p. 208. See *Hasi Kishan and State of Haryyana v. Sukhbir Singh & others.* A.I.R. 1988 SC 2127. The Supreme Court of Indian held that all courts should exercise the power of awarding compensation to the victims of offence in accordance with S.351 code of criminal procedure 1973, so as to achieve the goals of social justice.

This appeal is aimed at reviewing the objective of administration of Criminal Justice in Nigeria, which has hitherto focused on the principle of deterrence but which in its entirety has not been able to accomplish its targets of preventing and controlling the rate of criminal acts in the society. Thereby necessitating an appraisal of the most undeveloped area of our criminal justice system, i.e. compensation as a criminal sanction in addition to, or in substitution for other forms of sanctions. This will enable us to highlight the inherent deficiencies contained in our Criminal Justice System with regard to the question of compensation, restitution and remedies for victims of crime. Furthermore, the work will identify the categories of victims under certain criminal situations to determine those victims that deserve public sympathy depending on the role played by them in the commission of such crimes and the extent to which public fund that is grossly inadequate be expended on them in terms of compensatory remedies. In the final analysis we shall proffer suggestions on the subject matter in order to take care of the inadequacies in our Criminal Justice System as a supplementary effort to the various recommendations so far made in notable published works,[301] with particular emphasis on the need for the system to change its focus from punishing offenders to that of enforcing the rights of victims of crimes in accordance with the trend in modern times.

Justification for Crime Victim's Rights Policy

The neglect of victim's rights in our laws has the following negative consequences:

(i) victims are made to cope not only with mental trauma, physical injury, loss or damage to property, but also with insensitive investigation and legal processes;
(ii) mistrust in the state' s capability to protect the citizens;
(iii) reluctance of victims to invoke the criminal process against offenders which results in a growing tendency for victims and

[301]See the Report of the National Committee on Remedies for victims of crime *Ibid.* See also The Report of the commission on the Review of Administration of criminal Justice in Ogun State, June 1981 pp. 42-48. Hons Von Henting, The Criminal and His Victim (Mid-Hawan 1948) Mannhein, *Comparative criminology* Vol. 2. (Third Impression 1970).

the community to take the law into their hands;

(iv) greater emphasis on punitive and retributive rather than restitutive and compensatory sentencing;

(v) duplication of legal process, because criminal and civil causes arising from one event or transaction are pursued separately;

(vi) lack of faith in institutions of the criminal justice administration, particularly the Police and the Courts; and

(vii) general ineffectiveness of the criminal justice system.

From the foregoing, it is evident that the enhancement of victim's rights and remedies should be an important concern of our criminal justice system. Such a change in attitude will restore the citizen's confidence in the criminal justice system and will further assist in the attainment of social objectives as enshrined in chapter II of The Constitution of the Federal Republic of Nigeria, 1979. The rationale behind this proposition is based on the fact that the parties concerned will continue to live in the same small community with the fundamental objective to preserve and enhance social harmony otherwise referred to as "Social Equilibrium".[302] Indeed Radcliff Brown summed up the position in this way:

> "... a Judge is not regarded as having properly settled a case until all parties concerned are satisfied with the settlement".[303]

In the words of Adeyemi,

> "compensation is, by custom a measure known to, and accepted in virtually all African countries in the region ... it therefore becomes clear that the emergence of compensation in Africa was not a result of its being designed as an alternative to imprisonment, in as much as it predated imprisonment in the region. Rather, it is simply one of the measures provided for in the respective criminal justice system".[304]

---

[302]See the Sixth United Nations Congress Report on the Prevention of Crime and the Treatment of Offenders captioned "Caracas Declaration" (A/CONF 87/4/Revl) 1980. The seventh Report states that crime prevention and criminal justice be viewed within the context of the social, economic, cultural and political systems of member states.

[303]Primitive Law, 9 Ency. Soc. Sci, p. 294 (1933).

[304]See Professor Adeyemi A.A. ;"Personal Reparations in Africa: Nigeria and Gambia". P. 54 in *Alternatives To Imprisonment in Comparative Perspective* Ed. By U. Zvekio (United Nations Inter-regional crime and Justice Institute, Nelson Hall, Chicago 1993).

The State of the Nation

Before the advent of the British in this country, we had our own system of criminal justice; in the south, there were numerous systems of customary law, while in the North, Islamic law of crime applied.[305] In both systems, there were provisions for criminal law and procedure, with the native courts administering justice to all manner of people. Apart from punishment, there were provisions for compensation or restitution coupled with various rights for the victims of crime.[306] On the arrival of the British colonial administration in Nigeria, the common law of England was imposed on the people and consequently, there was the emergence of the criminal and penal codes, which were fashioned out of the English, and Sudanese criminal and penal laws respectively.[307] A cursory look at these codes reveals that there is no system o criminal justice, which does not provide for some form of restitution or compensation for the victims of crime in one form or the other.[308] In reality, not much has been done in the field of social or welfare development as the criminal law on the aspect has been almost static. As Karibi-Whyte J.S.C. has put it "the repression of anti-social conduct by means of punishment is the paramount objective of the criminal law."[309] Perhaps the English law reluctance towards recognition of compensatory remedies to the victims of crime also influenced Prof. Okonkwo view on this point when he remarked that:

> "the main object of a civil case is merely to compensate the plaintiff as far as possible for the wrong done to him. It is true that a criminal court has a power albeit very limited to provide for restitution or compensation in criminal proceedings . . . punishment is what the criminal law is about and compensation is what the civil law is about."[14a]

For example, the Criminal Procedure Act provides for compensation only in cases of probation orders, false and vexatious charges and damage caused

---

[305]See Adeyemi A.A., "Criminology in contemporary Africa", *Nigerian Journal of Criminology*, vol. 2 No. 1, pp. 1-29 see also Milner A., *The Nigerian Penal System* (1972) pp. 22-47.

[306]A. A. Adeyemi, *Op. cit.* p. 21.

[307]See Lord Lugard, Political Memoranda, 1913-1918, Memo 2, 3 and 5.

[308]See section 78 penal code, section 365 CPC. Section 3 CPC and sections 255-262, 435 (2) C.P.A.

[309]Karibi-Whyte, Ground work of Nigerian Criminal Law, p. 93.

by riot with the monetary compensation limit of twenty naira. Similarly, the Criminal Procedure Code provides for vexatious accusation, probation orders and damage by riot. The code limits the award at fifty naira. It is submitted that the maximum amount provided in the two statutes are grossly inadequate to be of any meaningful effect and it should therefore be reviewed upwards. However, Section 365 of the C.P.C. provides generally for award of compensation for criminal injury in addition to or in substitution for other punishments.

No doubt, the present positions in these statutes have become practically insufficient and unrealistic. Hon. Justice Mamman Nasir, the former President of Court of Appeal, appropriately described the situation as follows:

> "The Nigerian Society has developed immensely to such an extent as to ridicule in many respects all the known values of wealth or morality and even crime of yester years, when criminal procedure law was envisaging a total compensation not exceeding N20, as far back as the position in 1945 when the Criminal Procedure was enacted and is still so thinking, the society has progressed in all other spheres. May be we do not care, may be nobody cares. The first problem is that our laws are completely out of date . . .I believe it is now the time, not the year 2000 for us to seriously reconsider the whole field of criminal justice."[310]

With due respect, this writer agrees with the view of the learned judge to the effect that our laws are completely out of date. We should therefore fashion out new patterns and trends now prevailing in modern society.[311] Accordingly, a National Criminal policy is imperative in this country to cater for all the parties involved in a criminal process viz, the accused, the victim and his dependants and the society at large. In the words of Owoade:

> "In concrete terms, the compensation provisions in Nigeria are far from being adequate; they are deficient not only in respect of the amount to be awarded but also on the scope and circumstances of the award. For example, as has been seen the compensation and

[310]In his key note Address to the National Committee on Remedies for victim of crimes, presented in Abuja in 1989

[311]New Zealand, Australia, Germany, France, India, U.K. and U.S.A.

> restitution provisions are inadequate both in substance and in form that they would not have been tolerated even in England as of now and because Nigeria unlike England is rather slow at law reform, the situation becomes increasingly an unhappy one.[312]

In fact, Prince Bola Ajibola, the former Attorney-General and Minister of Justice of Nigeria realized the inappropriateness of the law on this point when he indicated the position of the government towards this aspect as follows:

> "the law has been silent for too long on adequate redress for victims, who may not only have lost their properties, but may also have been maimed or killed."[313]

Happily, the government of Nigeria realized the need for a re-examination of the penological policies in order to attain a fairer administration of criminal justice. Hence, the Federal Ministry of Justice, through its Law Review Series organized a National Conference at Abuja in June 1989.[314] **At the end of the Conference, participants issued a twelve point Communiqué, which *inter alia*** advocated the following suggestions:

> (i) That Nigeria's Criminal Justice system should no longer focus its attention entirely on the punishment of offenders but should also consider the rights of victims of crimes.
> (ii) At present the provisions of our penal laws and procedure codes on compensation and restitution for victims of crime are grossly inadequate and these should now be modernised and updated taking into consideration the principles and practices of our traditional criminal justice systems on compensation and restitution for victims of crimes.

---

[312]Dr. M. Adekunle Owoade, Reform of Sentencing in Nigeria: A note on Compensation, Restitution and Probation. P. 122 at 125-126. *Restitution, Compensation and Remedies for Victims of Crimes* Justice Law Review series of 1989) ed. Sade Adetina.

[313]See *The Guardian* vol. 5 No. 3 February 9, 1988 at p. 16 captioned "Government plans law to back Robbery Victims Compensation" being a proposal which was then receiving the attention of the Federal Government of Nigeria.

[314]The conference attracted the participation of eminent judges, lawyers, law teachers, professionals and a very wide range of interest groups.

(iii) A Criminal Injuries Compensation Board should be established in each of the states of Federation and Abuja and the Board should be funded from Federal, State and Local Government Subventions, Fines and proceeds of sale of assets seized from offenders.

(iv) Insurance Companies should play a more effective and supportive role in the compensation of victims of crime.[315]

It is noteworthy that the National Conference was a laudable and major attempt ever made in the history of administration of criminal justice in Nigeria to cover all the parties concerned in a criminal case.

After all, justice is not for an accused person alone, but a tripartite concept, to wit, the accused, the society and the victim. Our courts have on several occasions reiterated this cardinal principle of criminal administration. For example, Mr. Justice Oputa, Justice of Supreme Court (as he then was) expressed the judicial view point of penal policy in the following commendable way:

> Justice is not a one way traffic. It is not justice for the appellant only. Justice is not even a two-way traffic. It is really a three-way traffic- justice for the appellant accused of a heinous crime of murder; justice for the victim the murdered man, i.e. the deceased, "whose blood is crying to high heavens for vengeance" and finally, justice for the society at large – the society whose social norms and values had been desecrated and broken by the criminal act complained of.[316]

Similarly Nnamani J.S.C. in the case of *Ngwu Kalu v. The State* remarked thus:

> "it has to be emphasized that in these cases of murder, justice must also be done to the victim whose life has been cruelly cut short. Indeed this Court has said it on several occasions."[317]

[315]See The Report of the National Committee on Remedies for Victims of Crime. *Ibid.*

[316]*Godwin Josiah v. The State* (1985) 1 N.W.L.R. 125.

[317](1988) 4 N.W.L.R. 503 at 513.

Moreover, Aniagolu J.S.C. emphatically stated in *Nwafor Okegbu v. The State* that:

> "where else would this be more appropriate than a tragic case like this in which a young boy with a promising future was unceremoniously sent to the grave by hoodlums."[318]

In the light of the fore-going pronouncements, it is clear that this aspect of our criminal law and procedure has been neglected for quite a long time to the detriment of the interest of the victim in the administration of criminal justice. Perhaps, no other observation would illustrate this position, but that of Prof. Agbede who has this to say:

> "the most undeveloped area of our criminal justice is that of compensation as a criminal sanction in addition to or in substitution for other forms of sanction. A criminal justice system that is addressed solely to the criminal offender with little or no regard to the plight of the victim of the crime is certainly not in accord with modern notion of justice."[24]

To fully appreciate this point, a brief analysis of a typical criminal proceeding will be apposite. For example, when an accused person is arraigned before the court on a criminal charge of stealing certain goods worth several thousands of Naira, if the prosecution is able to prove the ingredients of this offence beyond reasonable doubt against him, the accused person is found guilty and convicted. In the eye of criminal law and procedure, justice has been done, but to the victim whose properties have been stolen and in most cases not recovered justice has not been done. The entire proceedings would have been meaningful to him, had it been that his main interest in the proceeding (i.e. his properties) are recovered and given back to him. The conviction and sentence of the accused person to term of imprisonment or fine has little or no significance to him. In practical terms, the victim is now left to recount his loss in terms of finance, time and energy expended going around the halls of justice from the inception of the case, which in Nigeria might span between

[318](1979) 1 S.C. 1.

[24]"Modalities for the enforcement of financial compensation for the victims of crimes" Vol. 5, Justice Law Review Series 1989 (ed. Sade Adetiba).

one day to 3 years or even more. Honourable Justice Karibi-Whyte who has observed as follows has stressed the need for the participation of the victim in the criminal process. The participation of that victim in our criminal process is limited to his role as a witness for the state in the prosecution of the offender. This passive role has been criticized as unsatisfactory and not sufficiently demonstrative of the interest of the victim."[319]

In view of the foregoing analyses, as well as the view of eminent jurist and judges so far expounded, it is clear that committal to prison for a criminal act is not always adequate in our contemporary society and as such there should be some ways of making the offender to indemnify the victim for his violence. In accordance with this position, the setting up of Criminal Injuries Compensation scheme[320] is imperative but before this is done it will be necessary to hold an investigation into the relationship between criminals and their victims, a fact which is important to be ascertained before we determine a deserving and undeserving victims to be compensated.

The Relationship between the Criminal and the Victim

There are situations when the *relationship* between the criminal and the victim is *crucial* in determining criminal responsibility. For example, provocation on the part of the victim has been treated for many Centuries as a mitigating factor in English law,[321] as well as under the Nigerian legal system. In cases of wounding, evidence of consent on the part of the victim will exonerate the person inflicting the injurious act from any criminal liability. Thus injuries received in boxing, wrestling, football and other sports as well as through surgical operations, sterilization, castration and artificial insemination will not necessarily be accorded any criminal responsibility.[322]

It is a common fact that crime always requires an object, personal or impersonal, the role played by this object be it active or passive should be

---

[319]"National Policy on Compensation to Victims of Crime: How Desirable? P. 262 Justice Law Review series *op. cit.*

[320]As recommended by the Report of the National Committee on Remedies for Victims of Crime *op.cit.* Similarly, the British Government set up the Criminal Injuries Compensation Board in 1960.

[321]See Hans Von Henting, *Punishment, Its Origin,* Purpose and Psychology (London, 1937). Gresham Sykes, *Crime and Society* (New York, 2nd ed.) 1967.

[322]See Kenny-Turner, *Outlines of Criminal Law* 16th Ed., Cambridge, 1902). 117.

submitted to clinical diagnosis as an essential part of our efforts to understand the criminal and the manner in which he should be treated.[323]

In recent years, there has been a growing recognition that a crime is a complex social event involving a pattern of interaction between the criminal and his victim in a socially defined situation. If we look only at the criminal, we leave more than half of the picture because the victim may play far from a passive role. Perhaps we can refer to this as "Criminal – victim situation", because criminology would be incomplete without the proper study of the victim, unlike criminal law that directs arsenals towards the accused person.

The distinction between criminal and victim has become vague and blurred in individual cases of recent, which in former days appeared as clear-cut as that of black and white.[324] Thus, an in-depth scrutinization of actions of persons will reveal a doubtful situation of who is to blame. Sometimes, it is a matter of mere chance who becomes the criminal or the victim. And as Pinatel[325] points out, the two roles may be exchanged either successively or simultaneously, for example one of the parties may be first the criminal and afterwards the victim; as in the case of a swindler who is killed by his angry victim. There are certain individuals, who either because of their personal characteristics or as members of certain occupations can be described as *Latent Victims* as they are more prone than others to become the object of crime e.g. the young, the old, females, the drunk (Clifford Shaw) the feeble minded, the illiterate, members of minority groups, drivers, and all persons handling large sums of money (Bank officials and police escorts blaring Sirens on the road), the social men and women spraying money at parties as well as those victims who are tired of life and provide the killer with every opportunity.[326] At times, a victim is not necessarily an individual it may also be a collective entity, a firm or a whole race or nation. The provisions of the substantive Criminal Law will usually indicate when they are intended to be protected. For example in cases of genocide, victims are not only those individual members of the national,

---

[323]See Hermann Mannhein. *Op. cit.* p. 71.

[324]Paul Cornil, "Contribution de la "Victimologie" auk sciences Criminologiques,' Rev. Droit Pon. Criminol, April 1959 in Hermann Mannheim *op. cit.* p. 673.

[325]Jean Pinatel, *Criminologie* pp. 345-350 in Mannhein *op. cit.*, p. 673.

[326]For example in Chicago Skid Row District USA, Donald J. Boque observed that criminals frequent such districts to rob the residents who are defenceless on account of age, infirmity etc. Similarly major cities like Lagos, Benin, Kano, Enugu and Ibadan in Nigeria attract criminals especially the pick pockets, area boys who easily find victims among the residents. It has also been claimed that Julius Ceasair belong to the category of those who are tired of live.

racial or religious groups whose destruction has been the object of the crime but also the group as whole.[327] Having established the relationship between the criminal and his victim, it is essential to examine the role of the victim in specific offences, in order to ascertain the quantum of compensatory awards such a victim deserves.

Homicide offences

These are types of offences where personal factors are most likely to play an important role. For instance, there are occasions when the victim precipitates the crime, like when the victim was the "first to commence the interplay of resort to physical violence." At times, the victim initiates the attack, but the accused over powers him and consequently attacks him in self-defence.[328]

In *State v. Agbo*,[329] it was held that this defence availed the accused that, having observed that the deceased inflicted a fatal hatchet on him, snatched the hatchet from the deceased and killed him. Under S. 282 C.C., killing in self-defence of property is also excused. Hence in R. V. Ebi,[330] it was held that on a charge of murder, the accused was entitled to be acquitted on the ground that the killing was justifiable in defence of his property against the felonious attempt to destroy it. It is further contended that in addition to death sentence imposed on the accused person convicted for an offence of murder,[36a] there is the need to compensate relatives of the victim (the deceased) in terms of monetary values based on standard of the deceased way of life.

---

[327]For example, the incessant clashes between the Ogonis and the authority, in Rivers State of Nigeria which consequently led to the execution of Ken Saro Wiwa and 8 other MOSOP leaders on their alleged roles in the murder of four Ogoni leaders. The frequent religious riots in the Northern part of the country is another vivid example. Examples are the Kano Riot, Bauchi Riot and the Zango-Kataf riot. See also S. 220 (a) of the German Penal Code 1954 enacted in conformity with the Genocide Convention of 1948, which purportedly classified Germany as the best race in the world. Similar situations led to wars in Bosnia Azegovinla, Somalia, Burundi and Liberia to mention a few.

[328]See section 32 (3) C.C., Section 59-67 Penal Code.

[329](1973) 3 E.C.S.L.R. 4.

[330](1958) 3 W.A.C.A. 36.

[36a]Note that at times, even if the accused is ordered to pay compensation the possibility of recovering it from him may be too remote.

Black-Mail Offences

The relationship between criminal and victim has to be particularly close since the former can operate only if he knows a secret of the victim. However, the criminal may have obtained possession of the secret by mere chance without having established any relationship with the victim. On the other hand, the criminal may be successful, even without knowing any secrets at all, provided his victim is in a position where he has to fear even the most groundless accusation. While accidental victims pass through this ordeal due to their physical inferiority to that of the offender in such a situation they do not consent to sexual intercourse. Even in a situation where the culprit is apprehended and prosecuted, the standard of proof required to prove this offence often makes compensatory remedy difficult. In this context, a Honourable Justice of the Supreme Court, Karibi-Whyte had aptly described the situation thus:

> "though crimes of physical violence feature prominently in compensation cases, there are crimes such as rapes and sexual assaults, the injury of which cannot be easily quantified. The nature of the damages resulting from the injury requires specific evidence which may not be adequately adduced in criminal trials."[331]

The revelation in the landmark judgment delivered by the Court of Appeal in the case of *Bodunrin Baruwa v The State.*[332] It must be emphasized that the main contention of this writer is that compensation to the victims of crimes in Nigeria is imperative in line with the various analytical issues that have been discussed above, so that an accused person must offer a certain monetary compensation or something of economic value to the injured party and if the latter accepts it, the injury is redressed, accordingly, the criminal procedure is complete. For the avoidance of doubt, this monetary compensation is due entirely to the victim and or his family to serve as a requital of the injury.[333] It is

[331]From survey conducted the Welfare Officer or Probation Officer claims that all these girls had been willing participants acting from boredom and the desperate need for some form of excitement and that sexual adventure had become vogue among them. In addition, it is discovered that some of them are molested by their step-fathers. As well as others that are sexually stimulated by the parents e.g. in extreme cases.

[332]Reported in the *Guardian*, Wednesday, August, 21, 2996.

[333]See Archibold: Criminal Pleading Evidence and Practice pp. 5-289-724 (42nd Ed. London, Maxwell 1985).

respectfully submitted that this is consonance with the notion of social justice. While the amount of compensation should vary according to the nature of the crime, the age, rank and status of the injured party should also be taken into account. However, the hitherto neglect by our courts of compensatory provisions in the Criminal Codes is out of tune with the modern trends now prevailing in several advanced countries. The pattern adopted in some of these countries shall be briefly examined.

Survey of Foreign Jurisdictions

The current world-wide interest in improving the situation of victim of crime was first considered in New Zealand which established the major comprehensive state crime-victim compensation programme, ranting awards to victims of violent crime in respect of medical and funeral expenses and for lost earnings and support.[334] In Australia, the South Australian government enacted a new law to increase maximum compensation available to victims with effect from 1st of September 1990. The government recognized the rights of victims by implementing the 1985 United Nations Declaration on the rights of the victims.[335] Similarly, the Attorney-General of new South Wales announced the Charter which gave recognition to the rights of victims and establish minimum standards for the fair treatment of victims by departments involved with justice, health and community services. The Charter further provided that a victim of crime covers members of the immediate family of the deceased, where an offence results in death.[336]

In U.S.A., compensation and restitution to victims of crime are treated separately under the Federal and various state laws. According to Prof. Leroy L. Lamborn "the United Nations has adopted the Declaration of Basic principles of justice for victims of crime and abuse of power, with the enactment of the

[334]See *The Statutes Amendment (Victims of Crime) Act 1990* Common-Wealth Law Bulletin Vol. 17 No. 1 January 1991 pp. 135-136.

[335]See Charter of Victims' Rights, Commonwealth Law Bulletin vol. 16, No. 2 April 1990 pp. 657-659.

[336]"Victims in the Criminal Justice Process: An American Perspective" ,p. 95, Fed. Min. of Justice L.R.S. *op. cit.* See also Hon. Justice Y.O. Adio J.S.C., O.F.R. "Victims of Judicial Process in Nigerian Law: Problem of Compensation 1994 Judicial Lectures Continuing Education for the Judiciary (M.I.J. Professional Publishers Ltd) pp. 41-53.

victims Bills of Rights, though it does not provide enforcement mechanism."[337] However the unenforceability of these rights coupled with a desire to give the victim the same symbolic standing as the accused led to a movement to amend the U.S. Constitution and the Constitution of various states in 1982. This has been achieved in various states, California Florida, Michigan and Rhode Island.[338]

In England, as earlier stated the development is of modern phenomenon with the setting up of the Criminal Injuries Compensation Board in August 1964.[339] Under the scheme, anyone who suffers personal injuries on or after that date as a direct consequence of a criminal offence or trying to arrest an offender or to prevent a crime can apply for compensation. The scheme further provides that compensation should be payable only if the injury was one for which compensation of not less than £150 would be awarded though subject to review. And recently, a white paper entitled "Crime Justice And Protecting The Public"[340] contained government proposals for legislation has been published. It states *inter alia:*

> "Encouraging more use of financial penalties, especially compensation to victims and fines which take account of offenders' means".[341]

It is interesting to note that the United Nations has set Regional and International standards regarding victims of crimes, the prevention of victimization, access of the victim to justice and fair treatment, restitution from the offender, compensation from the state and social assistance towards

---

[337]Lamborn, "Victim Participation in the Criminal Justice Process: The Proposals for a Constitutional Amendment", 34 Wague Law Review 125 (1987). See Toohey, "The Victim in Judicial Process" paper read at 6th International Appellate Judges Conference, 7th-11th September, 1992, Nigeria. Cal., Const. Art 1, No. 28, F1. Const. Art. 1 No. 16(b), Mich. Const. Art. 1 No. 24, R.I. Const. NO. 23.

[338]See Archibold *op. cit.*

[339]February 1990 (CM 965, Hmso), Common Wealth Law Bulletin Vol. 16 No. 2 April 1990. Furthermore the victims' Charter contained in Common Wealth Law Bulletin Vol. 17 No. 1 1991 has been adopted in Britain.

[340]See Common Wealth Law Bulletin Vol. 16, NO. 2, *ibid.*

[341]Victims of Crime: Survey of Redress, Restitution and Compensation for victims of crime; U.N. Document A. (CONF 121/14/1985) G.A. Res. 40/43/U.N.G.A. or Supp. (No. 53) at 213-15, U.N.D.C. A/40/53 (1936).

recovery.[342] Happily enough, the international standards set to improve the situation of the victim of crime has attained appreciable advances in many countries.[343] For instance, virtually most common law jurisdictions have been shifting their attention from the traditional view to the material problems of the victim of crime arising out of his misfortune.[344]

Time is therefore, ripe for the setting up of Criminal Injuries Compensation Board as suggested at the National Seminar to compensate the victims of violent crimes in Nigeria. It is further contended that setting up such a scheme is an indispensable and Constitutional duty of the government to provide appropriate remedy for its law abiding and innocent citizens.[345] First, this will ensure the protection of the right to private properties and the right to life provided under Chapter IV of the 1999 Constitution to be guaranteed in cases of its violation.[346] Secondly, a separate and distinct compensation provides in our criminal law will avoid the multiplicity of proceedings and at the same

---

[342]See Council of Europe, The position of the Latin in the Framework of Criminal Law and Procedure (Strasbourg 1985), council of Europe, Assistance to victims and Prevention of Victimization (Strasbourg, 1988). See also Adeyemi, "Basic Principles of Justice for Victims of Crime and abuse of Power and their Application in Nigeria", In Symposium, International Protection of Victims, 7 Nouvelles Etudes Penales 421 (188). Nkpa, "Victims of Crime in the Igbo section of Nigeria, in Victimology: A New Focus; 115 (1: Draplem & E. Viamoeds Lexington, Mass: Lexington 1975).

[343]See Fidelis Nwadialo, SAN, "Compensation to victims of Arson and other Offences to property" p. 212. Justice Law Review Series *op. cit.*

[344]For example, a similar scheme under the Emergency Relief Committee has been set by the Federal government to assist the victims of natural disasters like flood, drought incidents as well as religious riots.

[345]This is better appreciated from the jurisprudential school of thought that crime, against which the state undertakes and endeavours to protect the public, is a disturbance of some legally protected interest, which are worthy of protection. That crime gives rise to legal nexa between the violator and society, but between the violator and his victim, it upsets the balance not only between the criminal and society but between the criminal and the individual victims.

[346]Note that because of the existing distinction between civil and criminal wrongs, the individual victim is at liberty to seek redress as best as he can through the usually inadequate civil channels. In practice, where a victim in a criminal proceeding undertakes a separate civil action simultaneously with the criminal trial, the general principle of law and practice stipulates that the criminal trial should take precedence over the civil suit. The recent killings of six Apo traders in Abuja and the consequent setting up of judicial panel by the federal government headed by Hon. Justice Goodluck which invariably indicted the police for the wrongful killings and made recommendations for compensation for the dependant of the victims as further strengthen this alternative measure.

time protect the accused/defendant against harassment by double proceedings, thereby reduce the workload of the courts and minimize, if not eliminate the delay in the court legal procedures.[347] Another significant relevance of this concept is that it brings justice within the reach of the poor who would not have been able to afford the cost of civil proceedings to uphold their rights.[348] Furthermore, the scheme provides remedies for the victims of criminal acts where the criminal offender was never caught or where the properties involved have been disposed of and not recovered or where the accused is not a man of means. It is further suggested that towards the effective realization of compensation, restitution and reparation policy to victims of crimes, the government should involve the Insurance Sector, an arrangement which will relieve the government of the need to cater for victims' claims, for example in traffic cases compensation is payable by the Insurance Company.[349] In respect of cases of fraud and misappropriation of funds, the accused person should be compelled to pay the amount embezzled back to the actual owners.[350] Moreover, compensation scheme conforms to our traditional concept of dispute settlement and it is in consonance with our social values.

Finally, if the scheme is implemented, it will be effective in the speedy administration of criminal justice and it is considerably less expensive than civil process. In order to circumvent the technical point that the victim is not a party, it is suggested that the victim should become a party, by operation of law, on the conviction of the accused person so that he may be able to put his claims before the court properly for compensation.[351] Despite the laudable objective behind the pragmatic approach towards criminal law reforms the granting of compensation terms may probably hinder the success of criminal

---

[347]This is consonance with the agitation for social justice in Nigeria and other African Countries where the vast majority of the citizens are poor and uneducated and to compound their problem the state does not provide legal aid for such situations.

[348]See J.O. Iruku, "The scope and function of Insurance Industry in the Compensation of Victims" p. 222 at 232 Law Review Series *op. cit.*

[349]The current proceedings in the various Failed Bank Tribunals set up by the Federal Government serve as a veritable means of attaining modern criminal justice.

[350]The court should then take evidence fully as to the nature and extent of injury, loss or damage suffered, including the victim's/complainants contribution to the offence and consequent injury, loss or damage. Furthermore the question of compensation payable should be assessed purely on the basis on which a similar assessment will be made if it arose in a civil suit.

[351]Dr. A. O. Adelola Criminal Justice: Restitution, Compensation and Victims' Remedies: Some neglected views. P. 236 J.L.R.S. *op. cit.*

prosecutions. The opponents of compensation scheme have contended that the interests of the complainant/victim have not been obliterated, and that the underling intent of the present criminal justice system is the victim.[352]

This group has also canvassed that in certain situations if the victim receives private satisfaction in terms of compensation he may exhibit apathy and thereby become an ineffective witness. It is however submitted that even under this situation, the victim cannot get compensation until the accused is convicted. It has also been canvassed that the police may act as agents of the criminals in persuading victims' to accept compensating terms prior to or in the course of criminal trial. The criminals themselves may even make contact with the victim along with an offer of restitution or compensation or induce him not to testify and not to press for the prosecution.[353]At present, the only satisfaction the victim can get from criminal justice is the punishment inflicted upon the criminal.[354] Since the few indemnification provisions highlighted above are not sufficient, the victim of nowadays expects appropriate and reasonable indemnification of the damage caused to him and perhaps tends to think of criminal justice as nationalized vengeance, which to him is unsatisfactory.[355] But if the offender is not so treated, the victim to a large extent may not report

[352]The U.K. adopted victims' charter with moves to ensure that families of murder victims are consulted about the timing of a killer's release and whether restrictions should be placed on where he lives or works. One of the most striking rights established by the charter entitles the relatives of murder victims to be consulted by probation officers before killers are freed on life licence. The clause was framed after a series of incidents where murderers have ended up living close to relatives of their victims. In a number of cases the first the relatives have known of the release is when they have bumped into the killer in the street. Commonwealth Law Bulletin vol. 16, No. 2 April, 1990.

[353]See Bentham's concept of "Pain and Pleasure" Principle. See also Judge Freddie Pitcher, J.R. Court of Appeal First Circuit State of Louisiana, "Sentencing Guidelines: A Questionable Alternative to Discretion" a paper presented at the University of Lagos, Nigeria during a workshop on Democracy in Africa 1995.

[354]See also A.A. Oba, "Compensation orders under S. 78 of the penal code "In Justice, a journal of contemporary legal problems vol. 2, number 4, April 1991.

[355]W.G. Deonar and S.P. "The Impact of Criminal Compensation Upon Victims' attitudes towards the criminal justice system" Victimology: An International Journal. Washington D.C., vol. 5, No. 1. 1980 pp. 61-67. On the general attitudes of victims to report crimes to the Law Enforcement Agencies, see D.R. Singh, "The International Crime (Victim) Survey in Bombay" p. 95 published in the United Nations Inter-regional Crime and Justice Research Institute, titled Criminal victimization in the Developing World (No. 55 Rome 1995). See also Dr. R.R. Washila, "Problems of Victims in the Administration of Justice: the Law Enforcement Perspective p. 195 Law Review Series (*Supra*).

the offender to the police, who may be unable or unwilling to do anything. At times, he fears that the likelihood of retrieving the lost property might diminish if he reports the offence and that even if he reports it would not prevent future experience.[356] It is therefore the opinion of this writer that towards compensation to victims of crimes in Nigeria emphasis should be placed on the role played by the victim in the commission of an offence, with a view to distinguishing between deserving and undeserving victims. If we review the statistics of reports available, one can say that from the current crime rates almost everyone will be a victim of crime during his or her lifetime, hence the need to reappraise the plight of a victim in a criminal process.[357]The received criminal justice system and its inherent problems so far highlighted above have become most unacceptable in Nigeria on the ground that we can no longer afford to run criminal justice systems that have very few provisions for victim remedy. Suffice it to say that it is unfortunate that up till today, nothing beyond the submission of the National Committees Report has been heard. There has been total neglect or inaction on the part of the government on its implementation. Thus, our criminal Justice System remains as it were before the setting up of the National Committee without providing adequate machinery to redress the act of criminality against the victim.

Restitution

If one looks at the legal systems of different countries, one seeks in vain a country where a victim of crime enjoys a certain expectation of full remedies for his injury. The punishment of crime is regarded as the concern of the state, while the injurious result of the crime is regarded almost as a private matter. The Nigerian criminal law accepted and recognized remedies such as restitution, compensation and damages for victims of crime but in an unsatisfactory manner as emphasis is placed on punishment of the offender for various crimes committed against the victim as the most appropriate relief. Thus, for

[356]Hon. Justice Uwaifo in *Baruwa's case supra* analysed the plight of the accused thus: "all he seemed to have done was to report to the police, as a good citizen should that an unknown man had lain dead or dying unattended to in a public place near the water side . . . That earned the appellant his long incarceration and agony. The learned judge further observed that this unfortunate incident will be cited by some citizens as an excuse for their unwillingness to give information in the public interest to the police.

[357]

instance, restitution is made possible by the court if the property stolen is recovered and tendered as exhibit during trial but where such a property is not recovered restitution becomes almost an impossibility for the court to make and the "unfortunate victim" who loses his property by some criminal act has to content, if the offender be brought "to justice" with no other satisfaction for his loss than can be afforded by the punishment of the offender by the state, as one guilty of a public wrong, but not required to make restitution for the private loss which his action has caused. Alternatively, where such property is not recovered but the prosecution is able to prove the ingredients of theft beyond reasonable doubt against the accused upon which he is found guilty and convicted. In the eye of criminal law and procedure, justice has been done. But to the victim this is far from justice,[358] as he is left to recount his loss in terms of finance, time and energy expended going around the halls of justice from the time the trial began, which might span between one day to 5 years or even more. To him he ought to be compensated and/or awarded damages for his travails if the so-called justice is to have significant meaning to him. Thus the victim of criminality is habitually ignored. He cannot even himself seek satisfaction since the law of the state forbids him to take the law into his own hands. Unlike what operated in different communities before the advent of the British; restitution, compensation and damages featured prominently under indigenous court systems.[359] The position was wiser and more just than we are today, for the customary legal systems embraced the theories of restitution, compensation and damages to the injured while the present system have nearly abandoned this practice, to the detriment of all concerned. Yet granting these reliefs is more reformatory in its influence more deterrent in its tendency and more economical to the community.

The Current Legal Position

Restitution relates to the return or restoration of movable property either stolen or otherwise dishonestly acquired, or taken without permission, or property innocently obtained from such successor. This remedy relates to

[358]Justice is not a one way traffic. It is not justice for the accused only. Justice is not even a two-way traffic. It is really a three-way traffic – for the accused, the victim and the society. Per Oputa JSC in *Josiah v. The State* (1985) 1 NWLR 125.

[359]See The Future of Law in Africa (ed. Allot) Chap. 2.

property offences whenever any property, or proceeds of its sale or property brought with stolen money, is recovered, it should be restored to its original owner.[360] It is our opinion that restitution apart from property offences should cover violent crimes. Restitution *per se* is different from cases of compensation, damages but slightly similar to restoration. Restitution occurs where an offender is made to disgorge the benefit he has acquired through his own criminal act. While compensation is concerned with relieving the victim of a crime of any loss he might suffered physically or financially. On the other hands, restoration relates to restoring the possession of immovable property to a person dispossessed of it by means of, e.g. the offence of forcible entry.[361] Closely related to this relief is reparation which covers both compensation and damages. It ensures that the offender does not enjoy the fruits of his crime and also provides a form of remedy that tries to restore the party to the *status quo ante crimine.*

Survey of Existing Laws

There are different statutory provisions as between the northern and southern states on the issue of restitution for victims of offences, which are considered below:

Assault

In the case of injury to the body or health of another, or in the case of deprivation of liberty, the injured party may demand equitable monetary compensation for the transgression, though this has occasioned no pecuniary loss. This position is by analogy to be applied also to those interferences, which violate the right to free exercise of the will, the "inherent right to self-determination in the personal sphere of life".[362] Where death has been caused,

[360]See Archbold; Pleading, Evidence and Practice in Criminal Cases Editors Stephen Mitchell, P.J. Richardson 42nd ed. (London Sweet & Maxwell) 1985, 5-297 at pp. 732-736.

[361]See section 267 of the Criminal Procedure Act.

[362]By the reasoning, the Federal Supreme Court awarded to the injured person a compensation for the moral damage suffered in a case, in which a photograph was published for purposes of advertisement by a third party without the knowledge and consent of the person reproduced and without having obtained the latter's authority.

the person bound to make compensation must make good the deceased's funeral expenses to the person on whom the obligation to pay such expenses lies (the person bound to furnish maintenance to the deceased, or the deceased's heir). If the deceased at the time of the injury stood in a relationship to a third party by virtue of which he was or might be bound by law to furnish maintenance to such a third party, and if in consequence of the death such third party is deprived of the right to claim maintenance, the person bound to make compensation must compensate the third party by the payment of an annuity, to the extent that the deceased would have been bound to furnish maintenance during the presumable duration of his life. (The obligation to make restitution/ or compensation arises even if at the time of the injury the third party was only *en ventre sa mere*).[363] Similarly, in the case of causing death, or of causing injury to the body or health of another, or in the case of deprivation of liberty, if the injured party was by law bound to perform services for a third party (e.g. a husband or parent; not the employer of a domestic servant, this relationship arising not by the operation of law, but by virtue of a contract of service), the person bound to make compensation, must compensate the third party for the loss of service by the payment of a money annuity. It is the opinion of this author that the victim should be entitled to claim damages for any criminal offences even if the injury does not at the same time amount to a contravention of the criminal law. Thus, the hitherto procedure that the victim of a criminal offence can bring his claim for damages against the offender separately before the civil courts should be modified to enable the victim within the criminal procedure, bring a claim for material damage suffered as a result of the criminal offence. This suggestion will serve two ends, by compounding civil reliefs with that of a remedy under criminal proceedings will avoid the multiplicity of proceedings, at the same time protect the accused/defendant against harassment by double proceedings. This will also reduce the workload of the courts and minimize, if not eliminate the delay in the court legal procedures.[364] Invariably, the task of attaining speedy administration of justice will be further achieved, as this approach is considerably less expensive and brings justice within the reach of the poor who would not have been able to afford the cost of filling civil actions to uphold their rights.[365]

---

[363]See BGB – Art 844.

[364]See Margery Fry, "Justice for Victims" (The Observer, July 7, London, 1957.

[365]Second Seminar for Heads of Penitentiary Administration in African Countries, Report, Harare, Zimbabwe 29 February – 6 March 1988 (hereinafter referred to as "The Harare Report"), p. 2.

Homicide

There are situations when the relationship between the criminal and the victim is relevant in determining criminal responsibility. For instance, provocation on the part of the victim of murder mitigates degree of punishment against an accused person. Furthermore, the exercise of self-defence by the accused at times avails him on a charge of murder. But where an accused person is found guilty of murder, it is contended that in addition to death sentence there is the need to compensate relatives of the victim (the deceased) in terms of monetary values[366] based on standard of the deceased way of life to assuage material loss of the dependants. Both the State and the relatives of the condemned person should make financial contributions for the victim's dependants.

Assaults, Defamation, Bigamy and Sexual Offences

In cases of assaults, defamation and bigamy of which have been proved against an accused person it is desirable for the victim to be restored. This becomes more appropriate than fines or imprisonment made against the accused person in the sense that monetary indemnification by the accused for the benefits of the victim that has been unlawfully and unreasonably assaulted or defamed serves the end of justice and the quantum of financial award by the court should take into consideration the age, physical and mental condition of the person on whom it is inflicted.[367] As regards bigamy, restitution is not out of place in view of the position under family law which permits financial compensation in divorce petition brought on the ground of adultery. Perhaps, it is in respect of offence of Rape that restitution rather than imprisonment of the accused is more satisfactory to the victim. For example, where a woman has been raped sentencing the accused to imprisonment for life with or without whipping under Section 358 Criminal Code or to life imprisonment and fine under Section 283 Penal Code is of little relevance to the victim. In fact, punishment cannot fully compensate for the injury,

---

[366]See Commonwealth Law Bulletin vol. 17 No. 1 January 1991 pp. 5-7.

[367]See Section 373 Criminal Code. See also Adeniyi Olatubosun, "Double-Decker Marriage in Private International Law – A Dialectical Appraisal" in Indian Journal of International Law New Delhi, 2001.

which may be physical, emotional and psychological, suffered by a victim of rape.[368] Though, the evaluation of the injury is particularly difficult in the case of moral damage, but it is more reassuring to the psychology of the victim, if she gets financial reliefs. A clamour for this position was emphasized by the witnesses who testified at the Hon. Justice Oputa Panel on Human Rights violation sitting at Port Harcourt on complaints of assault and rape of women testifying as victims of various indecent assaults by the soldiers.

Stealing, Robbery, Burglary and Housebreaking

In respect of these offences, that restitution is more appropriate for the victims by the offenders according to the type of property stolen. Sentencing the accused to terms of imprisonment or fine without more serves no useful purpose for the victim especially in cases where property stolen is not recovered as the victim is left to bear economic burden arising from the exploits of the offender.[369]

Unlawful Assembly, Seditious Meeting, Riot, Affray Offences

As soon as the courts are determined to make an accused found guilty of these offences which result in wanton destruction of properties and goods and even lives indemnify the victims jointly and severally and prospective criminals would weigh the likely consequences of their plan if caught in an unlawful act. This will further guarantee safety of lives and properties. The enormity of loss incurred in such offences is better imagined where the victim is rich, or a big firm or the government.[370]

---

[368]In England victims of rape receive handsome compensation from the Public Fund. See *THE TIMES*, 15th December, 1993, p. 1.

[369]See Sections 411-415 CC.

[370]The country has witnessed several communal clashes and religious riots such as Ife/Modakeke wars, Ijaw/Itshekiris wars, Ogoni riots, Bauchi Riots, Maintaisaine Riots in Kano, Kaduna Riots, Zabo Katarf wars etc. where thousands of lives and millions of properties were lost and several citizens rendered homeless.

Perjury and Corruption

Wherever a person knowingly makes false statement of facts which invariably harm another person, he ought to bear financial burden by redeeming the untrue position to assuage the victim of injury emanating from the falsehood uttered by the accused. This will further promote fair comment and integrity of citizens. Corrupt practices no doubt demand indemnification by the culprits concerned as punitive sentence of an accused alone will not deter others from engaging in this acts. Perhaps, it is in realization of the danger being portended by corrupt activities both in the private and public sectors that the present federal government launder campaigns on anti-graft activities through the passing of Corrupt Practices Act by the National Assembly.[371] The foregoing and many other similar cases require state's assistance which u8nder the present legal system in this country is not satisfactory, not fully utilized and not available in most cases. In the words of Hon. Justice Y.O. Adio, JSC (as he then was):

> The Federal Government's or State's assistance is imperative because the State has a moral obligation to protect all citizens and to make reparations if the protection fails. A compassionate society should assist citizens who find themselves, due to no fault on their part, in circumstances of need.[372]

Compounding of Sentences

It should be pointed out that the punitive aspect of dealing with criminal offences predominates in the Southern States than in the Northern States. The Criminal Procedure Code applicable in the Northern State strictly speaking, do not provide for payment of compensation in the direct and clear manner in which some of the provisions of the Criminal Procedure Act have been considered do. Indeed, the Northern Criminal procedure Code makes provision for a kind of novel arrangement – *Compounding of Certain Minor*

---

[371]See The Corrupt Practices and Other Related Offences Act, 2000.

[372]Victims of Judicial Process in Nigerian Law: Problem of Compensation" in 1994 Judicial Lectures: Continuing Education, National Judicial Institute (Supreme Court).

Offences. A situation whereby the offender and the victim may by mutual agreement sort out their problem in circumstances in which the person that is hurt (victim) can obtain some sort of satisfaction which could make him become satisfied. Over twenty minor criminal offences can be compounded under the provisions of Section 339 of the Criminal Procedure Code. Though this provision seems strange in the South nevertheless it is desirable from the point of view of the victim who might have to go without compensation or financial benefit has to incur expenses of instituting a fresh civil action against the offender before he can get compensation. This approach promotes or encourages true reconciliation or payment of compensation to the victims of such crimes. Even in Europe, victims of minor crimes were dealt with in a recitative way. For centuries in Europe, for example in the Dutch Republic, a considerable number of cases were settled by composite or extra-judicial agreement. In England, settlement out of court were known, for minor matters, a fact attested to by the renowned jurist, Blackstone in his Commentaries on the laws of England (italics) as follows:

> It is not uncommon, when a person is convicted of a misdemeanour ... for the court to permit the defendant to speak with the prosecutor (sic) before any judgment is pronounced, and if the proscecutor declares himself satisfied, to inflict but a trivial punishment. This is done to reimburse the prosecutor his expenses and to make him some private amends, without the trouble and circuitry of a civil action."[373]

In the light of the foregoing, compounding of minor offences is more convenient and appropriate for certain offences.[374] As far as most Nigerians are concerned, if the injury, which they suffer, is not grave they will prefer to forget everything about it rather than be involved in court proceedings which are often protracted and prolonged. In other words, most of them are reluctant litigants or witnesses. Also, a similar practice is often allowed in the Magistrate Courts whereby a complainant or principal witness seeks to withdraw his complaint against the accused or his relations outside the province of the courts.

[373]See Lenman & Parker, "The state, the community and the criminal law in Early Modern Europe" in Crime and the law, p. 26.

[374]See Sections 78 Penal Code, 357 & 365 CPC.

Under the Constitution of Federal Republic of Nigeria, 1999 the provisions of fundamental rights and the special procedure for the enforcement of these rights include restitution, restoration, reparation, compensation and damages among either remedy upon infringement of fundamental human rights in appropriate cases.

Alternative Dispute Resolution (ADR) and Crimes

Nigerian criminal law derives from English common law. As a result the common law has played too dominant a role in the expounding of Nigerian criminal law by the courts. Essentially, the basis of English Criminal law has been the common law considerably supplemented by statutes.[375] Thus, the received criminal justice system in Nigeria operates on the underlying assumption that a crime is a dispute between the state and the criminal, on the one hand, and the state, the victim, on the other. Hence, the Nigerian penal system has operated mainly on the theoretical assumption of deterrence, reformation, elimination and incapacitation.[376] Over the years, the object of criminal justice is to protect the society against crime and to punish the offender. With the progressive changes in punitive approach in courts a new concept of individualization of sentencing has emerged. Consequently, the horizon of judicial consideration widened enough at the stage of determination of guilt as well as of passing sentence.[377] But with the present trend prevailing in contemporary society for the attainment of social justice, the state of administration of criminal justice need to be overhauled.[378]

In this regard concerted effort is being made to examine the possibility of integrating Alternative to Dispute Resolution (ADR) mechanism into criminal process and to evaluate the marked differences in the degrees, extents of its acceptability and utilization of this mechanism under the Conventional Criminal Courts and the Customary Courts.

[375]See the Future of Law in Africa (ed. Allott) cited in Okonkwo & Naish, Criminal Law in Nigeria (1980) (2nd ed.) (Sweet & Maxwell) at p. 3.

[376]See H.L.A. Hart, *Punishment and Responsibility*: Essays in the Philosophy of Law (1968) (Clarendon Press, Oxford).

[377]Mool Singh, Compensatory, Justice in Criminal Law: A goal of social Justice (Government College, Ajmer) (India)

[378]See the Report of the National Committee on Remedies for victims of crime of 23rd August, 1991 organised by the Federal Ministry of justice Law Review Series in Abuja. There is an ongoing process of improving on the administration of criminal justice in Nigeria.

Matters affecting the Civil Interests of the Parties

It has long been a principle of law and practice that disputes between parties are settled alternatively outside the court system or in some cases as supplementary to the traditional court mechanism.[379] The Practice of Dispute Resolution has been in existence from time immemorial and often made use of by parties to dispute because of its practical advantages of settling disputes with less formality and expenses compared to what operate in the court of law. Thus, customary legal system recognizes this mechanism as will be shown later in this work while states and federal laws recognize this mechanism as a form of resolving disputes relating to commercial transactions but exclusively reserved to civil proceeding. Of all the different forms of ADR – arbitration is the most developed and more often utilized by parties to disputes. In Nigeria, the law governing arbitration is contained in the Arbitration and Conciliation Act.[380] The enactment is modern, comprehensive and based almost substantially on the UNCITRAL model law on international Commercial Arbitration and its rules. This work acknowledges invariable contributions of learned authors on the arbitration law both within and outside Nigeria,[381] however, the thrust of this work examines alternatives dispute resolution in broader perspective with a view to determine the degree, its relevance and extent of its applicability in criminal matters.

---

[379]Hon. Justice Dolapo F. Akinsanya, "ADR – The New Trend for the Nigerian Legal Profession" in MPJFIL Vol.5 No. January, 201.

[380]See Arbitration and Conciliation Act Cap. 19 Laws of Federation of Nigeria, 1990.

[381]See Anthony Wlaton, *Russel on the Law of Arbitration* (2nd ed.) (1991) (London, Sweet & Maxwell). Rowland Williams, Alternative Dispute Resolution (ADR) Salvation or Chimeria' (in a journal in Arbitration May 1990, the author practiced initially as a barrister in general civil litigation in Winnipeg, Canada, and thereafter as a partner in a leading firm of London Commercial Solicitors now fellow Chartered Institute of Arbitrators, FCI Arb.) See J.O. Orojo and M.A. Ajomo, *Law and Practice of Arbitration and Conciliation in Nigeria* (1999) (Mbeki, Lagos). Gauis Ezejoifor, *The Law of Arbitration in Nigeria* (Longman) M.O. Ogungbe (Mrs) Associate Professor, "Alternative Dispute Resolution and the Arbitrator's Duty to Act in Good Faith" paper presented at the Faculty of Law, Olabisi Onabanjo University, Ago Iwoye on the 27th September, 2001.

Matters of Criminal Nature

The position of law under the received criminal law and procedure is that criminal causes are not arbitral, because they ought to be punished for the common good.[382] According to Western philosophy of criminal jurisprudence, if the offence is of a public nature no agreement can be valid that is founded on the consideration of stifling a prosecution for it.[383] Essentially, this rule seems to exclude arbitration in criminal trials. While this may still be correct with regards to all those offences which either were felonies of are of a public nature.[384] In considering whether a criminal matter or proceeding may be referred to Alternative Dispute Resolution for arbitration, mediation, conciliation, mini-trial etc. regard must be had to whether the matter or proceeding is one, which the policy of the law would or would not permit to be compromised. If not, then it would not be capable of being removed from the ordinary courts of the land. But in reality where a party injured has a remedy by action as well as by indictment, nothing can deter such a party from referring the adjustment of the reparation, which he is to receive to arbitration, although a criminal prosecution may have been commenced. It is our submission that many offences classified as misdemeanours may validly be resolved outside criminal court between the accused and the victim and the outcome of such arrangement is made the subject of reference, with the sanction of the court. There are instances where 'a complainant' at the magistrate court writes to withdraw his complaint on personal, family or religious reasons against an accused person. Procedurally, all what are expected to be done, is for the magistrate to invite such a complainant into the witness box to swear on oath, apparently to ascertain the veracity and genuineness of his stand on the matter and invariably the accused is discharged and the charge is struck out. The provision of section 284 Criminal Procedure Act supports this position:

> "If a complainant at any time before a final order is made in any case under this chapter satisfies the court that there are sufficient

[382]Nwabueze, *Machinery of Justice in Nigeria,* Parker, & Allerton, *The courage of his convictions* (London, 1961); Fitzgerald, *Criminal Law and Punishment.*

[383]See Hart, Punishment and the Elimination of Responsibility (1961) Hobhouse Memorial Lecture.

[384]Suggestions are sometimes made that the law should try to draw a line between such vastly different types of behaviour, and that the notion of crime should be limited to the more serious offences, with other terms being found for the less serious. In Okonkwo *op. cit.*

> grounds for permitting him to withdraw his complaint the court may permit him to withdraw the same and shall thereupon acquit the accused unless the court directs that the accused instead of being acquitted shall be discharged".

It is noteworthy to state emphatically that many jurists and lawyers that imbibed strict application of English criminal justice system in our legal system are adherents to the general belief that amicable settlement, conclusion, negotiation were hardly compatible with the tenets of the "received" western philosophy of criminal justice system.[385] Some eminent jurists also shared extreme extension of this idea to restitution, reparation and compensation in Nigerian courts.[386] From the plethora of judicial decisions on criminal matters available in Nigeria, it is remarkable to point out that at the stage of determination of guilt as well as of passing of sentences our judges have not deemed it important to consider or emphasize the personal circumstances of the accused while imposing sentences.[387] But it is a matter of great disappointment that victims of crime are still out of the scene.[388] The courts have not paid enough attention in criminal cases on the distress of the victims and their dependants. It is therefore strange that the courts have generally taken less into account the plight of the victim in criminal cases but concentrating on the routine 'backward looking' philosophy of punitive syndrome while sentencing the offender the victim and his dependants get nothing.[389] In the modern contemporary society, a changed in social environment is imperative, as economic hardship has become a vitally important matter deserving

[385]See the Utilitarian principles of punishment.

[386]They believe that criminals should be hated and severely punished by the application of maximum punishment.

[387]Though the courts have discretionary powers to choose from average of sentences all too often a punishment is imposed by the busy judge or magistrate without consideration of the value of this approach who have to effect sentences.

[388]Hon. Justice A.L. Balogun, OFR, 'Problems of Victims in the Administration of Justice: The Judicial view point; Agbede, Modalities for the Enforcement of Financial Compensation for the victims of crimes both in Justice Law Review series book entitled Restitution for victims of crimes in Nigeria, (ed. Sade Adetiba),. See Adeniyi Olatunbosun, Compensation to: Victims of crime in Nigeria; A critical Assessment of criminal – victim Relationship" M.Phil Seminar Paper, Faculty of Law, O.A.U., Ile-Ife.

[389]See Se Stephen Schafer, Restitution to victims of crime (1960) (London Stevens & Sons Ltd.) See also A.A. Oba, 'Compensation orders under section 78 of the Penal Code' in Justice, a journal of contemporary legal problems Vol. 2 No. 4 April, 1991.

attention. The important question to be addressed here is whether alternative dispute resolution in criminal litigation is in consonance with the goal of social justice? Would it not be deviation from the basic principles of administration of criminal justice? These issues and other related ones would be discussed hereunder.

The Need for Alternative to Imprisonment

The spate of congestions in the prison yards has been on astronomical increase in recent years. Several factors responsible for this upsurge are beyond the realm of this work.[390] Obviously, the over-dependence of the penal system on imprisonment has not deterred criminals and reliance on prisons has not reformed criminals as well as Prof. Adeyemi has rightly observed that imprisonment cannot cope with the crime problem.[391] Is it viable in Nigerian circumstances to afford to run prisons system with increasing financial burdens on the already deteriorating economy? This should be a source of worry for all. It is submitted that the time is now ripe in African countries to give serious thought to alternatives to imprisonment like the more traditionally accepted measures of restitution, reparation, compensation and fines on the one hand and negotiation, reconciliation, mediation and arbitration on the other hand in place of imprisonment as Africans cannot appreciate a treatment like imprisonment which, if it benefits at all, is benefiting only the government in total disregard of the victim and African juristic thought of maintaining social equilibrium.[392] Therefore, the English idea of the public nature of a criminal offence has certainly become inappropriate in contemporary criminal policy system. Prof. Ajomo emphasized this point thus:

> ... after several years of sustained ridicule of African concept of crime and punishment on the part of western legal writers, modern European states have now come round to borrow the idea.

---

[390]See *Law Development and Administration in Nigeria* Vol. (1990) (ed. Yemi Osinbajo & Awa. U. Kalu (Federal Ministry of Justice Law Review Series).

[391]"Personal Reparation in Africa: Nigerian and the Gambia" in *Alternatives to Imprisonment in Comparative Perspective* (ed. U. Zvekio) U.N. Inter-Regional Crime and Justice Institute, Nelson Hall, Chicago).

[392]A.A. Adeyemi, "Criminology in Contemporary Africa" Nigeria Journal of Criminology, vol. 2. No. 1.

> We were told that Africans have no law. Those who thought we have something resembling law felt that it was too vague and too fluid to be of relevance to modern man. In particular, the idea of compensation in criminal prosecution is now in vogue in modern Europe even though African states have presumed to abandon the practice by the European conquerors.[393]

Paradoxically, compensation and restitution which were more popular, effective and acceptable means of disposing of cases in many customary courts than ever they were in the British patterned Courts earlier rejected and denounced has now become the cornerstone of criminal justice system in most advanced countries.[394]

The Range of ADR in Criminal Trials

Aspects of viable alternative measures to criminal litigation exist in our criminal law and procedure though authorities involved in the administration of criminal justice in Nigeria rarely utilized them. At the pre-trial stage, public confidence in the competence of the police to investigate the case effectively and efficiently coupled with the weight of criminal activity from the perspective of its seriousness and quality of evidence influence the obligation of the victim to report such crimes.[395] Perhaps, the existence of alternative ways and means of dealing with those crimes outside the sphere of law enforcement agencies influence non-exploration of investigational process of such crimes at the police station.[396] In some cases, citizens resort to self-help measures like solve it myself, family, friends support, consultation, warning, plea of unreserved apology as alternative modes of seeking redress

[393]Comparative Analysis of Customary Law in Africa being a chapter in the book entitled *Integration of the African Continent through Law* (1990) (ed. Yemi Osinbajo) published by Federal Ministry of Justice Law Review Series.

[394]See Victims charter (U.K.) in Commonwealth Law Bulletin Vol. 16 No. 2 April 1990 at pp. 671-672.

[395]See Police, Citizens, Experience and Attitudes towards Punishment – An overview of the main fundings, A report on the International Crime (Victim) survey in Bombay, India published in the United Nations International Crime and Justice Institute, Nelson Hall, Chicago, 1993.

[396]See W. Skogan, Reporting crime to the Police: The Stages of World Research" in Journal of Research in Crime and Delinquency (1984).

from criminal acts inflicted.[397] Also, negative belief by the public in the ability of the police to detect and apprehend offenders especially in cases where the propensity to recover property involved is doubtful, exploring redress though the police may be viewed as non-beneficial and sheer waste of time, energy and resources.[398] Even, where crimes are reported timeously, long investigational methods coupled with logistics problems often encountered by the Nigeria Police invariably leads to abandonment of complaints at the police station. Closely related to this is the possibility of relations of the suspects reaching out to the complainant outside the police station making compassionate pleas, indemnification terms, religious and other consideration to dissuade the victim from pressing for criminal prosecution.

The Legal Framework of ADR in Technical Offences

There are basically two sources of criminal law in Nigeria, first criminal statutes namely the Criminal Code and penal code and secondly, there is a host of statutes, both federal and state defining what may be described as technical offences. Under the second category there are offences created under the law of the federation like the Dangerous Drug Acts[399] and at the state levels such as Bush Burning law[400] slaughtering of animals: Public Health law,[401] Burial in Houses[402] to mention a few examples. In all these offences stern warning and diversion from the criminal process are more often adopted in place of prosecution. Interestingly, the police authorities initiate pre-settlement of such a criminal breach instead of arrangement of suspects in court.

---

[397]See Singh, D.R., 'The International Crime (victim) Survey in Bombay" published by Tata Institute of Social Sciences, Bombay India 1992. See also Adeniyi Olatunbosun, Public Attitudes towards Reporting Crimes in Nigeria in Nigerian Law Practice Journal Vol. 2, No. 7, Nov. 1998 (Criminal Legal Education, NLS)

[398]See the Failure of Prosecution (1996) (CRP). A Report on the prosecution of criminal suspects in Nigeria) by Clement Nwankwo, Bonny Ibhawoh, Duluth Mbachu.

[399]Cap 91 Laws of Federation of Nigeria 1990.

[400]Ondo State Edict NO. 4 of 1989.

[401]Slaughtering of Animals Public Health Cap. 165 Laws of Federation of Nigeria 1958.

[402]Section 246 CC.

ADR and Specific Offences

Both the formal and the informal criminal justice systems provide for compounding procedures. Compounding mechanism consists of the receipt of some property or other consideration in return for an agreement not to prosecute or inform on who has committed a crime. This arrangement exists at common law and has been further modified by the English Criminal Act of 1967. Strictly speaking, the provisions for compounding certain offences exists in the criminal procedure code applicable in the Northern states and by common practice in certain criminal cases in the Southern states. The compounding of the criminal offences in question may involve payment of compensation to the victims of the crimes in consideration for their consent or agreement that the crime be compounded. The compounding of a crime occurs when a person asks for, or receives, as the case may be, money or other compensation on the understanding that he will abstain from pressing for the prosecution for the criminal offence.[403] The magnitude of this arrangement will be appreciated through the category of the offences compoundable by law, namely causing hurt, assault and use of criminal force, mischief resulting in injury, loss of damage to a person, criminal trespass, criminal breach of contract of service, criminal intimidation, enticing or taking away or detaining with a criminal intent a married woman, defamation, insult intended to provoke a breach of the peace, grievous hurt by a dangerous weapon, unlawful detention, burglary and house breaking.[404] In such situations for example, the person insulted may compound the offence of insult intended to provoke a breach of the peace and whenever any offence under the section is applied, it has the effect of an acquittal of the accused. It should be noted that arrangement for compounding offences allows the offender to use all legitimate means to persuade or induce the victim to agree that the criminal offence in question should be compounded. Thus we can rightly say that the punitive measure of dealing with offenders predominates in the southern states than in the Northern states. It is our submission that if the offender and the victim hurt by his criminal act may by mutual agreement sort out their problem in circumstances in which the injured

---

[403]See Aguda, *The Criminal Law and Procedure of the Southern States of Nigeria.*

[404]These offences punishable under the Penal code are described in the first column of Appendix C of the Northern Nigerian Criminal Procedure Code, Chap 30 subject to the Provision of Section 339 (i) Penal code. See also Gambian Criminal Procedure Code Section 145 (I) Tanzania Criminal Procedure Code, Section 176. See also Tudor Jackson, *The Law of Kenya* An Introduction (1976) (2nd ed.) KLB Nairobi at P101 – referring to Section 118 of the Penal Code, Kenya.

person can obtain some sort of satisfaction which could make him become satisfied and agree that the offence should be compounded the effect of which amounts to an acquittal, then no harm can be said to have been done to either side. Perhaps, those holding opposing views might say that the compounding of certain minor criminal offences is strange, archaic or unsatisfactory. We consider it to be desirable from the point of view of the victim who might have to go without compensation or financial benefit after the conviction of the offender or subsequently to incur expenses of instituting a civil action against the offender before he can get compensation. For centuries, even in Europe, victims of minor crimes were not satisfied with a punitive legal system of only fines and other punishments without promotion or encouragement of reconciliation or payment of compensation to the victims of such crimes.[405] In England, settlement out-of-court were known for minor matters as graphically stated by Blackstone,

> It is not uncommon, when a person is convicted of a misdemeanour . . . for the court to permit the defendant to speak with the prosecutor (sic) before any judgment is pronounced, and if the prosecutor declares himself satisfied, to inflict but a trivial punishment. This is done to reimburse the prosecutor his expenses and to make him some private amends, without the trouble and circuitry of a civil action.[406]

The desirability of this practice in Nigeria, has been justified by Hon. Justice Y. O. Adio, JSC (as he then was) in this way

> Nigerians are known to be reluctant litigants or witnesses. As far so they are concerned, they find compounding of minor offences more convenient. If the injury which they suffer as a result of the criminal act of an accused is not much they will prefer to forget everything about it rather than be involved in court proceedings. Even in matters affecting their fundamental rights they always seem to be satisfied once the act affecting them is declared illegal or unconstitutional.[407]

[405]In the Dutch Republic, a considerable number of cases were settled by composite or extra-judicial agreement.

[406]See His Commentaries on the Laws of England.

[407]Victims of Judicial Process in Nigerian Law: Problem of Compensation" in Judicial Lectures. Continuing Education for the Judiciary (1994). (MIJ Publishers) NJI Sc. P. 21 at 49.

Extending the range of offences compoundable beyond the realm of minor offences has been postulated by Prof. Adeyemi that

> an overwhelming number of crime are settled by the parties through the compounding procedure and are never brought to the attention of the authorities. In order words, these cases are diverted from the criminal process approximately 20 percent of unintentional homicide, 60 percent of theft (these also involve restitution), 40 percent of rape and defilement 67 percent of assaults, and so forth. In 1988, 72 percent of adultery cases in Nigeria (North & South) were settled by the compounding procedure without the invocation of the criminal process.[408]

It is clear from the foregoing views of eminent jurists that settlement of criminal disputes outside the forum of court is justifiable and should be encouraged. It is respectfully submitted that the position of law in the Southern states have not placed much emphasis on compounding procedure, a review of the criminal law in the Southern states should be undertaken, while there is still room for improvement in relation to the number of crimes in which compounding approach may be allowed. Within judicial province a reported offence may be compounded at any stage up to the conclusion of the trial, but before conviction and sentence, however, once trial has commenced in the court, the offence can be compounded only with the authorization of the trial court. Outside the formal system, parties can compound an offence in which case it will never be reported or recorded in judicial statistics. The practice of compounding is also prominent in road traffic offences.[409] In the latter situation the person charged with such an offence offers to indemnify the dependants of the deceased and takes up responsibility for funeral rites of the victim with the understanding that the relatives of the dead withdraw their complaints at the police station, even after the case is being tried in court

---

[408]Personal Reparations in Africa: Nigeria and Gambia Alternatives To Imprisonment in Comparative perspective Ed. U. Zvekio (1993) Interregional Crime & Justice Institute, Nelson Hall, Chicago. Note that in England victims of rape receive handsome compensation from the public fund see *The Times*, 15th December, 1993, p. 1. In Niger, a victim of attempted rape in Basaniwa demanded for a sum of N30,000 and a ram from a Gwari man as restitution for allegedly attempting to rape her while testifying before a magistrate's court in Jiwa, Abuja. See *The Punch*, Friday, October 12, 2001, at page 5.

[409]Adeyemi *ibid.*

compounding mechanism is adopted to resolve the matter beyond the frontier of criminal justice.

Ripeness of A.D.R. in Capital Offences

A clamour for alternative mechanism to the concept of punishment in criminal trials is not a recent phenomenon; it has long been canvassed as far back as 1895, when Prins during a discussion of the problem of restitution to victims of crime had this to say:

> The guilty man lodged, fed, clothed, warmed, lighted, entertained, at the expenses of the state in a model cell, issued from it with a sum of money lawfully earned, has paid his debt to society; he can set his victims at defiance; buy the victim has his consolation; he can think by taxes he pays to the Treasury, he has contributed towards the paternal care, which has guarded the criminal during his stay in prison.[410]

These were the bitter and sarcastic words of Prins, the Belgian when he could no longer contain his indignation at various practical and theoretical difficulties raised against his proposals on behalf of the victim. His was not the first voice claiming recognition and respect for the victim's injury, and it was by no means the last.[411] Adherents to the classic criminal law also increasingly voiced their concern; but, constrained by the legislation of states which has, in one form or another, tacitly allowed the principle of restitution, compensation, damages while the unfortunate victim of criminality was habitually ignored up to the present time. Obviously, the state of criminal justice as of now whereby a person who loses his property by some criminal act, and has to be content, if the offender be brought to justice, with no other satisfaction for his loss than can be afforded by the punishment of the offender by the state, as one guilty

[410]The Paris Prison Congress, 1895, Summary Report (London).

[411]See William Tallack *Reparation to the Injured; and the rights of The Victims Crime to Compensation* (1900) (London); Richard R. Cherry, *Lectures on the Growth of Modern Law in Ancient Communities Lectures on the Growth of Criminal Law in Ancient Communities* (1890) (London); M.J. Sethna, *Society and the Criminal* (1952) Bombay; Report of the Commission on the Review of Administration Criminal Justice in Ogun State June 1987. The Report of the National Committee on Remedies for Victims of Crime, August 1991 in Abuja.

of a public wrong, but not required to make conciliation for the private loss which his action has caused is to say the least no longer satisfactory to the public at large.

Alternative mechanism to criminal prosecution should be encouraged and allowed to thrive under our penal policy. The adoption of this concept is likely to generate some problems in penal legislation.[412] The problem however, may not be simple. It may entail several practical and theoretical complications; but these must not be allowed to break the ties, by which the victim, through his injury and loss, is associated with the criminal offence.

This book has tried to approach the problem from two angles in an attempt to serve not only the ideas of victimology (sort of resolving conflict between the victim and the accused), but also the task of the penology as well. Alternative dispute resolution is mean to carry out a mission not only in helping the victim of crime in his present neglected position but, at the same time, in refining the practical concept of punishment. Our approach differ from the current solutions among lawyers that if a criminal act results in personal injury, damage or loss, the victim, is at liberty to institute separate civil action to recover his loss outside the ambit of criminal trial which is entirely emphasizing punitive measures. A reappraisal of criminal philosophy is desirable not pity towards the victim, but appreciation of his claim is needed. Not thirst for revenge against the criminal, but a clearer understanding of his deed would help his reform and rehabilitation. Modern Criminal jurisprudence establishes a close relation between crime and its object, and the criminal and his victim.[413] Alternative approach to criminal justice transcends beyond the traditional concept that crime construes a relation between the criminal and society to a relation between the criminal and his victim.

The general principle of criminal procedure that a victim of crime is a competent and compellable witness and not a complainant at the High Court level is more or less a 'fiction', the victim is not just simply the cause of the criminal procedure, he has an indispensable role to play in the criminal process, while the 'state' is not the 'complainant' in its true form but 'a sort of trustee'. Our position can be further buttressed by a practical example that the death of a principal witness in a criminal charge before the commencement

---

[412]See Samuel J. Barrows, The Sixth International Congress: Report of its Proceedings and Conclusions (Washington, 1903).

[413]See Herman Mannheim, *Comparative Criminology* (vol. 1 & 2) (1970) Third Impression (London Routledge & Kegan Paul).

of hearing terminates the proceeding where the evidence of the deceased is the only proof of the allegation against the accused be that of murder, armed robbery and other offences. In this work we try to offer how an idea of Alternative Dispute Resolution may come nearer criminal process. We have no illusion that by this brief analysis we have succeeded in solving the problem of merging the concept of ADR with criminal law and procedure. But we have tried; to pave the way and the analysis so far made may help in the search for a solution to criminal justice devoid of time wasting (as justice delayed is justice denied), less technical in its procedural form and satisfactory in its sentencing mechanism. The tone of this work seems to be revolutionary as we have succeeded in solving the problem of merging the concept of ADR with criminal law and procedure. But we have tried; to pave the way and the analysis so far made may help in the search for a solution to criminal justice devoid of time wasting (as justice delayed is justice denied), less technical in its procedural form and satisfactory in its sentencing mechanism.

5

SENTENCING GUIDELINES AND JUDICIAL DISCRETION

In the criminal sentencing process, judges had almost infinite discretion to mete out a sentence on a criminal as long as the sentence imposed did not exceed broad statutory limits.[414] The prevailing view is that the past life or particular habits of an individual offender are relevant to the sentencing decision and the idea that every criminal offence in a specific legal category requires identical punishment is rejected. The winds of change began to blow against unfettered discretion in sentencing. Many jurists, criminologists, and judges persistently criticized the disparities in sentences meted out in the various court systems. This group of jurists argued that:

> Modern criminal justice process must not choose any longer to tolerate a regime of unseasoned, unconsidered caprice for exercising the most awful power of organized society, the power to take liberty and ... by process of what purports to be law.[415]

Their consensus is that:

> the prior sentencing practices of judges offered little hope for reform, because judges were not required to explain their sentences. Considering the fact that judges were not require to articulate reasons for sentencing, it became difficult, if not impossible, to discern if sentences were based on careful deliberation and objective factors, or whim and caprice.[416]

---

[414]This broad discretion was recognized by he United States Supreme Court as far back as 1947 in the case of *Williams v. New York*. 337 U.S. 241 (1949)

[415]See Frankel, Lawlessness in Sentencing, 41 U. Cin. L. Rev. 1 (1972).

[416]See Freddie Pitcher, JR.; Sentencing Guidelines; A Questionable Alternative to Discretion, being a paper presented at University of Lagos, Nigeria in a Seminar titled Democracy in Africa Workshop, 1995.

Principles of Sentencing

The call for a national commission to study disparate sentences began to develop momentum throughout the criminal justice system. Advocates of national commission suggested that the commission would be responsible for formulating laws and rules for the implementation of sentences and ensuring that the rules would be enforced effectively and objectively.[417]

As far back as 1984 in USA, congress heard the call of the reformers and passed the Sentencing Reform Act, which established the United States sentencing commission, the pre-cursor to erosion of judicial discretion, especially in the federal court system. Congress gave the sentencing commission the responsibility of changing the way federal district courts sentenced persons convicted of federal crimes. Before the Act, Congress was generally content to define broad sentencing ranges for various offenses, leaving the imposition of sentences within those ranges to the discretion of individual judges, to be exercised on a case by case basis.

The basic objective of conferences and seminars on sentencing is aimed towards advising government to promulgate a detailed sentencing guideline system, to enhance the ability of the criminal justice system and to reduce crime through a sentencing system that is fair as well as effective.[418] This goal is to be achieved by (1) abolishing parole, in order to achieve greater degree of honesty in sentencing; (2) imposing essentially the same sentences on similar offenders committing similar crimes, in order to eliminate unwarranted disparities and achieve a greater of uniformity in sentencing; and (3) varying the sentences imposed to reflect differences in the severity of the criminal conduct, in order to achieve a greater degree of proportionality in sentencing. This guideline system is capable or achieving the latter two purposes by establishing a large number of narrow sentencing ranges for various offences and offenders and generally mandating that sentencing courts impose sentences within the appropriate guideline range.[419] A sentencing court may depart from the applicable Guideline range only in specified circumstances, such as when it

---

[417]See the report of National Criminal Justice System REFORMS BY FEDERAL Ministry of Justice, Abuja in 1990. See also Nigeria's Criminal Justice System: The Way Out in Vanguard, Monday, August 22, 2005 at pp. 45-48. See also Ogletree, The Death of Discretion? Reflections on the Federal Sentencing Guidelines, 101 Harv. L. Rev. 1938, 1940 (1988).

[418]Am. Jur. 2d, New Topic Service: Federal Sentencing Guidelines, 4 (1993).

[419]*Ibid.*

finds that there exists an aggravating or mitigating circumstance of a kind, or to a degree, not adequately taken into consideration by the sentencing commission in promulgating the Guidelines.[420] The guidelines are intended to ensure certainty, uniformity, consistency and proportionality of punishment, fairness to victims, and the protection of society. The guidelines are also to assist courts in stating for the record the considerations taken into account and the factual basis for imposing sentence. It is important to note that the guideline are not mandatory, but are advisory and are only intended to assist courts in the sentencing phase of adjudicatory process.

The Development of the Guidelines

In an effort to carry out its national mandate, the Federal sentencing commission created categories of offence behaviour and offender characteristics, and prescribe guideline ranges that specify an appropriate sentence for each class of convicted persons. The sentence would then be determined by coordinating the appropriate offense behavior category with the appropriate offender characteristic category. In establishing categories of offenses for the sentencing guidelines and the policy statements, the commission will take into consideration:

1. The category of the offence;
2. The circumstances under which the offence was committed that mitigate or aggravate the seriousness of the offense;
3. The nature and degree of the harm caused by the offence,

[420]Several state legislatures in US caught on to the sentencing guideline idea and formed sentencing commissions to study the sentencing practices of their state court judges. The state of Minnesota was one of the first states to actually implement a sentencing guideline model for its judges. The Minnesota system allowed judges to depart from the sentencing guidelines only if they stated their reason in writing. The written reasons for departure allowed prosecutors and defence counsel an opportunity to challenge sentences they regarded as too severe or to lenient. The Louisiana Sentencing Commission, after several years of study, promulgated sentencing guidelines in 1992. The stated purpose of the Louisiana Guidelines is to recommend a uniform sanctioning policy which is consistent, proportional and fair for use by the Louisiana judiciary in felony cases in which the sentencing court must determine the sentence to be imposed. The guidelines do not apply to capital cases, cases punishable by a mandatory sentence of life imprisonment, or misdemeanor cases.

including whether it involved property, irreplaceable property, a person, a number of persons, or a breach of public trust;

4. The community view of the gravity of the offence;
5. The public concern generated by the offence;
6. The deterrent effect a particular sentence may have on the commission of the offense by others; and
7. The current incidence of the offence in the community and in the nation as a whole.

The sentencing commission should consider, in establishing categories of accused, the following:

1. Age;
2. Education;
3. Vocational skills;
4. Mental and emotional condition, to the extent that such condition mitigates the defendant's culpability or to the extent that such condition is otherwise plainly relevant;
5. Physical condition, including drug dependence;
6. Previous employment record;
7. Family ties and responsibilities;
8. Community ties;
9. Role in the offence;
10. Criminal history; and
11. Degree of dependence upon criminal activity for a livelihood.

The court should determine whether the following specific offender characteristics are not ordinarily relevant in determining if a sentence should be outside the guidelines:

1. Age;
2. Education and vocational skill;
3. Mental and emotional conditions;
4. Physical condition, including drug or alcohol dependence or abuse;
5. Employment record;
6. Family ties and responsibilities, and community ties;
7. Race, sex, national origin, creed, religion, and socio-economic status;

8. Military, civic, charitable, or public service, employment related contributions, and similar works; and
9. Lack of guidance as a youth or similar circumstances indicating a disadvantaged upbringing.

The sentencing guidelines are required to reflect the general appropriateness of imposing a sentence other than imprisonment in cases where the accused is a first time offender who has not been convicted of a crime of violence or an otherwise serious offense. Furthermore, the guidelines must include a determination of whether multiple sentences to terms of imprisonment should be ordered to run concurrently or consecutively. The guidelines must reflect the general inappropriateness of imposing consecutive terms of imprisonment for an offence of conspiring to commit an offence or soliciting the commission of an offence. The general policy limiting consecutive terms of imprisonment for an offense involving a violation of a general prohibition and for an offence involving a violation of a specific prohibition encompassed within the general prohibition. The guidelines are also required to reflect the appropriateness of imposing an incremental penalty for each offense in a case in which the accused is convicted of multiple offenses committed in the same course of conduct that result in the exercise of ancillary jurisdiction over one or more of the offenses.

The Imposition of the Sentence

In determining the particular sentence to be imposed under sentencing guidelines, the court should consider the need to reflect the seriousness of the offense to promote respect for the law and provide just punishment for the offense; the need to afford adequate deterrence to criminal conduct and protect the public from further crimes of the defendant; and the need for educational or vocational training, medical care, or other correctional treatment are to be taken into consideration in the court's determination of the sentence.

In determining the particular sentence to be imposed, the court must consider:

1. The nature and circumstances of the offense and the history and characteristics of the accused;
2. The kinds of sentences available;
3. The kinds of sentences and the sentencing ranges established

for the applicable category of the offense committed by the applicable category of the defendant as set forth in the guideline that are issued by the sentencing commission.

4. Any pertinent policy statement issued by the sentencing commission.
5. The need to avoid unwarranted sentence disparities among with similar records who have been found guilty of similar conduct;
6. The need to provide restitution to any victims of the offense.

Determining Criminal History

The future criminal behaviour of an accused is a paramount consideration in the sentencing process. Courts look at this behaviour in an effort to protect the public from further crimes of particular defendants. Sentencing Guidelines attempt to deal with this by taking into consideration, the appropriate sentencing range for the offense, the nature and seriousness of the offense and the criminal history of the offender. Criminal history simply means prior sentences and the term "prior sentence" means any sentence previously imposed upon adjudication of guilty, whether by guilty plea, trial, or a plea of *nolo contendere* for conduct not part in the instant offense, unrelated and related sentences. This is the method most often used by the courts in Nigeria when sentencing an accused person in a criminal trial. However, the police and the state in most instances are not with the up-to-date records of the accused persons.

Departures from the Guideline Range of Sentencing

Although the federal sentencing guidelines are mandatory, a sentencing court may diverge from the guideline sentence under certain circumstances. The sentencing Reform Act of 1984 provides that a sentencing court must impose a sentence of the kind and within the range established for the applicable category of offense committed by the applicable category of defendant as set forth in the sentencing guidelines that are in effect on the date the defendant is sentenced. However, if the court finds that there exists an aggravating or mitigating circumstance of a kind not adequately taken into consideration by the sentencing commission in formulating the guidelines, a different may be allowed.

Circumstances that may warrant departure from the guidelines cannot, by their very nature, be comprehensively listed and analyzed in advance. The courts can only make the decision as to whether, and to what extent departure is warranted. Some factors which they have not been able to take into account in the formulation of the guidelines,,

1. Harm caused by the defendant worsening the gravity of the offense committed;
2. The public welfare being significantly endangered;
3. The victims conduct invoking the offense;
4. The accused committing the offense to avoid greater harm;
5. The accused committing the offense as a result of coercion or dress;
6. The accused committing a non-violent offense while suffering from a diminished mental capacity;
7. The accused voluntarily disclosing the offense to authorities;
8. The accused substantially assists the authorities in investigating or prosecuting others.

Presence of any such factor may warrant departure from the guidelines, under some circumstances, in the discretion of the sentencing court.

The Failure of the sentencing Guidelines

The ministry has been quite explicit in setting forth the sentencing purposes that it expected the commission's guidelines to address. It is clear, in particular, that it wanted the commission to consider the full range of purposes for criminal sentencing, including deterrence, retribution, incapacitation and rehabilitation. Although the commission noted that it sought guidelines that would do justice for victims and the public, as well as offenders, the guidelines ultimately submitted for approval have failed to provide judges with much guidance in applying any particular purpose to any particular sentence. In fact the sentencing guidelines are permissive and non-binding.

The ministry urged the commission to consider a wide range of factors in determining the sentence to be imposed. The commission's determination of the factors which are relevant in determining whether a sentence fits within the existing guidelines have been disappointing. Other critics of the sentencing guidelines note that the system has failed to consider the offender's personal characteristics and has placed too great of an emphasis on the harm caused by the offender's act. It has also not taken much into consideration the circumstances that would serve to mitigate the punishment.

The commission has also failed to consider the impact of the sentencing guidelines on prison population and to take steps to ameliorate their likely adverse impact. Instead of concentrating on a solution in growing prison population, the commission noted that the increase was attributable, in large part, to preexisting sentencing statutes and concluded that the impact of the guidelines on prison population would be modest by comparison.

In the United States, the most important difference between the state and federal guidelines is not from structural or statutory factors; rather, it resulted from a United States sentencing commission policy choice. The choice was to develop a highly mechanical, "quasi-element" basis for federal sentencing guidelines instead of the more principled, conceptual "usual case" basis for state sentencing guidelines.[421]

The Debates on Death Penalty

Perhaps more words have been uttered – in public and in private-over the issue of capital punishment than over any other single issue of public or social policy. Virtually everything that can be said both for and against this unique penal sanction has been said and nauseam. Yet the debate rages on.

Evidence about the state and nature of murder, upon which one would imagine a rational judgment about the death penalty might be made, continues to accumulate, capital crimes such as murder, treason and treasonable felonies, sedition, even sexual offences and explosive attacks are frequently treated as the result of obscure influences and are regarded as point hereby savage. Over the years, homicide remains the arch typical crime in the minds of many people; Cain's slaying of Abel has been re-enacted and reinterpreted with endless fascination. Emergence of new facts about murder does not add much to the debate over the years. Why then this work, if there is little that is new or fresh to say on the subject?

[421]See Freddie Pitcher, ***op. cit.*** at p 15.

Issues on capital punishment became prominent in the 19th century in England,[422] United States of America[423] in the 20th century, while the debates are products of a new and emerging discourse of the 21st century in Nigeria.[424] This chapter analyses arguments for and against the practice of death penalty with a view to determine what should be the position of Nigeria within the ambit of the trends now prevailing in some foreign jurisdictions.

The Position in Britain

When the Homicide Act, 1957, which retained capital punishment for certain categories of murder, was repeated in 1965, Parliament decreed that the period of abolition should lapse on 31st July 1970 unless affirmative resolutions of both House of Parliament had been passed in favour of extending abolition, either indefinitely or for a further trial period.

The Howard League for Penal Reform, which has throughout its history been in the vanguard of abolition took bold step to bring the subject before the public through the symposium organized to bring together the thoughts of a number of eminent people from all walks of life. The wide range of the

---

[422]In Britain several views and opinions have been expressed in both Houses of Parliament during the last 200 years and several reports of Commissions and Committees have been compiled and published. The Royal Commission Report is the most significant in this field of study. CMD 8432 (1953). The Howard League for Penal Reform published a book: The Hanging Questions, edited by L.B. Lom Cooper (1969) (Gerald Duckworth & Co.) (London) (1949). See also Roy Calvert: Capital Punishment in XXth Century quoted by Gerald Gardiner Q.C., Capital Punishment and the Alternative (The Camelot Press Ltd.) (London and Southampton, 19560. The literature is enormous.

[423]The most illuminating American work is Sellin, the Death Penalty (Report for the Model Penal Code Project 1959) and Bedau, ed. Death Penalty in America 1961. See also Welsh, Capital Punishment in South Africa. (Duckworth & Co).

[424]Unlike Britain that has considered the abolition of capital punishment as far back as 1868. Nigeria has very little about it. Perhaps, the only Nigerian research work first recorded was that of Aguda's paper delivered at N.B.A. (Ibadan Branch) in 1964. Other eminent Scholars like Alan-Milner, Adedokun Adeyemi, D.A. Ijalaye have also made enviable contributions in the field. Alner Milner (1972), The Nigerian Penal System, London Sweet & Maxwell. A. A. Adeyemi, The Death Penalty in Criminological Perspectives. Nigerian situation, paper delivered at a National Conference on Death Penalty, 1990. D. A. Ijalaye; Capital Punishment: Quo Vadis Nigeria? In Law, Justice and the Nigerian Society, Essays in Honour of Ilori, Justice Mohammed Bello, CON, GCON ed. By I. A. Ayua (1995) (NIALS, Lagos pp. 188-200).

contributors' writers, academicians, judges and Magistrates, prison warders and medical doctors/ psychiatrists who made highly relevant and valuable contributions on the public issue, though the symposium is avowedly abolitionist, yet that is not to say that the arguments for retention of the death penalty are ignored; rather they are given the weight the writer feels they deserve.

Kenneth Younger

He traced the historical perspective of death penalty in Britain, which he described as the battle that had been long and hard in his words.

> The death penalty has long been in a category by itself in the British penal law, representing as it does the last remaining expression of an earlier philosophy under which punishment was physical, violent and irreversible. Because of this, even those who supported its retention agreed to its being continually narrowed down in its application, first by limiting it to murder, then by accepting a widening range of grounds for reprove by the executive, and finally reducing its incidence still further by passing legislation which attempted to distinguish kinds attempted to distinguish kinds of murder, which should incur the death penalty, form others which should not.[425]

Barbara Wooton

She condemned death penalty on the grounds of morality and mistakes. The writer behaved that to deprive another human being of life is, an inherently immoral action, except in certain cases of mercy killing. According to her,

> "No matter what justification may be preferred, killing, because of its ulter finality, is a uniquely destructive act, whether the killer is a soldier in battle, an executioner or a murderer".

---

[425]"Historical Perspective" in *The Hanging Question*, Essays on the death penalty (1969) (Gerald Duckworth & Co. Ltd., London) at 5-12.

Second only to the moral objectives to capital punishment, is the risk that a mistake can be made and that an innocent man can be convicted and hanged. The writer cited instances in which serious doubts have been raised as to whether the right man was convicted. The first was that of Timothy Evans, hanged for the alleged murder of his baby daughter largely on the evidence of the notorious murderer Christie. After two subsequent investigations it has been officially admitted and hanged. In case of Hanratty, hanged for the so-called A.6 murder in 1962. The BBC through its programmes made many attempts to induce the government to appoint an inquiry into the case. Also, a recent article in the People Magazine queried the conviction of Mohamoud Hassain Mattan, a Somali Seamen found guilty in 1952 of murdering a woman shopkeeper in Cardiff's Tigger Bay. In her conclusion, she made a sweeping remark that all murderers are horrible, but not all murderers are horrible characters through and through. At time a murder is an action quite out of keeping with the normal character of a man or woman who commits it. Sometime the crime is the result of a long period of domestic stress, frustration at work, economic stress in which one party suddenly reaches breaking point: Sometimes the crime is committed in a fit of wild youthful irresponsibility. Another typical example is the once famous case of the American, Nathan Leopold. In 1924, Leopold, aged nineteen, with his friend Loeb, aged eighteen, committed in Chicago a senseless murder. These two young men seized a schoolboy against whom they had no possible grudge, killed him and threw his body into a swamp where outside the city. Eventually, the "Perfect murder" which they hoped to accomplish was traced to them. They were convicted and sentenced to life imprisonment. Loeb was killed in a prison brawl some years later. But Leopold served thirty-three years in various prisons, from the age of nineteen to the age of fifty-two, when he was eventually paroled. Shortly before his release he published his autobiography- "Remorse". The man later became a person of great ability and he has used his gifts untiringly to help fellow prisoners who were less able or less educated than himself. During the war he volunteered to be infected with malaria in an experiment to find antidotes to this disease. Throughout his adult life he has tried increasingly to save his fellowmen; and now that he is a free man he works in a medical research laboratory. To execute Leopold would have done nothing to restore the young life that he destroyed, but it would have deprived the community of what, after one terrible episode, has been, beyond question, a good life. And there is no reason to support that Leopold's history is without parallel.

W.J.H. Sprott

Sprott argued that one's attitude towards the death penalty is a matter of one's scheme of values, which has to be weighed against other complicating values to determine which has priority. He raised doubts as to the deterrence strength and appropriateness of retribution of capital punishment. He further expressed his disgust at judicial killings and remarked that it lowers the moral standard of that whole community.

In furtherance of his analysis of priority of values, he argued that the claim that hanging of a murderer will satisfy vicariously the rage of the relatives and friends of the victim has little or no weight in terms of values because to console it by further killing seems not to be right.

Canon E.F. Carpenter

He viewed death penalty from the Christian context stating that nearly all communities in civilized time have practices it, usually without questioning its ethical validity. Some have felt its imposition a religious duty as Christianity was born into a world where the death penalty was customarily inflicted, and as such accepted it in the same way as slavery significantly, from the third century Christians increasingly dissociated themselves from its use on the rationale that it represented a resort to violence of a kind which the Gospel condemned.

David Darches

In his own view, David Darches described death penalty as a primitive sanction, that the deliberate taking of another person's life in cold blood is an appallingly uncivilized act under any circumstances; to do it accompanied by all the solemn panoply of the state apparatus is positively obscene. He further claimed that to add to these horrors by doing it by the brutal and primitive method of hanging is unspeakably disgusting.

Ruppert Cross

Rupert Cross in his own contribution addressed some secondary arguments against capital punishment. The risk of hanging the innocent and the risk of a mistaken view of the law were poignantly analysed. He cited the Evans case and argued that if Evans had been alive and in prison at one time of the Brabin report, it is reasonable to suppose that he would have been released. He also illustrated the case of Vickers, the first man to be hanged after homicide Act 1957, which the Court of Criminal Appeal described as "impeccable" a summing-up in which the jury was told that bodily harm is grievous "if it is such as seriously and grievously to interfere with the health or comfort of the victim.

Vickers was refused leave to appeal to the House of Lords, but, three years later, in another matter that House made it plain that the summing-up in Vickers' case had been far from impeccable because the jury should have been told that "grievous bodily harm" means "really serious bodily harm". He argued that Vickers was hanged in consequence of a mistaken view of the law taken by the trial judge.

Margaret Dribble

In her own contribution, Margaret Dribble attached emotional feelings to the issue of capital punishment, which she described as a corrupting influence in this way,

> A society that practices capital punishment involves every one of its members in a kind of corruption- The act itself arouses an interest so morbid and undesirable that the whole nation, during a celebrated murder trial, suffers from it. One cannot escape it: It is everywhere, in newspapers, on the radio, in conversations overheard on buses. We are no longer allowed to witness the kill, but we all share in the hunt, and the emotions of outage and the cries for revenge that are uttered to not seem to me to be in any way edifying... capital punishment is a punishment which gratifies, not one which cures or deters. It cannot cure the individual because it kills him: It does not cure society but corrupts it".

In the symposium of essays, Christopher B. Folwer deployed brilliant arguments in dispassionate opposition to capital punishment citing Ronald Manwood's case of 1959 as a pointless execution. The sequence of events was as follows:

Ronald Henry Marwood, aged 25, Scaffolder of Islington, celebrated his first wedding anniversary on 14th December 1998 by going out to a pub for a few drinks. After drinking ten half points of brown ace, Marwood accompanied the other four to a drinking Club in the Bow Road, where he consumed another nine or ten half pints of brown ace. At ten 'O' clock two or three carloads of young people including Marwood, left the club and went to a dance hall, another group of people came out of the dance hall and an affray broke out between the two groups. By the time the police arrived, Marwood's friend was manhandled; he went up to be the policeman who told him to "clear off" and struck him with his first. Marwood retaliated by striking the policeman, apparently with a knife, which he had in his coat pocket. The policeman died. Marwood fled the scene of the affray, throwing the knife over a garded wall, and hid in a nearly culde-sac. Six weeks later, on 27th January 1959, Marwood voluntarily went to the Caledonian Road Police Station and signed a statement admitting his guilt. He subsequently withdrew parts of his statement admitting his guilt. He subsequently withdrew parts of his statement which he claimed had been written by the police and which he mistakenly signed in a state of extreme tiredness after ten hours questioning.

On the 19th March 1959 Marwood was convicted of capital murder at the Central Crossroad court and was sentenced to death. His appeal was heard and dismissed by the Court of Criminal Appeal on 19th April.

One hundred and fifty members of Parliament of all parties wrote a six-point memorandum to the House Secretary in support of Manwood's plea for clemency, which was regretfully refused. The execution was fixed for Friday 8th May 1959, at 9a.m.

On the eve of execution, crowds gathered outside the prison to demonstrate against it. Prisoners staged a thirty-minute demonstration inside the prison and then threw lighted flowers out of their cell windows. By moving the crowd outside the prison was over a thousand. Strong and general demonstration were made against the police controlling the crowds. As nine 'O' clocks drew near, the noise subsided and people began to pray. The execution took place. She finally described the Marwood's execution as awful by perpetuating the practice of legal murder instead of educating citizens against violent reaction, which is more likely to serve the interest of the society.

Trevor Fish

Trevor Fish judged the issue of capital punishment in terms of its compatibility with a New Left ideology. He argued that the permanent abolition of legalized barbarity in the death penalty is a good opportunity to demonstrate that our society can behave in an ethical and civilized fashion. While reviewing the different modes of execution, John Maddox described all as indecent rituals. In his view, the aftermath of hanging in a l'Anglais seems in particular to have left much to be desired. He further expressed his view;

> If things were so arranged that the neck is broken, unconsciousness would be immediate, chiefly because of the way in which the spinal cord would be crushed between the separated vertebrae. In circumstance like these, the heart might go on beating for several minutes, but this is no more a sign of life than in those cases of clinical death associated with a beating heart upon which heart transplant surgeons must for the present rely for their raw material.

According to him, this phenomenon seems to have been the chief explanation of the practice of allowing the bodies of executed prisoners to hang for an hour before taking them down-"a needlessly literal interpretation of the passage in the death sentence which used to run "hanged by the neck until dead".

Hyatt Williams

The psychopathology of murderousness and the social pathology and epidemiology of murder were analyzed by Hyatt Williams in his contribution titled "Murderousness". He classified reasons why murder is committed into numerous types such as in a state of envy of the victim, in intense and perverse sexual desire, anger, disappointment, pain etc. He also referred to instances where there is a reversal of roles so that the victim designated becomes the murderer and there would be killer of the victim.

W.F. Roper

W.F. Roper brought his experience of murderers in the Prison Medical Service to his considered opinion that the lives of some of them would have been well worth preserving and that most of the others were not beyond redemption; although he referred to the isolated ones who might have been better out of this would because of their savage dispositions. However, the acknowledged a marked tendency for this kind of criminality to burn itself out in custody.

Macrae

Macrae described justice of capital punishment in an irrelevant penalty in terms of the moral and ethical issues involved and its effect on society.

S. R. Charles Cunningham

Some practical considerations to the issues of capital punishment were proposed by Sir Charles Cunningham reviewing circumstances in which so many murders are committed- fairly quarrels, pains in an unexpected situation, drunken or sexual frenzies, the carefully planned and calculated murder. According to him, there are too profound differences between murders, for example, between a man who murders his wife in a passion of jealously and one who murders her by a carefully calculated course of poisoning in order to get her money.

Hugh Klare

Hugh Klare, viewed relevance of capital punishment from the need to protect the prison officials. That people are ambivalent about prisons. He highlighted some general and undesirable aspects attached to prison work. According to him, if the post of public hangman becomes available, some very odd people are likely to apply. He argued that it is in the interest of the prison service that the death penalty should not be reintroduced in England. That prison officers need their self-esteem bolstered.

Louis Blom-Cooper

Louis Blom-Cooper addressed the issue of death penalty from the good moral reasons and concluded that it is an immoral practice which can be ended, in accordance with historical precedent, by the instance, induced by enlightened self interest, of those few public servants who to administer the penal system of modern Britain.

The U.S.A.

The Constitution Project, housed at Georgetown University in Washington, DC, seeks to develop bipartisan solutions to contemporary constitutional and governance issues by combining high-level scholarship and public education. In May 2000, the Constitution Project created a death penalty initiative to address the deeply disturbing risk that Americans are being wrongfully convicted of capital crimes or wrongfully sentenced to death. The Constitution Project convened the thirty members of the death penalty initiative's blue-ribbon committee to examine our country's present course, and to recommend ways to ensure that fundamental fairness is guaranteed for all. The committee's members are supporters and opponents of the death penalty, Democrats and Republicans, conservatives and liberals. They are former judges, prosecutors, and other public officials, as well as victim advocates, defense lawyers, journalists, scholars, and other concerned Americans. They have extensive and varied experience in the criminal justice system. They may disagree on much, including whether abolition of the death penalty is warranted, but they are united in their profound concern that, in recent years, and around the country, procedural safeguards and other assurances of fundamental fairness in the administration of capital punishment have been revealed to be deeply flawed. The members of the committee have brought a wide variety of philosophies, experiences, and perspectives to their work. They have deliberated long and hard about the recommendations presented here, seeking consensus because they recognized the need to overcome past divisions. For too long, society has cast the death penalty debate as one between "liberals" and "conservatives", those who are "soft on crime" and those who "care about victims of crime", or "abolitionists" and hard-line death penalty proponents. If we ever could, we can no longer afford to carry on the debate in this manner. Much is riding on our country's ability to put these stereotypes aside.

The committee's mission statement says that individual says that individuals who commit violent crimes deserve swift and certain punishment. Some of the members of the committee believe that the range of punishment may include death; others do not. But they all agree that no one should be denied basic constitutional protections, including a competent lawyer, a fair trial, and full judicial review of the conviction and sentence. The denial of such protections heightens the danger of wrongful conviction and sentence. In the months since the initiative was created, there has been a dramatic increase in the number of those released from death row because they have been shown – often at nearly the last minute- to be innocent. This is deeply disturbing to all of the committee's members, as it should be to all Americans. Committee members continue to be greatly troubled, as well by executions of persons with mental retardation and those who committed crimes as juveniles. While some states are considering reforms to narrow the application of capital punishment, especially with regard to persons with mental retardation others are enacting new laws that would actually increase its application.

Too often, cases of wrongful conviction involve defense lawyers who lacked the appropriate experience and resources. Sometimes, capital defense lawyers were also under the influence of alcohol or drugs, or slept through parts of a trial. These recommendations should not, however, be considered the final word. Capital punishment is an extraordinarily complex area of the law, and our nation's understanding of it and its problems have evolved with the accumulation of experience. The committee issues these recommendations because its members are confident of their wisdom and because a crisis in the death penalty system exists now and must be addressed as expeditiously as possible. Future recommendations may be expected as additional experience, study, and reflection bring to further consensus.

The philosopher Albert Camus, in Reflections on the Guillotine, wrote of a Burton Abbott, executed in California in 1957. "Today, as yesterday, the chance of error remains. Tommorrow another expert testimony will declare the innocence of some Abbott or other. But Abbott will be dead, scientifically dead, and the science that claims to prove innocence as well as guilt has not yet reached the point of resuscitating those it kills…. If justice admits that it is frail, would it not be better for justice to be modest and to allow its judgments sufficient latitude so that a mistake can be corrected"? Camus' statement, written in 1957, is as true today as it was then. No matter whether we support or oppose the death penalty, we must admit that the system is still fallible. The Committee took this fallibility into account in crafting these recommendations.

The Committee members present recommendations for reforms because they are urgently needed. In the name of justice, fairness, efficiency, and common sense the committee aged that the recommendations should command the support of all Americans, no matter what their views about capital punishment.

Nigeria

The genesis of pubic debate on capital punishment in Nigeria began unknowingly when the federal government made a last minute diplomatic effort to save the lives of a Nigerian, Nathaniel Jackson Ikpato Notibo and three Ghanaians sentenced to death in Libya. They were tried and found guilty for the murder of a Libyan, Mohammed Mustapha in Ghat in 1995. They were to be executed on Friday 28, 2002 by the Libyan authorities but the Nigeria's plea that the death sentence passed on them be commuted to prison terms yielded positive response, when the Libyan government acceded to this plea. Unknown to the Federal government, it has provoked a debate among its citizens over the retention or abolition of capital sentence in the country. On the 21st January 2003 Abuja, Federal Capital Territory under the auspices of the National Human rights Commission, Legal Resources Consortium, Human Rights Law Service and Vanguard, Lawyers, Journalists and sociologists conferred to discuss on the need to abolish capital punishment in Nigeria. Thus we have not only begun a public debate on capital punishment but that the president has gone even further to set up a committee to examine and advise him on the issue. This step shows that Nigeria finally inclining into the social mainstream of the 21st century. The government stance is viewed as pondering to the degenerate Liberalism of Europe and America where anything goes, including gay bishops. This national assignment has begun to generate suspicions and fears on its likely outcome going by President Obasanjo's pledge to a delegation of the European Union of his determination to seek for the abolition of capital punishment in Nigeria. It is difficult to convince the public that the government will not unduly influence the debate to tilt towards the promise already made to the European Union to abolish death penalty, a theme so dear to Europe's heart. That was one of the very much conditionality, which Turkey had to meet in order to qualify for European Union membership.

The issue of capital crimes is enormous; we must not take chances with our well being safety and security of our lives. The incidents of violent crimes are increasing on daily basis in Nigeria. We have had series of political assassinations, politically motivated murders, armed robberies resulting in brutal and cruel deaths, ritual killings, ethnic cleansing deaths, communal killings and religious murders unresolved, hate crimes, charade arrangement and burgled trials. Many times governments have played politics with celebrated murders thereby making the public feel indignant and lose confidence in the judiciary.

Improper handling of public debate on death penalty has the potential of even bringing down political leaders and their governments. Even great religions seem to endorse the vengeful instinct in affirming the principle of an eye for an eye and a tooth for a tooth.

If the President and the National Assembly with the support of certain Human Rights group are inclined to expunge death penalty provisions from our statute books, then constitutional conformity is imperative. The Constitution of the Federal Republic of Nigeria, 1999 does unequivocally recognize capital punishment. Section 33 provides,

> Every person has the right to life, and no one shall be deprived intentionally of his life, share in execution of a sentence of a court in respect of a criminal offence of which he has been found guilty in Nigeria.

Thus any law that runs contrary to the provision of the Constitution in null and void and of no effect whatsoever. The first step to validate abolishing capital sentence is to amend the constitutional provision and subjecting the matter to a referendum for the public to approve or disapprove it. The conflict of laws situation will further emerge from the position that is invariably arrived at the end of the day, in view of the fact that the application of Shariah law in some states of the Federation would retain death penalty in their respective jurisdictions.

Death Sentences and Execution

During 1994, 2,331 prisoners are known to have been executed in 37 countries and 4,032 sentenced to death in 75 countries. There figures are cases known to Amnesty International, the true figures are certainly higher. As in previous years, a small number of countries accounted for the vast majority of executions recorded. Amnesty International received reports of 1.791 executions in China, 139 executions in Iran and over 100 in Nigeria. These three countries alone accounted for 87% of all executions recorded by

Amnesty International Worldwide in 1994. Amnesty International received reports of several hundreds executions in Iraq but was unable to confirm most of these reports or to give an exact figures. Death penalty data in the United States shows that about 13,000 people have been legally executed since colonial times. By the 1930's up to 150 people were executed yearly. Lack of public support for capital punishment and various legal challenges reduced the execution rate to near zero by 1967. There are a number of federal offences that can lead to the death penalty. About 21 prisoners are housed in death row at the federal Tenre Hante, in facility. One was executed in 2001. This was the first federal execution in 36 years. Texas holds the record for the largest number of executions since the death penalty was reinstated in 1976.

As of 1 January 2002 there have been 784 executions in the US. About 30 to 60 prisoners are currently killed annually, mostly by lethal injection. There were about 3,690 prisoners sentenced to death in 37 state death rows, and 31 being held by the U.S. government and military. About 1.5% are women. Recent laws have expanded the number of crimes for which capital punishment can be applied. Other legislations have reduced some of the appeal mechanisms available to those on death row. Public approval of the death penalty is currently about 70% while about 90% of those executed could not afford a lawyer when they went to trial. They had to rely upon a court-appointed lawyer. A study revealed that the homicide rate in those states with the death penalty is almost double the rate in states without the death penalty. The reason is partly due to the fact that use of death penalty by the state cheapens the value of life, and causes a higher homicide rate and that people in high homicide states demanding the death as a perceived deterrent.

Some few other developed countries in the world relatively impose the death penalty. Japan and South Korea are the only established democracies in the world, other than the U.S. which still conduct executions. The execution rate in Japan is a small fraction of that in the U.S. Some Christian denominations like the Southern Baptist Convention, the largest protestant denomination in the U.S. reaffirmed its support for the death penalty. Also, the Presbyterian (USA)'s General Assembly reaffirmed their opposition. Russia and many more countries not listed above retain capital punishment statutes on their books but have not executed criminals in many years. Russia and many more countries not listed above retain capital punishment statutes on their books but have not executed criminals in many years. In Kenya, its last prisoner on death row was executed in 1984. The government of Kenya plans to abolish the death penalty and has an informal moratorium on executions.

Racism and Capital Punishment

There are those that state that capital punishment is unfair to people of other races, classes, or mental abilities. I say that these aspects are not an issue. Murder has no colour, class, or IQ murderer is a murderer. When a loved one is killed, one doubt anyone could take comfort in the fact that the perpetrator had a low IQ, was black instead of white, or poor instead of rich. Ernest van den Haag wrote:

> If and when discrimination occurs it should be corrected. Not, however, by letting the guilty blacks escape the death penalty because guilty whites do, but by making sure that the guilty white offenders suffer it as the guilty blacks do. Discrimination must be abolished by abolishing discrimination – not by abolishing penalties. However, even if … this cannot be done, I do not see any good reason to let any guilty murderer escape his penalty. It does happen in the administration of criminal justice that one person gets away with murder and another is executed. Yet the fact that one gets away with it is no reason to let another one escape.

A 1991 Rand Corporation study by Stephen Klein found that white murderers received the death penalty slightly more often (32%) than non-white murderers (27%). And while the study found murderers of white victims received the death penalty more often (32%) than murderers of non- white victims (23%), when controlled for variable such as severity and number of crimes committed, there is no disparity between those sentenced to death for killing while or black victims 'Patrick A. Lanagan, senior statistician at the Dept. of Justice Bureau of Justice Statistics has studied the system in its entirety, and reports:

I don't find evidence that the justice system is treating Blacks and whites differently.

In a recent crime bill, the Racial Justice Act was proposed. The Act, had it been implemented, would have established a penalty-by quota system. As a precondition for applying the death penalty, it would have required that all races be proportionally represented in the execution chamber. This practice would have allowed judgment to be made, not the facts of a particular case, but on the facts of a defendant's race.

Also, does not the fact that the death penalty is optional make it seem more prone to racial discrimination? It has been called racist since a prosecutor can seek a death sentence against an African-American for a capital crime but not a white person for the same offense. One never hears prisons called "racists" because they are mandatory for many crimes. If the death penalty were the same way, race would be a non-issue and the court would be forced to concentrate only on the crime committed, as it should be. For capital punishment to be applied equally to every criminal, rich or poor, black or white, it must be mandatory for ALL capital cases.

Use of the Death Penalty against Juveniles

International human rights treaties prohibit anyone under 18 years old at the time of the crime being sentenced to death. The International Covenant on Civil and Political Rights, the American Convention on Human Rights and the UN Convention on the Rights of the Child all have provisions to this effect. More than 100 countries have laws specifically excluding the execution of juvenile offenders or may be presumed to exclude such executions by being parties to one or another of the above treaties. In Nigeria Juveniles are exempted from execution under the Criminal Procedure Act and Criminal Procedure Code. A small number of countries, however, have executed juvenile offenders. For example, five countries since 1990 are known to have executed prisoners who were under 18 years old at the time of the crime-Iran, Pakistan, Saudi Arabia, USA and Yemen. The majority of known executions of juvenile offenders were in the USA (6 since 1990).

The Scientific Studies

Scientific studies have consistently failed to find convincing evidence that the death penalty deters crime more effectively than other punishments. The most recent survey of research findings on the relation between the death penalty and homicide rates, conducted for the UN in 1988, concluded that

> This research has failed to proved scientific proof that executions shave a greater deterrent effect than life imprisonment. Such proof is unlikely to be forthcoming. The evidence as a whole still gives no positive support to the deterrent hypothesis.

Effect of Abolition on Crime Rates

Reviewing the evidence on the relation between changes in the use of the death penalty and crime rates, a study prepared for the UN in 1988 stated that

> "the fact that all the evidence continues to point in the same direction is persuasive a priori evidence that countries need not fear sudden and serious changes in the cure of crime if they reduce their reliance on the death penalty".

Recent crime figures from abolitionist countries fail to show that abolition has harmful effects. In Canada, the homicide rate per 100,000 population fell from a peak of 3.09 in 1975, the year before the abolition of the death penalty for murder, to 2.41 in 1980, and since then it has remained relatively stable. In 1993, 17 years after abolition, the homicide rate was 2.19 per 100,000 populations, 27 percent lower than in 1975. The total number of homicides reported in the country fell in 1993 for the second straight year.

5.10 International Agreements to Abolish the Death Penalty

One of the most important developments in recent years has been the adoption of international treaties whereby states commit themselves to not having the death penalty. Three such treaties now exist.

(i) The second Optional Protocol to the International Covenant on Civil and Political Rights, which has now been ratified by 28 states. 4 other states have signed the Protocol, indicating their intention to become parties to it at a later date.

(ii) The Sixth protocol to the European Convention on Human Rights, which has now been ratified by 23 European States and signed by 3 others.

(iii) The protocol to the American Convention on Human Rights to Abolish the Death Penalty, which has been ratified by 3 states in the Americas and signed by 4 others.

It should be noted that the Sixth protocol to the European Convention on Human Rights is an agreement to abolish the death penalty in peacetime. The other two protocols provide for the total abolition of the death penalty but allow states wishing to do so to retain the death penalty in wartime as an exception.

Execution of the Innocent

The greatest argument against death penalty is the likelihood of executing the innocent. As long as the death penalty is applied, the risk of sentencing an innocent can never be eliminated with the attendant irreparable loss. Out of the number of people convicted of capital crimes in the USA from 1900 to 1985, 350 persons were innocent of the crimes charged, while some of these prisoners escaped execution by minutes, 23 of them were actually executed.

The US Congressional report by the House Sub-Committee on Civil and Constitutional Rights in October 1993 listed 48 condemned men who had been freed from death row since 1972. The report blamed inadequate legal safeguards to prevent wrongful executions and listed numerous inherent flows in the criminal justice system. The report concluded:

> Judging by past experience, a substantial number of death row inmates are indeed innocent, and there is a high risk that some of them will be executed.[1]

If America can experience such disheartening events, Nigeria cannot be immuned against such occurrences. However, there is no empirical survey to ascertain the number of innocents that were wrongly executed. But from the synopsis of cases already highlighted in this work there are similar events in Nigeria. For example, the case of ***Nosiru Bello v. The State***, where the appellant convicted of armed robbery was hurriedly executed before the appeal he filed was heard is akin to executing an innocent, though in legal parlance it amounts to executing a condemned person without due process. Also, the conviction of Ken Sarowiwa and 7 others are their hasty execution which denied them of exercising their rights of appeal within 30 days as provided by the Decree under which they were tried was contrary to the rule of law and legal process.

[1]See A1 *ibid* p. 32.

> As for the penal system accidentally executing an innocent person, one must point out that in this imperfect world, nothing that is worth having comes without risk.

Also, the death penalty is not the only institution that contains risks in exchange for social benefits. We, in fact, mindlessly use far more dangerous institutions that take the lives of innocents by the hundreds every day, like the three or four tons of lethal metal we call automobiles for example. After all, how can we accept the average 45,000 people a year death toll arising from car wrecks for our personal conveniences when the very slim risk of wrongful executions is so unbearable?

Following the lines of that logic, we not only would have to sacrifice our vehicles, we would have to sacrifice the personal conveniences of using electricity and fire because of the lives they cost by accidents. We would have to go back to living in caves because of our fear of taking risks for social benefits. Indeed, we accept and use far too many evinces and institutions that kill far too many hundreds of innocents each and every day to justify focusing this much paranoia on the slimmest and unlikely of risks. In fact, it seems that the only time a human device or institution cannot get away with risking innocent lives is when it threatens murderers.

To enjoy the privilege of using cars, airplanes,[426] or any other device that improve the quality of our lives, we accept the risks and deaths that are caused by them completely in order to reap their full benefits. The same concept applies for the death penalty only on a far less scale. As long as we are entitled to recklessly endanger hundreds of innocent lives daily for our personal conveniences, then surely we should be allowed to take on lesser risks for something far less selfish and self-serving like public safety. Every institution that is of great benefit to society always contains risks so that we may enjoy a better world. The death penalty happens to be the least dangerous of them, yet it is focused on with the most paranoia. Such an attitude is completely irrational. The Syndicated columnist Charley Reese stated: I favour a fair trial, one quick appeal and prompt execution. I don't think murderers ought to live much beyond 12 months from the day their victim is buried . . . (and) as for not being able to correct a mistake, so what? Virtually all-accidental deaths are deaths by mistake. Why impose a standard of perfection, as a sentence for

[426]Recently between October – December 2005, Nigeria witnessed two domestic air plane crashes, the Bellview Airline involving about 127 passengers and the Sosoliso airline involving over 100 passengers including secondary school pupils.

a crime, is neither cruel nor unusual? In another case of note, the court said:

> The punishment of death is not cruel, within the meaning of that words used in the constitution. It implies there is something more inhuman and barbarous, than the mere extinguishments of life.

There are those who insist that the Constitution does not support the death penalty. This is simply not true. The Fifth Amendment states:

> No person shall be held to answer for a capital, or otherwise infamous crime, unless on a presentment or indictment of a Grand Jury, except in cases arising in the land or naval forces, or in the militia, when in actual service in time of War or public danger; nor shall any person be subject for the same offense to be twice put in jeopardy of life or limb, nor shall be compelled in any criminal case to be a witness against himself, nor be deprived of life, liberty, or property, without due process of law; nor shall private property be taken for public use, without just compensation. . . . a capital, or otherwise infamous crime . . . be twice put in jeopardy of life or limb . . . nor be deprived of life . . . without due process of law .

So the Constitution does allow capital punishment through indirect references such as these. Former Justice Marshall McComb of the California Supreme Court wrote in 1972:

> It is my opinion that the death penalty is constitutional, as determined ... in innumerable cases. Therefore, since it is the duty of the legislature of the electorate, and not the judiciary, to decide whether it is sound public policy to empower the imposing of the death penalty, it is my opinion that if a change is to be made, it should be effected through the legislative process of the people through the initiative process.

The U. S. Supreme Court Justice Antonin Scalia confirmed this analysis in 1997 when he said:

> No fewer than three of the Justices with whom I have served (Justices Brennan, Marshall, and Blackmun) have maintained that the death penalty is unconstitutional, even though its use

is explicitly contemplated in the Constitution. The Due Process Clause of the Fifth and fourteenth Amendments says that a person shall be deprived of life without due process of law; and the Grand Jury Clause of the Fifth Amendment says that no person shall be held to answer for a capital crime without grand jury indictment.

Country Status on the Death Penalty

The country status on death penalty worldwide is as follows:[427] Eight seven countries have abolished death penalty, they are:

Andorra, Angola, Armenia, Australia, Austria, Azerbaijan, Belgium, Bermuda, Bhutan, Bolivia, Bosnia-Herzegovina, Bulgaria, Cambodia, Canada, Cape Verde, Colombia, Costa Rica, Cote d'Ivoire, Croatia, Cyprus, Czech Republic, Denmark, Djibouti, Dominican Republic, Ecuator, Estonia, Finland, France, Georgia, Germany, Greece, Guinea Bissau, Haiti, Honduras, Hungary, Iceland, Ireland, Italy, Kiribati, Liechtenstein, Lithuania, Luxembour, Malta, Marshall Islands, Mauritius, Mexico, Micronesia (Federated States of), Moldova, Monaco, Mozambique, Namibia, Nepal, Netherlands, New Zealand, Nicaragua, Norway, Palau, Panama, Paraguay, Poland, Portugal, Romania, Samoa, San Marino, Sao Tome and Principle, Senegal, Serbia and Montenegro, Seychelles, Slovakia, Slovenia, Solomon Islands, South Africa, Spain, Sweden, Switzerland, Tajikistan, The former Yugoslav Republic of Macedonia, Timor Leste, Turkey, Turkmenistan, Tuvalu, Ukraine, United Kingdom, Uruguay, Vanuatu, Vatican City and Venezuela.

While ten countries have abolished death penalty for ordinary crimes, they are:

Albania, Argentina, Brazil, Chile, Cook Islands, El Salvador, Fiji, Israel, Latvia and Peru.

Thirty-five countries are *de facto* abolitionist as they have not carried out any executions for 10 years; date of last known execution in brackets: Antigua and Barbuda (1991), Barbados (1984), Belize (1985), Benin (1993), Brunei Darussalam (1957), Burkina Faso (1988), Cameroon (1988), Central African Republic (1981), Congo (1982), Dominica (1986)(Eritrea (no death penalty since independence in 1991), Gabon (1979), Gambia (1981), Ghana (1993),

[427]http://www.handsoffcain.org/bancadati/index.php?tipotema=arg&idtema=6000632. 9/28/2005.

Grenada (1985), Jamaica (1988), Kenya (1987), Laos (1989), Madagascar (1958), Malawi (1992), Maldives (1952), Mauritania (1987), Morocco (1993), Myanmar (1988), Nauru (no executions since independence, 1968), Niger (no executions or death sentences since 1976), Papua New Guinea (1957), Saint Vincent and the Grenadines (1995), Sri Lanka (1976), Suriname (1982), Swaziland (1982), Tanzania (1994), Togo (1978), Tonga (1982) and Tunisia (1991).

Russia is committed to abolishing the death penalty as member of the Council of Europe while five retentionist countries are observing a moratorium on execution bay are; Algeria, Guatemala, Kazakhstan, Kyrgyzstan and Mali.

Fifty-eight countries have retained death penalty, they are Afghanistan, Bahamas, Bahrain, Bangladesh, Belarus, Botswana, Burundi, Chad, China, Comoros, Cuba, Democratic People's Republic of Korea, Democratic Republic of the Congo, Egypt, Equatorial Guinea, Ethiopia, Guinea, Guyana, India, Indonesia, Iran, Iraq, Japan,. Jordan, Kuwait, Lebanon, Lesotho, Liberia, Libya, Malaysia, Mongolia, Nigeria, Oman, Pakistan, Palestinian National Authority, Philippines, Qatar, Republic of Korea, Rwanda, Saint Kitts and Nevis, Saint Lucia, Saudi Arabia, Sierra Leone, Singapore, Somalia, Sudan, Syria, Taiwan, Thailand, Trinidad and Tobago, Uganda, United Arab Emirates, United States, Uzbekistan, Vietnam, Yemen, Zambia and Zimbabwe.

Findings on Death Penalty in Africa

Eleven African countries are abolitionists for all crimes and another ten are abolitionists in practice.[428] The states that are abolitionists for all crimes are Angola, Cape Verde, Djibouti, Guinea Bissau, Cote d'Ivoire, Mauritius, Mozambique, Namibia, Sao Tome and Principe, Seychelles and South Africa. The states that are abolitionist in practice are Burkina Faso, Central African Republic, Congo (Republic), The Gambia, Madagascar, Malawi, Mali, Niger, Senegal and Togo. In 2004, Amnesty International recognized Algeria, Benin and Tunisia as abolitionist states as well.

Thirty-two countries retain the death penalty, though not all of these

[428]The figures were supplied from information provided by Eric Prokosch of Amnesty International and Nicola Browne of the Centre for Death Penalty Studies at the University of Westminster in March 2003 to Prof. Dirk Van Zyl Smit in his article "The death penalty in Africa in African Human Rights Law Journal, vol. 4 No. 1 2004 at pp. 1-16. See also <http://web.amnesty.org/pages/death penalty-abolitionist 3.org.> (accessed 2 April 2004.)

countries perform official executions every year. For example, in 2001, death sentences were imposed in twenty-three countries, but executions took place in only six. However, at least one African country not included amongst these six resumed executions in 2002.[429]

At the international level most African states appear to be committed to the retention of the death penalty, as at 2002 only two African states Mauritius and South Africa, were prepared to sponsor the cautiously abolitionist resolution of the United Nations (UN) Commission on Human Rights on "the question of death penalty; While 23 states signed a formal statement of dissociation.[430] Also, only six African states are parties (and a further two signatories only) to the Second Optional Protocol to the International Covenant on Civil and Political Rights (CCPR), aiming at the abolition of death penalty.

As rightly observed by Dirk Van Zyl Smit, 'there is no escaping the reality that the majority of the inhabitants of Africa live in countries where official policies support the maintenance of the death penalty and which are prepared to implement it from time to time.'[431]

This author agrees with the learned Professor, the reason is not far-fetched official policies are not the only factors that determine the imposition and implementation of the death penalty in Africa. In Nigeria, for example, there are mechanisms of informal justice system such as gangland killings, political assassinations, ritual killings, communal killings and religious riots whereby persons are "sentenced to death" by unofficial ethnic militia, political things, lured assassins, ritualists, ethnic groups, religious fanatics, Nigeria has recorded series of unresolved murders in the past and even of recent, some victims of these unfortunate incidents were Alfred Rewane, Kudirat Abiola, Layi Balogun, Dikkibo, Bola Ige to mention but a few. The sudden death of Basorun M.K.O. Abiola in detention at the verge of the much publicized plan of his release has been allegedly traced to world organized complicity of the United Nations with some Nigerian collaborators in power and the widely denunciation of the judicial murder of Ken Saro Wiwa and others by the Military Tribunal. These incidents are not peculiar to Nigeria alone, it is wide-spread in some parts of Africa informal 'justice' has manifested itself in greater dimensions ranging from brutal killings, mass executions and even genocide in Rwanda, Sierra Leon e, Liberia, Congo, Angola, Cote d'Ivoire, Algeria and Sudan. Even in states where there is no formally an internal or an external

[429] Uganda; See http://web.amnesty.org/report 2003/2 cif.index.eng (accessed 2nd April 2004.)

[430] E/CN 4/RES/2002/77.

[431] *Op. cit.* at p. 2.

armed conflict, some countries have major problems that impact directly on the death penalty. Frequent violent crimes and insurgencies that result not only in temporary breakdown of law and order but the fatal weakening and emergent criminalization of the state itself by the deep institutionalization of corruption and arbitrary rule need to be dealt with decisively. In such countries, official abolition of death penalty by the authority may be of little significance to their citizens. For example, during Abacha era in Nigeria, incessant killings sponsored by the state or by highly connected citizens made many people to be worried about the death penalty and the official pronouncement towards abolition of death penalty policy was treated as an abstract moral issue which made them to be apprehensive of its abolition that it has capable of being capriciously applied to the powerless citizens by the state itself or by those in the corridors of powers.

The picture is, however not entirely gloomy, for there are limits on capital punishment in Africa. The first is at the level where direct international internet intersects with African law enforcement. A good example of this happening is through the International Criminal Tribunal for Rwanda (ICTR). Another potential restraining influence of the new-quasi-international tribunal in Sierra Leone, which is a hybrid institution, in the sense that it was created by the United Nations to try both offences under international criminal law and domestic offences.

Also, the pan-African human rights instrument – the African Charter on Human and Peoples' rights limits the application of death penalty in countries where it is practiced. This charter is the body responsible for propagating the principles of the African Charter and enforcing them. However, several scholars have commented generally on the relative inefficiency of the commission. Times may change this hitherto position. But for now, the commission has never been presented with a direct challenge to the death penalty in an individual case. The African Commission potentially may have had more impact where the challenge to the death penalty was on procedural grounds.

The Commission held that the trial of the Nigerian activist Ken Saro-Wiwa violated the due process provisions of article 7 of the African Charter and was thus arbitrary and in contravention of article 4 of the Charter. Unfortunately, the Commission only released this well-reasoned judgment in October 1998. While Saro-Wiwa had been executed in November 1995 and the Nigerian authorities had ignored the request of the Commission for his execution to be staged while it considered his petition. Similarly, in 2001 the authorities in Botswana went ahead with the execution of Mariette Bosch before she could fulfill her intention of appealing to the Commission. Though death penalty thrives in Africa and the

African Commission has done much to curb executions of condemned activists in these high-profile cases, yet they have set procedural benchmarks in capital cases by making underlined decisions that expedited appeal procedures and summary executions infringe both Articles 7 and 4 of the Charter.

At the national constitutional level there may be limits on the death penalty like those of Namibia, Article 6 of the Constitution and Mozambique, Article 7(2) of the Constitution. The political dynamics at the time these post-independence constitutions were drafted necessitated outright and express abolition of the death penalty as a bold-step to breakaway from what was seen as a symbol of Colonial Repression.

South Africa while recording historic moments in the early 1990 through President De Klerk in his historic speech of 2 February, 1990 first signaled real change. The speech was remarkable, not only because he espoused effectively his government's commitment to radical change by lifting the ban on the liberation movements and releasing from prison of its leaders including Nelson Mandella, but also stated with an announcement that the question of the death penalty would be revisited. As a follow-up to this political statement, no further executions took place after November 1989 until the law relating to Capital Punishment was amended in 1990.[432] It retained the death penalty but did away with mandatory sentences of death and restricted the potential application of death penalty to the most serious crimes. A great lesson could be learnt from the South African experience in the sense that at such historic moments when a constitution is setting down new national values and atmosphere of freedom explicit espousal of an abolitionist position is viewed as carrying high political costs. No political party that later emerged seems to have pushed for inclusion of a clause outlawing death penalty in the constitution.

The stakeholders in South Africa adopted a careful egg dance around the question of capital punishment when the drafters of the New Constitution provided in the "interim" constitution of the Republic of South Africa, Act 200 of 1993 in Article 9, which recognized the right to life. In the "Final" Constitution of the Republic of South Africa, Act 108 of 1996 provides without qualification in Art. 11 that

> "[e]very one has a right to life".

[432] See the Criminal Law Amendment Act 107 of 1990. The formal abolition of the death penalty was effected by the Criminal Law Amendment Act 105 of 1997 which followed the decision of the Constitutional Court discussed earlier.

The task of ascertaining the true intendment of the legislature on the question of death penalty was left for the Constitutional Court to interpret and pronounce upon. The opportunity then came in the case of *S. v. Makwanyane & Anor*[433] for the Constitutional Court to make pronouncements on the purport of Article 11. The Court articulated arguments of counsel on both sides carefully and very extensively, and anchored them in the fundamental values of the right to life, human dignity, equality and legality that are the cornerstones of the whole constitutional order.[434]

The Constitutional Court by the majority decision held that death penalty was unconstitutional in South Africa. Both Chaskalson P. who read the leading judgment and O'regan J. remarked specifically that the framers of the constitution failed to expressly state either that the death sentence is not a lawful penalty or that it is permissible in circumstances sanctioned by law. According to the Court, the drafters of the Constitution adopted the terse formulation of the right to life that is not one which has been used in the Constitutions of other countries or in international human rights conventions. In addition by the strategy adopted, the drafters have; not used the language so common in other constitutions that provides that no one may be deprived of life arbitrarily or without due process of law.

Thus, the formulation of the right to life is different from that adopted in other jurisdictions and to that extent their jurisprudence will be of less value in South Africa. In the end the strategy adopted by the politicians was highly successful. Invariably, the Makwanyane decision is a strong precedent that will be very hard to overturn. It is also relatively invulnerable to upset it by constitutional amendment. In fact, former President Mandela preferred to support the Court decision as a general inviolable judicial pronouncement on death penalty than to test explicitly abolitionist position in public based on a simple provision outlawing the death penalty that could be replaced by a referendum.

One cannot but agree with the underlying philosophy of South African position on death penalty, being a country that had just emerged from the age-long racism and apartheid that recorded that deprived thousands of citizens of their freedom and their lives. The need to breakaway from this tradition became so compelling that a new constitutional order being put in place by the evolving democracy must be seen to be pragmatic and revolutionary in its characteristics and operations. However, for about a decade now that new democracy has been

---

[433] *Op. cit.* at p. 391.

[434] See B.E. Harcourt, 'Mature adjudication,: Interpretative Choice in recent death Penalty cases" (1996) a Harvard Human Rights Journal 255.

put in place, violent crimes, brutal killings and murders have been rampaging the country in a larger proportion than in any other African country. It is therefore a matter of time when South Africans would converge to reappraise the re-introduction of death penalty through constitutional amendment.

In Tanzania, the constitutionality of the death penalty was upheld and a judgment of a lower court overturned on the basis that while the death penalty was an inherently cruel, inhuman and degrading punishment offending Articles 13 (6)(d) & (e) of the Tanzanian Constitution, it was saved by a constitutional limitations clause that allowed derogations for legitimate purposes. Thus, if society decided the death penalty was a legitimate form of deterrence that was sufficient. Therefore, the South African strategy is not always successful. The citizen of every country is the ground-norm of its legal order, if the state through its citizen affirms its belief on death penalty through the referendum whatever judicial decision has been in existence prior to this political standpoint becomes inoperational and not binding.

In Zimbabwe, the constitutional specifically endorses the death penalty nevertheless a corresponding provision provides a basis for restricting its use. The amendment in 1990 provided safeguards against the application of death penalty and to ensure that the death penalty could not be challenged directly.

Pakistan introduced the so-called Hadood ordinance, which punishes adultery with death by stoning, in 1979. In accordance with this law, Zamfran Bibi was sentenced to death by stoning on 17 April 2002. However, she was acquitted by the Appellate federal Sharia court on 6 June 2002. On 5 July 202, the 40-year-old Zahid Shah was stored to death by a mob in the check Jhumra village near faisalabad, because he had called himself "the last prophet of Islam". The prayer leader Maulvi Fakir Mohammed had incited the people in the mosque to kill the mentally ill Zahid shah for blasphemy. In this case, it must be mindfully said, that the phenomenon of illegal stoning occurs.

In Sudan, summary executions have been adopted in some capital offences. Also the 18-year-old Christian Abok Alfa Akok was sentenced to death also by stoning on 8 December 2001 in the West-Sudanese Darfur. The punishment was commuted to 75 lashings in March 2002. In the United Arab Emirates, a young Indonesian house aid called Kartini was sentenced to death for alleged adultery in the emirate of Fujairah on 200. The sentence of death was later commuted to one years imprisonment and deportation.

Further, Iran is a country, which is known for death sentence in recent years. Since May 1997, when Khatami became the President, 25 death sentences by stoning have been executed, 17 of the convicted persons were women. On 26 October 1997, the Associated Press reported on the public execution of three men and three women in Northern Iran, after a court found them guilty of adultery and prostitution.[435]

On 11 July, 2001 a woman called Maryam Ayubi was sentenced to death because she had committed adultery and had murdered her husband with the help of her lover. In May, 2001 a woman was sentenced to death in the Evin prison in Teheran, because she had acted in pornographic films and was engaged in extra-marital relationship.

It must be noted that instances and case of death penalty are not exclusive to Islamic countries. Countries of secular instinct also have its on tale of the incidence of death penalty.

Death penalty applies for various offences in Ghana. Condemned prisoners have the right to lodge an appeal with Court of Appeal. If this is refused, they can appeal to the Supreme Court. The last executions in Ghana date from July 1993, when 12 people were shot for armed robbery or murder. On 12 February 2002, one Edward Anim Densu was sentenced to death by hanging by the Koforidva High Court. His sentence was later commuted to life imprisonment. The Minister of Justice of Ghana, Mr. Nana Akufo-Addo, declared on the 27th day of February 2001, that he was not personally in favour of death penalty, while emphasizing that this was not necessarily the government's position. In fact, the government has never expressed a wish to abolish the death penalty. However, in recent years, there has been a relaxation of penal policy: IN February 1997, seven people sentenced to death were released on health grounds and 15 had their sentences commuted to life imprisonment. In 2000 Amnesty International published a report and took action requesting President Kufoor to initiate a national debate on the total abolition of death penalty.

In Gambia, death penalty was abolished in April 1993, and it was re-established in August 1995, by the Armed Forces Provisional ruling Council, although it never came into force. Surprisingly enough, there has only been one execution since independence in December 1980, Mustapha Danso was convicted of the murder of a deputy commander in chief and was executed in September 1981. The most recent death sentence in Gambia was in June 1997 where four man were convicted of treason and sentenced to death by the high court, after an armed attack on Farafenni military camp in November 1996. Their sentence was quashed on Appeal in October 1997. Also three soldiers arrested in July 1997, after an armed attack on Kartong military post, were sentenced to death by the High Court in 1998.

In Zambia, the United Nations Human Rights Committee examined a

[435] See *Amnesty International & Others v. Sudan* (2000) AHRLR 297.

communication from Bernard Lubuto in *Lubuto v Zambia Communication*[436] alleging that his rights under the International Covenant on Civil and Political Rights had been violated. The author of the communication was arrested in February 1980 and sentenced to death on 4 August, 1983, for aggravated robbery. On 10 February, 1988, the Supreme Court dismissed his appeal. The author claimed that the death sentence imposed on him was disproportionate since no one was killed or wounded during the robbery. The Human Rights Committee also considered that the length of the proceedings against the author might raise issues under Article 14(3) (c).

The Commission thus took the view that the facts before it disclosed a violation of Articles 6(2) and 14(3(c) of the International Covenant on Civil and Political Rights and that the author was entitled, under Article 2(3)(a) to an appropriate and effective remedy entailing the commutation of sentence.

In Cote d'ivoire, the current legislation is the Article 2 of the Constitution of Cote d'ivoire of 23 July 2000, which abolished death penalty.

Until 2000, the Cote d'ivoire penal code provided for the death penalty for murder and aircraft hijacking. However, this punishment was never used after independence in 1960. In 1975, President Houphouet-Boigny himself ordered that all death sentences be commuted to terms of imprisonment. In 1995, an attempt to extend the scope of the death penalty failed. On 16 March, 1995 in response to a rising waves of crime, the council of ministers drafted a bill extending the death penalty to cover the crime of robbery with violence and providing for executions "by firing squad" in presence of the public. In April and September 1995, President Henri Konan Bedie prevented the bill from becoming law. In the end, the President never promulgated the law.

However, in Guinea death penalty is maintained for several offences; on 31 July, 2001, 22 people convicted of murder were sentenced to death by Kankan criminal court, they are currently imprisoned in Kankan civil prison. In the same vein, in Liberia, death penalty is maintained for several offences. The most recent execution was in November 1995, seven commanders of the armed group, conseil de paix an Liberia (LPC)-Liberian Peace Council, were shot after a specially constituted court sentenced them to death for atrocities committed against civilians. It is possible that other execution have taken place in the conflict that has raged in Liberia since 1989.

In Nigeria, capital punishment exists under criminal and penal codes and in all the states practicing Sharia legal system.

---

[436] Suit No. 390/1990.

Criminal and Economic Crimes Reported to the Nigeria Police: 1975-1996.

Year	Total Crimes reported	Violent Crimes Reported	Economic Crimes Reported	Armed Robbery	Theft or Stealing	Burglary	Unlawful Possession and Receiving Stolen items	Fraud	Assault	Grievous Wounding
1975	193,635	59,978	107,509	1,182	73,260	18,673	8,643	4,933	50,265	6,905
1976	214,286	63,404	113,790	2,000	74,272	21,792	9,361	5,297	53,292	5,946
1977	219,112	74,031	94,907	2,075	56,324	19,001	9,075	7,238	61,511	11,485
1978	220,475	70,102	104,753	2,775	65,159	18,886	10,078	6,747	56,626	10,571
1979	203,733	67,747	103,294	2,197	63,363	19,918	9,476	7,393	51,987	11,559
1980	210,908	51,768	89,427	2,381	61,915	12,027	6,690	5,728	37,203	15,507
1981	253,952	54,560	78,921	1,643	48,912	16,256	7,862	3,659	39,402	16,463
1982	271,240	75,251	90,921	1,311	63,067	15,364	6,039	4,627	55,153	15,671
1983	311,961	72,233	102,916	1,430	63,161	20,012	10,590	7,240	52,204	16,892
1984	372,558	70,188	128,573	1,415	78,615	21,457	15,462	10,539	50,001	15,671
1985	350,606	64,975	133,895	1,194	81,378	22,983	16,850	12,890	43,824	16,892
1986	311,422	70,955	134,895	1,308	82,308	25,983	13,173	11,981	50,009	15,965
1987	326,838	78,899	131,052	1,260	79,750	20,609	16,104	12,890	59,219	15,938
1988	352,861	81,687	162,514	1,338	101,062	29,265	17,289	13,236	61,708	15,938
1989	308,973	72,111	152,787	1,577	90,882	29,626	16,243	14,158	52,595	15,846
1990	334,767	71.093	145,636	1,644	90,071	26,947	13,822	12,855	52,007	15,359
1991	306,057	69,816	120,159	1,064	72,294	23,484	11,067	11,936	51,312	14,775
1992	300,383	73,525	134,469	1,568	78,807	28,826	11,232	13,899	53,320	16,491
1993	320,950	72,343	159,675	1,975	105,972	27,516	10,408	13,845	51,987	16,369
1994	278,366	67,037	119,702	2,044	69,347	26,392	13,546	10,018	45,877	17,167
1995	253,098	66,724	113,755	2,109	70,542	23,258	13,524	8,942	46,543	16,300
1996	239,572	74,150	111,814	2,419	71,338	15,627	13,057	8,.794	52,741	17,650

Trend of Imprisonment and Prison Conditions in Nigeria						
Year	Total Crimes Recorded by Police	Total Prison Admission	Convicts as % of all zinmates	(Natural)	Firing Squad	Judicial Execution
1975	193,635	87,947	37.54	146	*	*
1976	214,286	108,733	46.95	94	-	77
1977	219,112	112,713	432.58	86	85	61
1978	220,475	128,713	34.15	69	9	41
1979	203,733	129,618	37.20	108	60	28
1980	210,908	165,506	39.65	115	4	4
1981	353,952	135,465	30.16	361	-	14
1982	271,240	202,153	27.0	147	-	58
1983	311,961	243,293	32.20	205	-	11
1984	372,558	238,005	34.61	381	232	123
1985	350,606	230,328	34.0	501	255	46
1986	311,422	202,024	33.0	620	233	42
1987	326,838	269,121	36.5	N.A.	259	**
1988	352,248	113,412	31.34	1,615	207	41

Arguments for and Against Death Penalty

Jurists and the public have expressed several views and opinions on the practice of death penalty over the years. Majority of these views and opinions have been tailored on the effectiveness of death penalty towards controlling commission of capital crimes and the imperatives for its abolition upon the perceived failure of this mode of punishment in the society. The positions are of two major groups; one supporting it in the rationale that it deters criminals from venturing into heinous crimes, though many in this group admit that the death penalty is not totally deterrent than other forms of punishment. Another group opposing it on the basis that it is immoral and being incapable of correcting any possible error of conviction, though many in this group agree that its abolition cannot completely eradicate incidents of murder and other capital crimes from the society.

There are several reasons in support of death penalty. As earlier stated, it serves as a deterrent and helps in reducing crime, though it is irreversible. Eminent advocates of death penalty like John Stuart Mill, Sir John Anderson, St. Augustine, Thomas Aquinas and host of others have argued extensively and pungently too, that it is hard to kill a wrong person due to the several chances/procedures at the disposal of the convicted to challenge his sentence. The proponents of death penalty have argued that the risk of executing the innocent is so small, indeed so infinitesimal, that the consideration can be dismissed".[437] In fact, the punishment being an extreme one, the judicial system takes a lot of care in arriwing at its decision. Available judicial records have shown that there are several safeguards guaranteeing protection of the rights of those facing the death penalty. Indeed, trials are more likely to be fair when life is at stake. In Nigeria, the judicial system is very careful with death sentences. The courts more often strictly apply the requirement of "proof beyond reasonable doubt, in murder cases, to such an extent that the general public feelings towards such judgments have been that of rage and mixed feelings. While hanging the wrong man is a mistake of unparalleled gravity, this likely problem is with the trial, and not the punishment. When an innocent person is sentenced to death, it is not the fault of the punishment itself, but the trial that led to this punishment.

The proponents of death penalty have further canvassed the argument that it ensures the safety of the society, brings justice to those who have suffered and most importantly helps in reducing crime and criminals in the society. They claim that this punishment is important to keep the brightness of justice and public safety shining brightly in our society. According to them, it is not the penalty whether death or prison – which is unjust when inflicted on the innocent, but its imposition. They further argued that even in cases of rare mistakes, this is not peculiar to death sentence alone; offence carrying prison terms is susceptible to similar situation. Therefore, allowing those who cause death of innocent victims to walk around free on the streets and the premise that the court might make a mistake in just a bleak assumption.

Extending the frontiers of their propagation the advocates clamour that death penalty is not revenge, rather, it is a matter of putting an end to a life that has no value for other human lives, so that if one cannot value the life of another human being, then one's own life has no value. They further argued that while some people might think that death penalty is inhuman and barbarians, so is murder, citing the plights of those people who have lost their beloved or whose lives have been tied to a hospital bed because of some acts of barbarous persons. Going by the background of their arguments, sentencing a murder to death is in fact a favour to the society.

---

[437] See House of Commons Proceedings, 14th April 1948.

In serving this purpose, they argued that unlike terms of imprisonment in which there is always a chance for the accused getting out no matter how long, with execution, there is no parole and there is no way they can come back. In furtherance to this reasoning, it has been said that capital punishment would help clear out the crowded prisons a lot better. For example, in Nigeria, prisons are always congested and no new prisons are springing up to accommodate the large number of criminals; therefore by getting rid of the really bad people off the streets for good, we would free up some space in the prisons.

From the realm of theology, the advocates justify capital punishment by referring to some scriptural passages;

Whoever sheds the blood of man; by man shall his blood beshed, for God made man in his own image.

That God is sometimes portrayed as putting evildoers to death.[438] Also, in the Old Testament, murder, adultery, idolatry, incest, rape, kidnapping, pederasty, witchcraft, blasphemy, bestiality and other wrongdoing is punishable by death. In the New Testament as well, there are passages that seem to affirm the right of the state to administer the death penalty. Governmental authority "does not bear the sword in vain; for he is the servant of God to execute his wrath on the wrongdoers".[439] Also, Jesus commended the good thief on the Cross next to him, who had admitted that he and his fellow thief are receiving the due reward for their deeds.[440] Similarly, the right of the state to put criminals to death seems taken for granted in the New Testament. This view is certainly taken for granted in the patristic tradition and later in the work of Thomas Aquinas. The patristic tradition is fairly united in support of it and St. Augustine argues that the fifth commandment does not forbid the taking of any human life, but only the taking of innocent human life. By this interpretation, Augustine offered what became the standard understanding in the West, making room for both a theory of just war as well as capital punishment. St. Thomas Aquinas followed Augustine and argued that the death penalty satisfies the four purposes of punishment. He compared state execution to individual self-defence by arguing that the body polities like an individual, has the right to protect itself against criminals. He compared capital punishment to amputation of a

---

[438] Genesis 9:6; Numbers 16.

[439] R.L. Young, Religious Orientation, Race and Support for the Death Penalty; Journal for the Scientific study of Religion, 31 (1982) pp. 76-87 cited in the General Social Survey Data and Information Retrieval System (GCS) at http://www.icpsr.umich.edu/G88/bib/bib2977.htm.

[440] Romans 13:4.

diseased limb in which someone protects the common good of the body by removing the affected limb. According to him, the death penalty serves the purpose of rehabilitation by ensuring that the sinner cannot commit further sins. Thomas believed that facing imminent death could efficaciously stir a person to repentance. A letter asking for clemency for someone on death row by Samuel Johnson precisely corroborated this view:

> When a man knows he is to be hanged in a fortnight, it concentrates his mind wonderfully.

Thomas Aquinas further argued that capital punishment deters others from sinning and that only the unjust and never of the innocent may be executed. Invariably, the position articulated by Thomas who also reflected in approved manuals of moral theology, the consensus of theologians, and the writings of pontiffs well into the twentieth century.[441] The late Pope John Paul II has made significant statement in his work titled Evangelism vitae;

> It is clear that, for these purposes to be achieved, the nature and extent of the punishment must be carefully evaluated and decided upon, and (the state) ought not go to the extreme of executing the offender except in cases of absolute necessity; i.e. when it would not be possible otherwise to defend society.

On the other hand, an almost solitary voice against death penalty was recorded by St. John Chrysostom in a sermon on the wheat and the weeds,[442] when he remarked *inter alia* a great care must be taken to respect every life, even that of criminals and unjust aggressors.

The most intriguing argument for the abolition of death penalty is that in the administration of death penalty, the experience of the horrid abuse of human life at the hands of the state in the 20th century has led to an increasing awareness that justice is sometimes not well served as not only are the innocent sometimes put to death, but sadly sometimes the holiest of saints. Those canvassing for the abolition of death penalty often argue that the state

[441] See James J. Megwern, The Death Penalty: An Historical and Theological Survey (Mahwah, New Jersey: Paulist Press, 1997).

[442] Homily 46 on Mathew 13:24-30 Nicene and Post-Nicene Fathers of the Christian Church, ed. Philip Schaff (Grand Rapids, Michr: Wm. B. Gerdmans, 1975 report) 10-288f.

should not have jurisdiction over life and death and cite details of the ways the state have been particularly abusive to religious believers, political opponents, social crusaders to such an extent that in the exercise of power of death sentence, the state does a very poor job in the discernment of innocent from guilty[443] may further argue that if the good cannot be distinguished from the bad, then it is better to spare both than to lose both. It is submitted that today, however the criminal justice system has undergone steady improvements in its organization as such cases are very rare, if not practically non-existent.

Arguments against Death Penalty

Most academic writers including prominent criminologists have through the ages discredited the death penalty. These abolitionists say that the death penalty is a relic of barbarism. That it is a backward looking approach to punishment. They argue that instead of concentrating on the criminals, lawmakers should identify the social causes of crime and eliminate them rather than just punish for the sake of punishment. Even in classical times, moralists and philosophers rejected the death penalty and the theories advanced in its favour. Plato denounced the theory, Thomas Hobbes, in his Leviathan decried it. Gandhi, in criticizing the bases of the death penalty said that an eye for an eye would soon make the whole world blind. The abolitionists argue further that the deterrence capacity of death penalty and indeed all vindictive justice is not provable, that people who take crime as a career are less likely to be deterred and most crimes including murders are not the results of reasoning or of weighing considerations for or against the intended crime and are not act to be repressed by the force of example.

Lord Ellen Borough's claim that the imaginary terror of the gallows on men's mind was enough to retain capital punishment was met by the assertion of Mary Wollstonecraft who said that "Executions, far from being useful examples to the survivors have a quite contrary effect by hardening the heart they ought to terrify".

The abolitionists also argue that it is improper and immoral to use a human life to show example. Life is so cheapened and by so doing, it has been said that society diminishes itself. According to Cesare-Beccaria, a criminologist of the abolitionist school: "To me, it is absurdity that the law which represents

[443] Robert Royal's Cathistic Martyrs of the 20th Century (Crossroad Publishing 2000).

the common will and detest and punishes homicide, should itself commit one and in other to keep citizens from committing murder, order a public one committed."

Society evolves with time and most societies in the highest plane of civilization have done away totally with the death penalty. It is a mark of civilization that we treat life with respect. One agrees with the sociologists and criminologists who say that no baby is born a criminal. That everybody, except the retard, is born with a promising, innocent, and positive disposition, but social conditions as he grows which leads to a low self-esteem turns him into a criminal/animal. Rather than cutting the stem by vindictive justice, we should examine the root cause of this aberration in order to correct it.

A very thorny case came up in 1976 in the American State of Utah. It involved a certain young man called Gary Gilmore. At 14 years, he spent most of his time behind bars. He entered reformatory after breaking a school window. He was later jailed for auto theft, armed robbery and assault. After his release from prison at 35 years, he started a new life. He got a job and fell in love with a girl who somewhere along the line left him. She returned to her former husband. Suddenly, Gary Gilmour snapped. He went to a petrol station and without provocation killed the attendant. The following night, he confronted the night manager of a motel and shot him dead. He was sentenced to death by firing squad. Against his wishes, an appeal was filed for him. Gilmore sent a note to the Supreme Court asking that he be allowed to die with dignity. The authorities prevaricated after the sentence was confirmed. Gary Gilmore complained that "to prolong the execution when I don' ask for it to be prolonged puts me through the stress of cruel unusual punishment." At his execution, he was asked if he had anything to say. He looked up for a long time, looked ahead of him and said unrepentantly, "let's do it." A kinsman of his made a statement which was classic, "Things might have been different if Gary had not been "caged" in different institutions on and off since the age of 14, going from juvenile trouble-maker to a hardened killer in 22 years."

Obviously, he was one who was a victim of his circumstance and experiences. Perhaps if his descent into crime had been nipped in the bud by reforming or rehabilitating him, there would not have been an occasion that called for his cold-blooded execution. It is not proved that the death sentence has deterred other would-be criminals from committing similar crimes. The upsurge in armed robbery cases in Nigeria was attributable to the after-effect of the civil war where many able bodied men were left without any means of livelihood.

Perhaps the better approach to meeting the disaster would have been to address the issue of under-employment and unemployment rather than setting up Armed Robbery Tribunals to deal speedily with such cases without the right of appeal. As statistics showed, the courts kept experiencing an ever-increasing deluge of cases that threatened to ground the machinery of justice despite public executions. The deterrence effect of such public executions, if ever, were very negligible, thus giving credence to the observation of Justice Burton Robert, a former Queens District Attorney that between 1891 and 1963, when the electric chair at Sing-Song terminated the lives of 584 victims, there was no discernible effect of eliminating crimes.

An eye for an eye never stopped any time. This vindictive principle has not helped to stop the endless bombing of the Israeli land by Palestinians despite revengeful counter-attacks by Israelis. In fact, it was postulated by some psychologists in America that the mere thought that they could be executed trigger off a deadly and frenzy behaviours from would-be criminals. Fear of execution has never proved as a deterrent to crime and like it has been said earlier, it has lost place amongst civilized societies. A case that occurred in Warri opened one up to appreciate the nobility in abolishing the death penalty. A certain Catholic nun, Sister Irene Conelle was murdered by her steward and his other conspirators and her car and other property stolen.

After much investigation, the suspects were arrested and tried at the Robbery and Firearms Tribunal, Effurun. The suspects were found guilty and sentenced to death like our law prescribed.

As soon as death sentence was handed down, the Vatican wrote, saying that they do not subscribe to the killing of the convicts and pleaded passionately that the convicts should not be killed. The Irish government also wrote through their embassy (The nun was an Irish), expressing their desire that the convicts be spared from execution because they did not believe in taking life for whatever cause. The family members of the fallen woman also visited from Ireland to see the graveside of their loved one and wasted no time in raising an objection to the convicts being executed. Thus the ball was passed on to our bully-like, obsolete laws, which cried more than the bereaved and needed to keep abreast with the trend of civilization. One wonders the effect it would have on the convicts to learn that their lives were being spared on request from the persons whose loved one they have snuffed out.

As regards the arguments to justify death penalty on the grounds that it is necessary to protect society, one thinks life imprisonment does offer the community ample protection.

Another troubling fact based on analysis is the unequal application of the death penalty, which finds most of its victims among the poor. It is seldom if ever used against the wealthy. This has been proven as a fact in America. Majority of those executed are the poor – not the rich killers. To add a little levity to an otherwise serious issue, even in Nigeria there has never been heard of a rich man being executed for murder or armed robbery, even though they commit such crimes. Dele Giwa and kindred cases are germane and very instructive in this regard where we have seen murder of the most heinous nature being perpetrated by the untouchables. The ones who are arrested at all one way or the other protract the cases and get the smartest lawyers that invariably get them out based on technicalities.

As to the religious scholars who say that "an eye for an eye", is a sacrosanct injunction. It is submitted that the Nazarene was considered superior to Moses the giver of that law and at his execution for an offence he never committed; he prayed that the Creator forgave his killers. The same attitude, which the Vatican and the Irish Republic prayed, we do in earlier cited case. The more humane Prophet Ezekiel gives a broader picture of the creator who said. "As I live saith the Lord, I have no pleasure in the death of the wicked, but that the wicked turn from his way and live.[444]

Perhaps, no justice would be done to this subject without a consideration of the plight of the hangsman – the doer of the state's dirty job whose identity is often concealed. Why encourage such an infamous and cold-blooded profession? Most of our law givers and law interpreters who hand out the death sentence cannot even kill a chicken, yet we expect someone over there to carry out such monstrous orders. A certain humane and repentant American hangs man by name Clinton T. Duffy, after seeing the flesh torn from the condemned's face by the rope and his swollen tongue, swinging legs and odours of urine, defecation, sweat and caking blood had this to say: "It would do the people good to know exactly how their mandate was carried out. Every juror who ever voted for the death penalty, every judge who ever pronounced sentence, every legislator who helped pass the law that made it necessary for us to go through this ordeal should have been with me today."

It is believed that the revenge theory upon which the death penalty was based has lost its place in modern thinking. Rather than be extremely judgmental to those convicts, products of a wild society without the cushioning effects of welfarism, most of whom were dragged up rather than being properly brought

[444] See Ezekiel 33:11.

up, we should consider the prayer of the SIOUX Indians who say "O Great Spirit, keep me from ever judging and criticizing a man until I have walked in his moccasins for two weeks" or as the Nazarene would say "Love your enemies, bless them that curse, do good to them that hate you, and pray for them which despitefully use you and persecute you."

Death penalty can kill innocent people and some argued that it should be abolished. It has also been said that to take another man's life away from him can be very cruel, because what give somebody the right to destroy another person's life. Prime example is that of David Kealm, Samuel Poole and Wilbert Lee who are just a few men on death but were released from death row a little bit before they were set to die.[445]

That death penalty is harsh from several different ways to perform an execution already analysed above in chapter one. Some of the outdated forms of capital punishment such as hanging, firing squad and beheading somebody, which are not used boldly in many advanced countries and have not been used for quite a while in countries that still permit it like Nigeria. Also, the more recent forms of killing people, which are by Electric Chair, a Lethal Injection and the Gas Chamber, are more often used when an execution is necessary, are cruel. For example, the Electric Chair is being used less and less due to the fact that it sometimes fails to kill a person instantly. It will often fry them until they catch on fire and burn up. It is on account of this narration that it is now being classified as cruel and criminal punishment.

Thus eminent people have canvassed that all these forms of execution have been used one time or another and firmly believe that it should never be used, and for many reasons because it carries many opinions and moral concerns. Furthermore, administering capital punishment involves a number of economic implications because to execute someone actually costs more than keeping him in jail for the rest of his life. For example, in U.S., it would cost $34,200 for life in prison without parole, for 50 years in prison, while to execute someone would cost $60,000 or just six years of executions. In Nigeria, it is hard to have an estimate of what it would take to expend on someone sentenced to life imprisonment due to uncertainty in the prices of goods arising from persistent inflationary trends and unstable cost of living, however it is doubtful whether the cost of executing a condemned prisoner will be as much considering the fact that hanging is most often used in this country. Perhaps, the only comparable aspect is the years that a condemned person spends on

[445] See http://www.death penalty info.org/Innocent % 20 list.html

death row awaiting execution, which ranges from five to twenty years. The death penalty need not be imposed for justice to be preserved. While the death penalty absolutely excludes the chance of the criminal harming society again, in contemporary society, imprisonment serves to defend society against the aggression of the criminal.

The goal of deterrence may also be retained even with an abolition of the death penalty. It has been argued that study of the issue has not determined a definitive answer to the question of whether capital punishment is a better deterrent than other forms of punishment. Some anti death sentence advocates argue strongly that no discernable deterrent is provided by capital punishment. Some even argue that crime increases with its use.

Furthermore some studies argue that although the death penalty keeps the sinner from committing more sins, and although imminent death may prompt conversion that it is better to foresee and prepare for death than to be surprised and unable to prepare as happened with Jeffrey Dahmer. They further argue that capital punishment completely excludes rehabilitation in any ordinary sense. This is because even if there is an end of life conversion, the death penalty does not allow acclaimed conversion to bear fruit. Many grave sinners, even murderers, have later led exemplary lives and brought many closer to God. In the Old Testament, Moses killed a man but then gave the commandment of God protecting life to the people of Israel. David committed adultery with the wife of Uriah and later facilitated the death of Uriah but he became the greatest Psalmist that ever lived and through his lineage, Jesus Christ emerged. In the New Testament, St. Paul persecuted and consented to the death of Christians but later went on mission to the Gentiles and offered his own life rather than hurt that Body of Christ he once persecuted.

In our time, Dr. Bernard Nathanson performed or oversaw some 75,000 abortions, including killing his own child, and co-founded the National Abortion Rights Action League (NARAL). However, God touched him, and he has spent more than 20 years in exemplary service of human beings in the womb through lectures, books and movies such as *The Silent Scream* and Eclipse of Reason. Even in Nigeria, an armed robber and ex-convict Kayode Williams later converted and became pastor and set up preaching ministry rendering services to prisoners and winning their souls for Christ.

Admittedly, not all criminals experience this melanoma, but our world is a better one because some have. Even from the concept of retributive justice upon which death penalty is thrusted, there is never a perfect correspondence between crime and punishment. For example, we could not put McVeigh to death 168 times to correspond with more than 168 murders of innocent people, including children. But clearly, lifelong imprisonment is an extremely serious punishment that is proportionate to extremely serious crimes even like that committed by the admitted killer, McVeigh. Before the execution of Timothy Mcveigh on June 11, 2001 Pope John Paul II demonstrated rare principle of love by calling and leading the entire people of God to show that we should be in love with a person, the person of Christ. He tried to save Mcveigh because he believes that that is what Christ would do. At Loyola Marymount University, a flyer advertised a talk on the death penalty, which featured pictures of John Paul II and Timothy Mcveigh with the caption; "Why is this man (the Pope) trying to save this man (Mcveigh)?" The discourse analysed why John Paul II a man who has fought against the taking of innocent human life in his youth resisting Nazi oppression, to his maturity fighting Soviet Communists, through his Poplay fighting against a "culture of death," try to save an irresponsible and guilty for more than 168 murders of innocent people and why would the victim of attempted murder try to save a converted, indeed, admitted killer.

For want of the penalty of death, increased numbers of victims are dying at the hands of murderers, when the fear of the death penalty would have deterred. Although, statistics being so hard to interpret with confidence, it would require the evidence of a significantly increased murder rate to be clear and convincing to show beyond doubt that the increase was of a kind, which the continued infliction of the death penalty might reasonably, have been expected to present.[446]

[446] Christopher Kaczor; Why the Death penalty? Capital Punishment and the Catholic Traditions, Department of Philosophy Local Marymount University.

6

OVERVIEW OF DEATH PENALTY

Death penalty is the supreme penalty exacted as punishment for murder and other capital crimes in Nigeria. There is perhaps no single class of offences that varies so widely both in character and in culpability as the class comprising those, which may fall within the comprehensive definition of murder. The consideration of the subject has been on from ages and the topic is stimulating and interesting with enormous literature of eminent experts and stakeholders. The work has analyzed arguments for and against the practice and virtually everyone knows so much by heart, logic and religious norms about the subject.

> Even statistical figures put forward by both sides are educative and informative and on a comparative basis are likely to balance almost evenly. For centuries now, appreciable change has been made in the attitude towards capital punishment at the international level though, its scope has been gradually restricted but its validity has never been successfully impugned. While many countries have abolished capital punishment altogether, some of these countries keep alternating between abolition and re-introduction and many countries have retained death penalty completely/totally.

As earlier stated, crime cannot be wholly extinguished by legislation, as it crime and punishment bore a measurable relation to each other. Law is a curb not a solvent. Outlawing or abolishing death penalty will not reduce the waves of murder and other capital crimes, rather it will make would be offender to find this act of criminality less risky and perhaps make such to be worthy of being undertaken.

Outside the realm of law, religion offers an interesting food for thought; here are many believers who in the reality of Hell commit acts, which they know to be sinful, and which they know to be violations of the commandments/tenets of their faith. Yet, some believers do still commit acts that have been so proscribed by their religion as well as by the authority of law. The reason for an ever-going controversy on death penalty is embedded on the views of people towards the conception of punishment, proper. Arguments on death penalty or capital punishment usually turn upon three major forms:

(1) Deterrence: the effect it produces upon others;
(2) Retaliation: the satisfaction of society's injured sense of justice; and
(3) Reform: the process of normalizing the offender.

That all the three have a place in the scheme of punishment, but not on an equal place. Punishment has only one logical basis, and that is Retaliation the other two-Deterrence and Reform are subsidiary factors. Deterrence rightly belongs to the system of prevention, planning and forecasting of crime. Reform relates to educational life after crime and social approach to crime. To make deterrence, the chief element in punishment is to violate the principle of equity. It is not ethical ever to use a human being, which is an end in itself, as a means. It is also ineffective, as crimes, especially major crimes, are committed mostly from passion or instinct, forces which more with directness. To make Reform, the chief element is to violate the principle of justice with its implication of retribution. He who does wrong must be made to bear the consequences. It is also mostly futile, since chronic mental deformities can no more be rectified than chronic bodily diseases can be cured. If it were in man's power to reform a human being, then reform might well be assigned the central place in the high grounds of humanity. Also, Retaliation alone is the true method of punishment. But it must be exercised within human limits. It is not for man ever to apply absolutes. This inevitably defeats its purpose.

It has been said that Capital punishment is no punishment; as it is an evasion of punishment. If the dead (convict) were to know that they are dead, then capital punishment would carry meaning. As it is 'Oh, death where is thy sting; oh, grave, where is thy victory?"

Furthermore, it has been said that the safety of the state in countenancing the death penalty would be better served before capture, but to put to death one securely held is like killing war prisoner for safety. In the same vein, the attitude of those who would spare the life of one who was reckless with the life of others has been described as Pacifism. On other hand, it is humanism; as such one may not know what he was doing.

Death Penalty on war crimes and humanitarian law has its own psychology and its own morals, for example a deserter from the battlefield has got to be executed on the sport; because a deserter is one who runs away for fear of being killed himself, as distinguished from a "conscientious objector" tag Jehovah witness group) who refuses to enlist from evasion to killing others. Thus, the certainty of being dealt with summarily is the only effective way to check desertion, with the resultant disintegration of the ranks.

Under the military law as well especially in Nigeria in the past, people freely shared, the philosophy during the aborted bloody coup d'etat of Col. Dimka in which Murtala, the then head of State was assassinated, people wept openly and called for the trial and execution of the coup plotters, however subsequent aborted coup d'etats of Mamman Vatsa, Gideon Orkah and Oladipo Diya met the last deep in peoples' hearts as they felt on the enormity of inflicting death upon human beings.

Similarly, the agitation throughout the entire civilized world against the execution of Sacco and Vanzetti was bared upon an inborn repugnance to taking human life as there was nothing about these men to call forth tender feelings.

Generally, an inveterate bad character who's any given act be insufficiently proved done away with an otherwise decent character whose sudden violent passion plunged him into the commission of a self confessed heinous act. On the question of whether it is right to hang a man, it has been simply said that because we all hang together, therefore it is not justifiable to hang one separately.

More importantly, punishment must never assume absolute form. This is because human judgment is fallible and may lead to a miscarriage of justice. But it is more than these reasons, our own share, past or present, direct or indirect is the influences that surround the individual being (victims and accused) in murder cases, all of these factors which more or less adventitious factors in the makeup of our being. People say, it is rare for a man in his normal reasoning to take sole credit to himself for his achievements, then why should he, then be held solely responsible for his abnormal actions? We are our brothers' keeper even the Holy Scripture say so.

Society is an organic thing. For in the words of mused Richard Baxter of old as he saw a doomed man led to the gallows: "there, but for the Grace of God, go." A man should be held accountable for his actions; it is by virtue of his being endowed with a sense of alternative, which, in the language of ethics, means an ability to distinguish between right and wrong.

In this sense, a man is a free agent with enabling capacities to confront and by sustained resolution to resist his environment and his hereditary impulses. This makes him different from an animal because an animal lacks the sense of alternative and we cannot connect responsibility with an animal.

A human being loses that sense in becoming a lunatic. He is then virtually on the animal plane, which has no crossroads it is a 'one-way' arrangement.

The epigraphs we have presented in the preceding Chapters drive home the challenge which the federal governments plan to organize a national debate towards the abolition of capital punishment in Nigeria which is to what extent will the position further expand and complicate the already critical conflict of laws problems within the Nigerian legal system. The broad equities underlying human existence must be given due regard if we are to have a civilization which is not merely mechanical. This is not to advance sentimentalism. If one disapproves of the eye for an eye concept of justice, neither does one believe in turning the other cheek. Life is a stem affair. Were it so that capital punishment would have a deterring effect, one should be in firm support of its as a social necessity. After all, who would not willingly sacrifice the wicked to serve the innocent? One might with as much reason be against cutting off a gangrenous limb, when it is a question of saving the rest of the body just as with the case of euthanasia. But are the reasons of those supporting this concept free from the allurements of self-rectitude!

Others say capital punishment has no deterring effect, as it could be shown psychologically that it does not have. He who is reckless of others is reckless of himself; he is reckless by nature; he is included that way. He is the sort that would stop at nothing. For instance, a burglar would kill as well as rob, if the death penalty for murder were removed. But why does he provide himself with a pistol? To use it only if necessary: why, of course. If no need for resorting to it arises, the most desperate burglar would stop to shoot, increased penalty or not as a matter of economy of effort. Again, if fear of the death penalty were really in his heart, then he would never deliberately put himself in a position to be able to make use of the weapon, for, in act of burglary, even if he kills to resist capture, he becomes guilty of murder. Thus, fear of extreme penalty in a reckless individual is an arrant nonsense. Rather it fascinates him.

Indeed, one is of the opinion that most criminals are irrational men and to being to argue for their irrationalities amounts to forecasting and permutations, which should not be the concern of law, but that of law-enforcers and lay-researchers. Perhaps to canvass reasons or make logical few rational criminals who are selfish and greedy to profit from their criminality by reducing the highest punishment for the heinous crimes may use thinking for criminals.

In Nigeria[447], for example, assassinations is rampant and once committed, the assertion cleverly go into hiding, not for any other reason but for the fear of death, the prospect of being caught by the arms of law and the likelihood of being descended upon by an infuriated mass of bystanders and being torn into fragments to check publicly committed. Murders make them to be faceless felon and at times turn out to be feign sympathizers.

The mystery may never be 'solved'. It will not be the first time, nor ours is the first, or only nation where a high profile murder has been filed away, marked unsolved. Such dossiers, however, are not thereby marked unsolvable, and relegated to musky vaults, sealed up for eternity. From time to time, an unexpected event, a misdirected word or seemingly insignificant act, "a fallout among thieves", a social re-ordering, a clink in the armour of impunity occurs, and light pierce the darkness of deception and obfuscation. Then the files are brought out for dusting, reviewing, and – possibly – revelation.

At times, the assassins have developed series of accentuated frenzies and in such situations, who say, death penalty has no useful role to play in curbing fratricide crimes and other violent criminalities resulting in deaths. This explains why the state safeguard a murder suspect from committing suicide in order to avoid public ridicule and shame attached to trial. Even, where such suspects are eventually tried, convicted and sentenced to death, they struggle hard to have the death sentence-committed to life imprisonment through proceedings to enforce their fundamental Rights while on Death row. That in cases of a gang of well organized homicidal maniacs rampaging students hostel, hunting and mowing down their own colleagues like they do in the blood-soaked Mafia cinema who with the applaud of the bravery and sense of solidarity of the students rallied, pursued and tracked down the perpetrators. That subsequent arraignment before the court and the eventual discharge of the accused is one of the most bizarre court decision which is likely to discourage the public in having faith in the legal process as many would regard the judiciary as collaborationist in the perversion of justice.

That the corrosive dagger of influence by highly placed individuals has found its place in the least of the collegial body and so aptly captures the criminality of elitist influence. Our universities have become too

---

[447] In Nigeria, the list of personalities assassinated is endless, Alhaja Kudirat Abiola, Alfred Rewane, Toyin Onagoruwa, Bole Ige, the then Attorney General and Minister of Justice of the Federation, Dikibbo etc.

commonplace to catalogue cases of murder; brutal killings of academic staff by disgruntled students on the motive of results or grades where such lecturers refused to succumb to pleas and threats. However, all blame must not be heaped on student cultism; this undeserving cultic ascendancy has been nurtured and encouraged by some academia in order to settle scores against some of their colleagues. Thus, in a nation that has produced some of the finest minds in all disciplines whose achievements are envied and lauded all over the world-behold the worship of the barbarian at the very pinnacle of the collegiate community. These barbarians can be kept at bay and properly nip in the bud by a commitment to the exercise of the collective will of the collegial community.

This death phenomenon has been described as the result of a changed mentality brought about by the disciplinary effect of detention. While awaiting execution, their passions have cooled off during that period and they have come to be used to their surrounding with the elementary instinct of self-preservation reasserted. Can the condemned persons really be entitled to this so-called "Right to life", can they complain of indignity, torture etc. Did they consider all these when they were pulling the trigger or hatching the hatchet that struck and sent the innocent victim to journey of no return. They should imagine what would be the position or plights of the deceased-victims underground, especially those who are going to be in the position of the dead in Hades having been denied of the opportunity to repent their sins and turn to God worse still, the dead shall not be redeemed after death even if it is untimely or unnatural.

Let us be firm but fair, civilization has one unfailing mark – sympathetic understanding "Tout comprendre, c'est tout pardonnor" which is one of the noblest sayings uttered and the truest. It points to the ideal course but cannot be made a practical rule. Thus, if we have to disregard the ideal to our own moral undoing let us do so. Some have argued that capital punishment is a mode of brute reaction, degrading in its effects upon the spirit of organized society: savages retaliate in kind but the retentionists say in Nigeria let it be.

There are several biblical principles which, when in place, would make the death penalty eminently more effective than it now is. It ought to be administered with absolute fairness. Neither race, money, influence, nor any other trivial factor should have any influence upon the facts of the case. If there is any doubt about a man's guilt, grant him the benefit of that doubt, and spare his life. However, in many cases where there is no doubt about the guilt of the perpetrator, there is no excuse for not demanding the full penalty in such instance.

Punishment of the convicted murderer ought to be implemented speedily. The policy of an endless string of appeals, which can stretch out over a dozen years, is a mockery of the law. Ecclesiastes 8:11 state "Because sentence against an evil work is not executed speedily, therefore the heart of the sons of men is fully set in them to do evil." While it may seem insensitive to those who view themselves as refined products of our modern world, executions would be significantly more effective, if they were carried out publicly. The secluded manner of the current process of executing condemned persons undoubtedly neuters the effect of capital justice. In Deuteronomy 21:22, "offenders were put to death in view of all the people; and the criminal's body was hanged upon a tree till evening."

Also, God whose foolishness is greater than the 'wisdom' of man (I Cor.1:25) apparently feels that public execution is a deterrent to capital crimes. Thus, for those who regard the Bible as a divine revelation, its instruction must be sought, and it is not silent on this matter.

Islam has a place for death penalty for a variety of offences as contained in the Penal Code and the States' Sharia'h Penal Code of some States of the Federation in the North that have adopted application of shariah law. Nevertheless, both applicable laws; the Penal Code accommodates compounding of sentences even for grave offences of homicide and the shariah Penal Code accepts compensation and indemnification of funeral expenses of the victims by the accused persons.

African Traditional Religion has a lesson to offer the mainstream of Anglo-saxon jurisprudence and philosophy of punishment relating to death penalty. It has its roots from the inception of African society, thus the practice of death penalty is not imported to Africa. History has shown that death penalty applied to the categories of crimes so regarded as serious especially those that involved loss of lives of the victims. Interestingly, the emergence of crimes against humanity which has just been a new development at the international sphere in modern times have been recognized under the various indigenous empires that have reigned before the advent of modern system of government introduced by the Europeans.

The famous Oyo, Benin and Songhai empires for examples recognized trials of sovereign rulers that committed atrocities of different dimensions against their subjects through application of forms of punishments such as hangings, banishments, exiles and suicides.

Modern developments have also witnessed contributions from many scholars, jurists, professionals, experts and stakeholders making copious viewpoints for its retention and its abolition. For too long, countries of the world have cast the death penalty debate as one between "liberals" and "conservatives" i.e. those who are "soft on crime" and those who "care about victims of crime", the "abolitionists" and the hardliner death penalty proponents. But the United States has gone beyond this classification as it believed that society can no longer afford to carry on the debate in this manner.

The US has put these stereotypes aside arising from the Constitution Project, housed at Georgetown University in Washington DC, which seeks to develop bipartisan solutions to contemporary constitutional and governance issues. The Constitution Project in May 2000 crated a death penalty initiative to address the deeply disturbing risk that Americans are being wrongfully convicted of capital crimes or wrongfully sentenced to death.

The Thirty Members Committee's Mission Statement states that individuals who commit violent crimes deserve swift and certain punishment. While some of the members of the Committee believe that the range of punishment may include death, others do not. But they all agree that no one should be denied basic constitutional protections.

The Committee evolved the third group on the question of death penalty - MANDATORY JUSTICE, consisting of Eighteen Reforms to the Death Penalty, notable Effective Command that an independent authority to screen, appoint, train and supervise lawyers to represent accused persons charged with a capital crime. It should set minimum standard for these lawyers' performance. That defence lawyers should be adequately compensated, and the defence should be provided with adequate findings for experts and investigators. Prohibiting Execution in cases involving Questionable Categories of Accused and Homicides: That persons with mental retardation and those under the age of eighteen at the time the crime was committed should not be eligible for the death penalty. Also persons convicted of felony murder, and who did not kill, intend to kill, or intend that a killing take place, should not be eligible for the death penalty.

Expanding and Explaining Life without Parole (LWOP): That life without the possibility of parole should be a sentencing option in all death penalty cases in every jurisdiction that imposes capital punishment.

Safeguarding Racial Fairness: That all jurisdictions that impose the death penalty should create mechanisms to help ensure that the death penalty is not imposed in a racially discriminatory manner.

Proportionality Review: That every State should adopt procedures for ensuring that death sentences are meted out in a proportionate manner to make sure that the death penalty is being administered in a rational, non-arbitrary and even-handed fashion to provide a check on broad prosecutorial discretion.

Protection against Wrongful Conviction and Sentence: That DNA evidence should be preserved and it should be tested and introduced in cases where it may help to establish that an execution would be unjust. Furthermore, all jurisdictions that impose capital punishment should ensure adequate mechanisms for introducing newly discovered evidence that would more likely than not produce a different outcome at trial or what would undermine confidence that the sentence is reliable even though the expense would otherwise be prevented from introducing the evidence because of procedure barriers.

Duty of Judge and Role of Jury: That if a jury imposes a life sentence, the judge in the case should not be allowed to "override" the jury's recommendation and replace it with a sentence of death. The judge in a death penalty trial should instruct the jury at sentencing that if any juror has a lingering doubt about the defendant's guilt, that doubt may be considered as a "mitigating" circumstance that weighs against a death sentence.

Role of Prosecutors: That prosecutor should provide "open-file discovery" to the defence in death penalty cases. The prosecutors' offices in jurisdictions with the death penalty must develop effective systems for gathering all relevant information from law enforcement and investigative agencies.

Application of Death Penalty in Nigeria: Facts and Figures

The record of capital punishment in Nigeria like that of any society is as old as the society itself. As earlier pointed out, in the traditional societies of the past, the many societies that constitute the present day Nigeria practice capital punishment, death penalty at that time was the punishment for offences like witchcraft, murder, adultery, sacrilege and repeated stealing. Although, death sentences were carried out under African Customary criminal justice process, there were no available records of condemned persons that were executed in view of the fact that the entire system was unwritten. Yet, Nigerian customary penal system had unrecorded data of executions carried out in different communities that made up the nation before the advent of Europeans.

The advent of British rule introduced capital punishment through criminal and Penal Codes as part of the Nigerian criminal justice system. The British rule ushered in the advent of capital punishment as a prescribed penalty for some defined offences: murder, culpable homicide, treason, sedition, controlling or presiding over an unlawful trial by ordeal, which results in death. The advent of military rule and the emergent culture of violence precipitated the high rate of armed robbery, which was later made a capital offence after the civil war. Furthermore, the incursion of military into politics in Nigeria has increased the number of capital offences and also witnessed the execution of many accused of plotting to overthrow the very military governments that were brought in through unconstitutional means. Apart from treasonable felonies punishable by death for conspiracy and coup d'etat, the Buhari/Idiagbon promulgated Decree No. 4 of 1984 which made drug trafficking a capital offence and also for the retroactive effect of this unusual and the unusual penalty which recorded the gruesome execution of three such offenders. The Abacha regime's law that culminated in the execution of Ken Saro Wiwa and other Ogoni leaders only rivaled the public outcry of the unpopularity of this law.

Results

One of the arguments commonly used against the practice of death penalty is that executing criminals is not a deterrent to violent crime. Is capital punishment a deterrent to violent crime? While all sorts of "arguments" are proffered on both sides of the controversy, several facts appear rather obvious from the research undertaken in this work.

First, this is not an issue that may be measured accurately in terms of statistics. No one can ever know how many potential murderers have refrained from taking human life due to their fear of prosecution, conviction, and ultimate execution. It will not do to ask those on death row: "Did a fear of the death penalty have any bearing on your inclination to commit the crime which brought you here?" This writer undertook preliminary research work on condemned prisoners in Abeokuta Prison but little was achieved as they were not ready to respond to questionnaires on the basis of so many reasons ranging from inability to understand English Language, impatience to interpretation of questions from English Language to Yoruba, the common medium of expression among the convicts, impaired state of mind, psychological problems, hatred and frustration. Thus, one can hardly expects an unbiased answer from convicted persons. However, from little interactions I had with some of the convicts, (though not too willing), I discovered that a fear of execution may well have been resident in their minds, only to be overpowered by other urges, stronger at the moment of their violence. Further research undertaken reveals that many of the convicts committed an offence of murder for example, because of the following factors, hate, rage, greed, lust, and ill-tempter among others.

It is therefore incongruous to say, "death penalty does not deter murder, and ought not to be employed". To admit this postulation is to say also that "imprisonment does not deter any type of crime, hence, ought not to be utilized either". From the informal interaction with the convicts, it is obvious that every lawbreaker knows there is the possibility that he may be apprehended, convicted, and incarcerated. It therefore defiles any sort of logic that argues that simply because men are reckless in terms of crime's consequences, the government ought to neglect an appropriate penalty for criminal activity. While it is most frequently argued that our legal system is so flawed that injustice frequently prevails. It is quite true to some extent, that justice system in the country is fundamentally flawed, which allows some powerful and rich men to circumvent the course of law, this has nothing to do with the death penalty rather it is the process of criminal justice that has been hampered by some few but highly connected law-breakers, this has apparently flawed the system in the sense that the "teeth" have been prevented from the law. But the solution is not to "throw the baby out with the bath water", rather resolute stakeholders need to "fair" the flawed system.

On a comparative trend, a wealth of empirical evidence has revealed that capital punishment deters crime in America. Some States that have adopted this means of deterrence have experienced a substantial drop in their average homicide rates. Empirical evidence has also shown that a vast majority of Canadians support the death penalty[448]. The incidents and rates of violent crimes are not directly proportional to the penalty or punishment that accompanies the violation. There are other variables, which are determining factors for the changing crime waves. These include among others, the material condition of the people, unemployment level, drugs and alcohol, availability of guns and other weapons and cultural tolerance of violent behaviours. For murder and armed robbery which are among the offence that attract the death penalty, studies have shown that the award of capital punishment does not in any way affects the incidents and rate. There is rather a fluctuation as shown by Professor A.A. Adeyemi in a study carried out between 1967 and 1986.

[448] See Wayne Jackson, "Christian Corner: Pen points" July 3, 2000.

Table 1. Comparatively True Case Figures and rates for Murder and Robbery actual Executions (1967 – 1986)

	Murder: True Cases		Robbery: True Cases		Total capital offence	Total Number of Execution
Year	Figure	Rates per 100,000 unit of population	Figure	Rates per 100,000 units of population	Total capital offences	Total Number of Execution
1967	415	0.68	969	1.59	1,384	9
1968	466	0.74	672	1.09	1,135	10
1969	580	0.90	525	0.82	1,105	7
1970	952	1.45	1,809	2.75	2,761	25
1971	828	1.22	1,344	1.99	2,172	130
1972	902	1.30	997	1.44	1,899	115
1973	959	1.35	924	1.30	1,883	91
1974	995	1.37	883	1.21	1,878	75
1975	999	1.34	1,065	1.43	2,064	74
1976	1,388	1.82	1,577	2.04	2,965	77
1977	1,573	2.82	1,944	2.44	3,517	180
1978	1,760	2.18	2,326	2.82	4,086	109
1979	1,698	2.04	1,965	2.30	3,663	53
1980	1,633	1.90	2,381	2.70	4,014	8
1981	1,520	1.71	1,747	1.92	3,267	10
1982	1,786	1.95	1,310	1.39	3,096	11
1983	1,857	1.96	1,430	1.47	3,287	6
1984	1,668	1.66	1,410	1.40	3,078	338
1985	1,432	1.37	1,194	1.15	2,626	301
1986	1,539	1.43	1,308	1.21	2,487	376
1987	3,944	0.68	1,972	1.09	5,916	615
1988	3,132	0.74	1,566	0.82	4,698	276
1989	3,721	0.90	1,861	2.75	5,582	187
1990	3,855	1.45	1,928	1.99	5,783	174
1991	5,463	1.22	2,732	1.44	8,195	155
1992	6,249	1.30	3,124	1.30	9,373	242
1993	6,277	1.35	3,139	1.21	9,416	373
1994	8,491	1.37	4,245	1.43	12,736	472
1995	5,445	1.34	2,723	2.04	8,168	467
1996	5,707	1.82	2,853	2.44	8,560	512
1997	5,841	2.82	2,921	2.82	8,762	525
1999	5,973	2.18	2,987	2.30	8,960	548
2000	5,181	2.04	2,591	2.70	7,772	528
2001	4,961	1.90	2,481	1.92	7,442	521
2002	3,495	1.71	1,748	1.39	5,243	200
2003	3,415	1.95	1,707	1.47	5,122	488
2004	3,257	1.96	1,629	1.40	4,886	484
2005	3,183	1.66	1,591	1.15	4,774	482

Source: Nigerian Police, Lagos State Command (computed form annual crime statistic table).

Criminological literature and research show that violence is predominantly a male dominated crime, and that urban areas and cities tend to have higher rates the violent crimes than rural areas. One crucial factor that promotes violence is urbanization. Although this study shows the relationship between capital punishment and the rate of violent crimes that attract the death penalty, below does the police record a data of criminal violence in Lagos State and Nigeria.

Table 2. Crime Related Deaths in Lagos State, Nigeria

Year	Murder and Manslaughter	Suicide	Grievous Harms and Wounding	Unnatural Offenses	Other Personal Crimes	Arson	Other Property offences	Vehicle (traffic)	Armed Robbery	Total
1986	100	16	29	14	3	4	2	39	95	302
1987	102	28	1	9	3	1	2	52	57	255
1988	76	8	-	1	3	-	13	86	44	231
1989	65	32	-	-	1	6	2	104	25	235
1990	73	28	-	-	27	-	-	58	52	238
1991	60	16	-	4	52	-	-	278	53	463
1992	92	12	-	6	105	1	-	359	40	615
1993	117	7	-	-	232	-	-	329	32	717
1994	114	11	-	1	155	-	-	243	79	603
1995	174	10	-	-	184	-	-	173	91	632
1996	173	19	-	-	124	-	-	186	85	587
Total	1146	187	30	35	889	12	19	1907	653	4878

Source: Nigerian Police, Lagos State Command (computed form annual crime statistic table).

The general pattern is characterized by fluctuation, which shows that in spite of the fact that some of the offense attracts the death penalty; people are still involved in it without consideration of the punishment. The following tables show there was increase in armed robbery cases from 1992 – 1996 as well as armed robbery deaths.

Table 3. Case of Armed Robbery in Lagos State and Nigeria

Year	(1) Total Cases Recorded in Nigeria	(2) Total Cases Recorded in Lagos	(3) Col. (2) as % of Col.
1986	1,308	340	26.0
1987	1,260	163	12.9
1988	1,338	140	10.5
1989	1,577	84	5.3
1990	1,700	95	5.6
1991	1,064	68	6.4
1992	1,568	107	6.8
1993	1,975	112	5.8
1994	2,044	272	13.3
1995	2,109	375	17.8
1996	1,419	563	15.0
Total	18,362	2,119	11.5

Source: Nigerian Police, Lagos State Command (computed from annual crime statistic tables)

Table 4. Arrests for Criminal Violence in Lagos State, Nigeria

Year	Total Arrest Recorded in the State	Grievous Harm and wounding	Assault	Armed Robbery
1986	73,694	3,768	7,900	370
1987	72,941	5,315	9,512	601
1988	84,439	4,458	13,992	240
1989	64,161	5,405	12,413	177
1990	64,067	5,409	11,694	174
1991	37,785	5,298	8,040	155
1992	52,998	7,914	9,131	242
1993	54,231	6,844	9,043	373
1994	50,565	8,022	12,264	472
1995	34,328	5,120	7,701	467
1996	34,547	5,956	8,048	512

Source: Nigerian Police Force, Lagos State, Command (Computed from Annual Crime Statistics Table.

From these statistics it is clear that armed banditry is on the increase including homicidal cases. The award of capital punishment may not have deterred people as said above but we have equally accentuated the fact that the sanctity of life is not diminished when a murderer is killed after the due process of the law rather it shows appropriately that people should not experiment with the life of others and greater still the revulsion that the society holds for the crime of murder.

The pathetic case about Nigerian situation is that violent crimes can be traced to, among other things, political instability that has produced some militant armed youths among ethnic nationalities that feel marginalized, unemployment, poverty, and population explosion. To a rational person, there is no doubt that the death penalty can be an adequate restraint and deterrence.

Crime is everywhere. In our neighbourhood, in the neighbouring States, wherever we look, we find criminals and crime. Criminals have become a part of our daily lives. The question then is does this mean we let them be the darkness of our society? No, definitely not. Eliminating crime and criminals from our society is our duty, and we cannot ignore it. Getting the rightly accused to a just punishment is very important. Some criminals commit crimes, because they have no other option to survive, some do it for fun. Even for capital offences, no one advocates death sentence for every offence. On a charge of murder, for example, the criminal procedure empowers the judge to convict an accused person for a lesser offence, even though such an accused person is not charged with that lesser offence provided the evidence adduced by the prosecution establishes a lesser offence. Thus our criminal justice recognizes the fact that not everybody deserves to die, but some definitely do.

We support the view that Nigeria still needs death penalty for now, so far it serves as a deterrent and helps in reducing crime. Although, it is true that death penalty is irreversible, but the present criminal justice system makes it hard to kill a wrongly convicted person due to the several safeguards given to the convicted to prove his innocence.

Obviously, death penalty is one of those extreme punishments that would create fear in the mind of any same person. Besides, the scripture states:

> "There is, in every soul (not liberated by the promises of the gospel of Christ) to, some degree, the fear of death.[449]"

Perhaps, the phrase, whistling in the graveyard was not born in a vacuum. The teachings of Jesus frequently emphasized the punishment of hell – where men will weep and gnash their teeth – which is the ultimate capital punishment. It is submitted that there is ample biblical evidence to establish the fact that the practice of executing criminals, especially those who commit premeditated murder, is consistent with the will of God. Divine authority in all dispensations of history has implemented such judgment. Everybody fears death, even animals. Ernest Van den Haag, in his article mentions:

> "One abstains from dangerous acts because of vague, inchoate, habitual and, above all, preconscious fears."

Most animals would think twice if they knew their own lives were at stake. Advocates of life imprisonment without parole as the maximum punishment cannot debunk the possibility of situations where prisoners serving life sentence without parole to commit another murder in the prison. In the words of Paul Van Slambrouck:

> "Assaults in prisons all over us, both against fellow inmates and against staff, have more than, doubled in the past decade".

[449] Hebrew 2:15

Empirical evidence has shown that trials are more likely to be fair when life is at stake – the death penalty is probably less often unjustly inflicted than other forms of punishment. Statistics[450] reveal that there is far less number of death sentences than life imprisonment sentences without parole given out every year. According to crime statistics compiled by the Nigeria Police there were approximately 5,000 criminals sentenced to life imprisonment and other terms of imprisonment as opposed to about 400 criminals sentenced to death. This shows that judicial system itself is very careful with death sentences.

Assuming without conceding that there are chances that an innocent person is executed, it is the problem with the trial, not the punishment. It is not the penalty – whether death or imprisonment – which is unjust when inflicted on the innocent, but its imposition on the innocent.

Just as there have been cases in which a person has been sentenced to death, and then after several years, it was revealed that the person was innocent, of which there is nothing that can be done to undo the punishment inflicted. So also is a situation whereby a person has been sentenced to life imprisonment, no court or compensation in this world can return the horrifying years spent in the prison by that innocent person. Thus, the judicial system has minimized the chances of mistakes. It is almost impossible to sentence a wrongly accused person. Then, why cause death of several innocent victims just on the bleak assumption that someday we might make a mistake. How far shall we continue to live in sins and expect grace abound, God forbid.

Conclusion

Death penalty has attracted stormy controversy in the administration of criminal justice. Perhaps, no other aspect of criminal law has been plunged into the stream of controversy more than capital punishment.

Some are insisting that execution of a convicted murder is wrong, contrary to right to life and against the norms of human rights. Others have further argued about the futility of combating violence with more "violence" i.e. that you cannot fight fire with fire. Now in the course of this work, we have established that there is a difference between violence and law enforcement, or punishment. Law enforcement and punishment is to crime as water is to fire,

[450] According to statistics gathered by the Criminal Justice Institute in Middletown, Connecticut – in Christian Science Monitor.

where fire fighters spray water on a burning building with such force that the flames have no choice but to back down. But the rate that we are executing murderers is analogous to trying to quench a bonfire with an eyedropper.

Some are also saying "violence does not solve anything". Thus labeling capital punishment as a form of violence in order to rationalize that shortsighted proposition. This idea is historically untrue and immoral doctrine. These people forget the basic truth that "reverence for human life" has nothing to do with the practice of death penalty, rather the only people they are interested in preserving are those who display the least of it … the very least reverence for human life.

Perhaps, most sophomoric clichéd argument is that executing a murderer will not bring back his victim. This school never explains how putting murderers in prison is any more capable of such a miracle. Capital punishment is not about bringing back the dead, that is not the object of executions and it never was. Capital punishment is about enforcing consequences for one's own actions to endorse personal responsibility. The society cannot expect anyone to take responsibility for their own actions of these consequences are not enforced in full.

Under the present criminal justice system, death penalty is not applicable to all killings. Those criminals who commit murders relying on self-defence or during times of passion (provocation) do not deserve death penalty. A plea of self-defence properly proved and established exonerates an accused person from a charge of murder. While unlawful killing in the heat of passion, reduces murder to manslaughter. Also, murderers who plead insanity shield themselves of criminal responsibility for their acts. Insanity means a failure to respond to the usual sort of incentives in the usual ways. However, we need to draw the line between mentally incapable and criminally insane in order to determine those who are to resume the responsibility for their actions. There needs to be a limit to which society should put up to. I believe every criminal, no matter how cruel he is, should be given at least one chance to change himself in countries whose legal system permits that, however there have been cases in which people have committed several murders e.g. serial killers or have committed crime even after imprisonment for example Canada. For such people advocating death penalty is not out of place. If somebody does not understand that going around killing people is wrong, then letting such people live is not only a great threat to the society, but also a great burden. Some people have argued that death penalty is in human and barbarous. So is murder. Death penalty is not revenge. Consider the agony and against anguish those people who have lost their beloved or whose lives have been tied to a hospital bed because of some barbarous person would be if they see the person who ruined their lives just getting a few years of imprisonment of mere rehabilitation. It is submitted that death penalty is not revenge; rather it is a matter of putting an end to a life that has no value for other human lives. Sentencing a murder to death is in fact a favour to the society. In spite the moral argument concerning the inhumane treatment of the criminal while awaiting execution via Death row phenomenon, we must revisit the "nature" of the crime committed. Can society place an unequal weight on the tragically lost lives of murder victims and the criminals? The issue is beyond the subject of philosophy but a divine conundrum at the core of perhaps the most intriguing issue facing the Nigerian legal system today. Of all ages, punishment is meted out because of the nature of the crime, devoid of any reference to the social identity of the victim. As Adam Bedam wrote:

> "even in the tragedy of human death there are degrees, and it is much more tragic for the innocent to lose his life than for the state to take the life of a criminal convicted of a capital offence."

One strongly believes that if one cannot value the life of another human being, then one's own life has no value. Death penalty is good and serves a definite purpose of reducing crime as well as bringing justice to the criminals and innocent. In order to serve its purpose, it must be improved and made more effective and efficient. The Nigerian justice system must ensure that the rightly accused is brought to justice. The rate of criminality in the country in the past forty-five years has been upsurged dramatically and so one believes that death penalty should not be abolished, as it ensures the safety of the society; brings justice to those who have suffered and most importantly helps in reducing crime and criminals in our society. Death penalty is important to keep the brightness of justice and public safety shining brightly on our society.

7

REVIEW OF DEATH-ROW PHENOMENON

The hard earned civil rule of the fourth republic, which ushered in General Obasanjo, has brought sanity to the manner of execution by reviewing the plights of condemned persons on the death row in the various designated prisons nationwide. Consequently, the death penalty imposed on many convicts was commuted to life imprisonment and terms of imprisonment. However, the death penalty is still retained under the existing criminal laws in the country.

In October 2002, Obasanjo told a meeting of an Ad Hoc delegation visiting Nigeria that he was committed to saving lives and not eliminating them. He said he adhere to HOCs campaign for a moratorium on executions that he was committed to it "here in our country and internationally". Accordingly, Obasanjo set up two groups to look into how the prison system could be reformed and decongested. The National Study Group on death Penalty, established in 2004, and the presidential Commission on Reform of the Administration of justice, established in 2007, recommended a moratorium on executions because the criminal justice system could not guarantee fair trial. Until June 2013, Nigeria had maintained a self–imposed moratorium on death sentence. This is apparently in conformity with the resolution of African Commission on Human and Peoples Rights calling for a moratorium on executions, though the issue of moratorium still remains an unofficial policy in Nigeria. In the same vein, the United Nations General Assembly Resolution 62|149 and 63|148 of 2007 placed a moratorium on the implementation of death penalty on member states is not automatically binding on Nigeria. Strictly speaking, it is not legally accorded the status of operating statute in Nigeria unless its details are enacted into law by the National Assembly. The moratorium is not binding and enforceable in the same manner as a treaty would be under international law, until it is domesticated into our national laws[451]. Though the terms of the supposedly agreed UN moratorium and the extent of Nigeria's commitment is not in public domain, nevertheless, a moratorium in legal parlance is suspension of action for a period of time to enable the authority to appraise its impact on a subject matter, it cannot be permanent.

For instance, Texas in the United States implements the death penalty in spite of the 2006 UN moratorium and the fact that the US has a seat on the UN Security Council. Also a 58-year old Black American was executed in the USA in compliance with a court judgment[452].

In Ogun State, Governor Ibikunle Amosun granted amnesty to seven prisoners, including two condemned prisoners, Messrs Rasidi Yisau and Saburi Adebayo, whose death sentence was commuted to life imprisonment in January, 2012.

Ondo State Governor Olusegun Mimiko, to mark the democracy Day in 2011, commuted the death sentences passed on three people, Sunday John, Ayodele Ikuomenihan and Oluwatimilehin Ifaramoye, who were to die by hanging for murder, and have been awaiting execution since September 2006, to life imprisonment. The Governor of Katsina State, Ibrahim Shema commuted the death sentence on eight prisoners to life imprisonment in commemoration of Ramadan on August 21, 2011. They were Musa Dauda, Sheu Idi Magaye, Nura Sabo, Samanu Salisu, Shitu Jubrin, Aminu Sada, Abdulkarim Mohammed and Friday Patrick due to good behavior, their length of stay in prison, and the fact that they had not killed anyone. In Delta State, Governor Emmanuel Uduaghan on February 2012, at a town hall meeting in

---

[451] See Section12, 1999 Constitution. See also Mrs. Funke Adekoya SAN interview in the Nation of July, 3 2013 where she said that it was unfortunate that Nigeria has decided not to comply with the UN moratorium on executions after it gave an undertaking to do so to the international community. But she noted that each country has to take whatever decisions it believes to be in the best interest of its citizens. Texas in the United States implements the death penalty in spite of the 2006 UN moratorium and the fact that the US has a seat on the UN Security Council. According to her, our Foreign Affairs Minister would have to make the case to the UN as to why we have reneged on our understanding

[452] While this was going on in the USA, the NGOs and human rights organizations did not pull down the Government concerned. But always exhibit double standards by passing down orders on other sovereign states, like Nigeria. This is a flagrant disregard to the norms of public international law. Also, unlike other climes, Section 33 of our Constitution clearly permits death sentence. Without amending these provisions, how can we suddenly start following the superpowers willy-nilly? I mean that this posturing is most annoying and smacks of neocolonialism. I detest it without apology," he said

Umeh Community, Isoko South Council Area, said he would not sign death warrants[453].

Non-Execution of Warrants

As at December 2012, there were about 970 inmates on death row. The figure comprises 951 males and 19 females. They are alive because of the refusal of past governors to sign their execution orders. This is because it seems the governors are reluctant sign such warrant since the return to civil rule in 1999. This non-signing of death warrants have translated into increasing number of prisoners awaiting execution in all designated condemned prisons nationwide[454]. According to official figures from the Nigeria Prisons Service, there were 1,039 inmates on death row. Many of them had been sentenced for over 10 years, but governors have not been too keen to have them executed. Their reason was reinforced by the civil societies and non-governmental organizations (NGOs), who have remained at the vanguard of life of condemned prisoners. Under the Criminal Procedure the President and the Governors are saddled with the functions of execution of death warrants of condemned persons in respect of federal and state offences. The federal and state Attorneys-Generals usually advise the President or Governors on whether or not to execute death warrants. The President or Governors are required to sign death warrants for the executioner to carry out the death sentences. Over the years the Governors, have not signed death warrants, these situations have exacerbated the numbers of persons awaiting death and invariably increasing the numbers of convicts on death row phenomenon nationwide. The former President of Nigeria, President Goodluck Jonathan during the 2013 Father's day service at Aso Rock, Abuja bemoaned the attitude of many Governors of states of not signing execution warrants of convicts in their respective states. In his view, there are good and difficult aspects of duties of states executives but enjoined them to live up to expectation by discharging their duties on both sides. It is believed that the President issued the directive to hasten the execution of the over 900 convicts awaiting the hangman's noose and to decongest the prisons. Jonathan said governors must be willing to carry out

[453] He said as a medical doctor he was trained to save lives and not to kill.

[454] See The Nigerian Tribune, Monday 1 July,2013 Features-at p35-36 reported by Sulaimon Olanrewaju Editor,featurestribune@yahoo.com 0805 500 1708.

their responsibilities "no matter how painful", in accordance with the law. The Criminal Procedure laws of states provide that governors should sign death sentences of condemned criminals before execution. Of the 36 governors, only two, the former Governor of Kano State, Ibrahim Shekarau and Adams Oshiomole of Edo State, have confirmed the sentences passed by the court on some convicts, since 1999.

As if Edo state government heeded the call of President Jonathan, the state government executed four convicts by hanging[455]. On June 24, 2013 the Edo State Government confirmed the execution of four convicted criminals[456]. The convicts were reportedly executed by hanging. The State Attorney-General and Commissioner for Justice, Henry Idahagbon confirmed the execution explaining that their convictions were secured years ago from the Supreme Court and that three of the executed criminals were convicted outside the state, but had been in prison in Benin. The appeals of the condemned prisoners were said to have gone through the Court of Appeal and the Supreme Court of Nigeria before the Edo State governor, Comrade Oshiomole signed their death warrants.[457]. The Governor further stated that the rule of law is different from resolutions by some NGOs and nations are not governed by NGO resolutions.[458]

On claims that there was a stay of execution order, Idahagbon said his office got the stay of execution papers, but that the execution was not carried out by his office. This is a fundamental issue that cannot be swept under carpet. If it is true that the processes had been served on the office of Attorney-General of Edo state then it would amount to a grave infraction of legal process and breach of law. The case of *Nosiru Bello v Attorney -General, Oyo state* had laid down the judicial condemnation of execution of a convict, while his appeal is

---

[455] According to a reported feature in the Tribune, 1July, 2013 the signing of the death warrants of the convicts executed in Edo state in June predated President Jonathans admonition as former Edo state Governor, Lucky Igbinedion had signed the death warrants of both Ijiofor and Igagu before he left office in 2007 while Oshiomole signed both of Nsofor and Aiguokhian in 2012.

[456] The Punch News on Tuesday, June 25,2013 reported by James Azania and Adesomoju that Edo Executes Four Convicts by hanging.

[457] Governor Oshiomole stated that God can have mercy on them, but I am unable, having regard to the overall circumstances of the case,namely,killing and dismembering the body of your victim and wanting to sell some parts and you ask me in the name of human rights to let him live.

[458] In his words, I am convinced that those people need to die under the law. As a Governor, I subscribed to an oath of office to obey the Constitution of the Federal Republic of Nigeria without fear or favour. I cannot be afraid to sign the death warrant of a man who has been found guilty of murder.

pending. The prison authorities, however, claimed they did not receive any stay of execution order.

This development has elicited condemnation from Amnesty International. The international human rights group, in a statement, had called for restraint on the part of the Nigerian government in carrying out the exercise[459]. The group further remarked

> We again urge the Nigerian authorities to stop all executions immediately and return to the moratorium on execution in the country. We oppose the death penalty in all cases without exception, as it is the ultimate cruel, inhuman and degrading punishment.

In the same vein, a legal rights group, legal Defense Assistance Project, condemned the execution. The group's national Coordinator, Chino Obiagwu, said the execution of the inmates was in violation of the appeal he filed on behalf of all death row inmates in the country.
According to him,

> Today the LEDAP frowns on the execution of four death row prisoners- Chima Ejiofor, Daniel Nsofor, Osarenmwinda Aiguokhan and Richard Igagu in Benin, Edo state.

The group further claimed that the Attorney General of Edo State and prison authorities were duly served with the court processes, comprising the notice of appeal and motion for stay of execution. In the midst of this controversy, it is obvious that legal action may eventually ensued by dependants or relations of the executed prisoners. However, the proprietary of the claim by the group that a general notice of appeal was filed on behalf of all condemned prisoners awaiting execution in the country may call for determination. This is rather a strange procedure as the court may not be inclined to deem such a process as properly covering all condemned persons nationwide.

---

[459] The Deputy Director for Africa, AI, Lucy Freeman, said "If confirmed, these executions mark a sudden brutal return to the use of death penalty in Nigeria, a truly dark day for human rights in the country.

European Union and use of Death Penalty

Noted for its long standing rejection of the EU to the use of death penalty and reiterating the UN Resolutions calling for the establishment of a moratorium as a first step towards abolishing death the death penalty in retentionist states, the High Representative in Nigeria, Catherine Ashton admonished Nigeria to join the majority abolitionist trend now prevailing in the African continent. According to her, executions can never be justified[460]. She expressed her sadness that Nigeria had broken its seven year moratorium on death penalty. She advised the country to amend its laws with a view to abolishing the application of death penalty. In the same vein, the United Kingdom's Minister for Africa, Mark Simmonds condemned the recent executions in Edo state against the backdrop of the Universal Periodic Review of Nigeria by the UN Human Rights Council that came up in the 3rd quarter of 2013.

Perspectives on the practice of Death Penalty

Death penalty usually generates important questions for the general support for or opposition to its application in jurisdictions where it is operational, Nigeria inclusive. However, one significant aspect of application of death penalty in Nigeria is the constitutional rights of appeal guaranteed condemned prisoners to explore, the process which checkmate the frequency of its application that invariably accounted for the death row situation. This can only be imbibed subject to their relevance to the contemporary security challenges facing Nigeria and until premium is placed on human lives and the tenets public safety is adhered to.

The phenomenon arising from due compliance with the rule of law cannot be totally discarded in spite of long standing pressure from International organizations on Nigeria to adopt international norms on basic human rights. In actual fact, Section 33 of the Nigerian Constitution clearly permits death sentence. Without amending these provisions, we cannot start following the superpowers willy-nilly; to do otherwise is to promote neocolonialism. The application of the death penalty has been expanded in its scope with the introduction of sharia law in some states of the federation. Several crimes ranging from apostasy, adultery, rape, and theft attract corporal punishments.

[460] See The Nigerian Tribune, 1 July, 2013 at p35.

The sharia legal system permits capital punishment by the authority of prescribed law both at municipal and international levels. The declaration of sharia as the state religion in some parts of the country and Nigeria being a member of Organisation of Islamic Countries further complicates the likely outcome of the on-going debate on the abolition of the death penalty.[461] The Islamic states advocate for the death penalty and corporal punishments in obedience to Islamic law and the structures of sharia. Thus, a strong case can be made in principle for and against capital punishment. The argument in favour is based on justice and the nature of a moral community, which requires that each person respect the life and liberty of others. Those who commit vicious crimes destroy the basis on which a moral community rests and forfeit their rights to citizenship and even to life itself. On the other hand, the argument against is based on love and the nature of an ideal community in which forgiveness and the hope for redemption are guiding principles. The protection of the innocent requires that criminals be isolated, perhaps permanently. Just punishment is appropriate, but love never gives up even on those who show no love.[462]

---

[461] See Prof. Prof. Yahdudu's comments in The Guardian, Sunday August 24, 2003.
S. Idris "Sharia and the 1999 Constitution: Is there a Cause for Alarm? In Law, Human Rights and the Administration of Justice in Nigeria, Essays in Honour of Justice Muhammed Lawal Uwais (M.T. Ladan, ed.) (Dept. of Public Law Ahmadu Bello University, Zaria) (2001) at p. 396.

[462]Kenneth Cauthen: Capital Punishment, Death Penalty, in Toward a New Modernism, (Lanham, M.D: University Press of America 1997) 151-165 and in The Ethics of Belief: A Bio-Historical Approach, 2 vols. (Lima, OH. CSS Publishing Co. 2001).